Pictures About Extremes

9/14/07

To Doug!
Thanks for all
your help!

Pictures About Extremes

The Films of
John Frankenheimer

STEPHEN B. ARMSTRONG

McFarland & Company, Inc., Publishers
Jefferson, North Carolina, and London

LIBRARY OF CONGRESS CATALOGUING-IN-PUBLICATION DATA

Armstrong, Stephen B.
    Pictures about extremes : the films of John Frankenheimer /
Stephen B. Armstrong.
        p.   cm.
    Includes bibliographical references and index.

    ISBN-13: 978-0-7864-3145-8
    softcover : 50# alkaline paper ∞

    1. Frankenheimer, John, 1930–2002 — Criticism and
interpretation.   I. Title.
PN1998.3.F7327A76   2008
791.43'0233092 — dc22   2007024970

British Library cataloguing data are available

On the cover: (top) John Frankenheimer on the set of the 2000 film
Reindeer Games (Dimension); (bottom) Rock Hudson in the 1966
film *Seconds* (Paramount)

Manufactured in the United States of America

McFarland & Company, Inc., Publishers
  Box 611, Jefferson, North Carolina 28640
  www.mcfarlandpub.com

Acknowledgments

I would like to thank the following people for their expertise and kindness: Doug Fowler, Deborah Coxwell Teague, Ernie Rehder, Virgil Suarez, John Fenstermaker, Robert Powell, Gale Bard, Karen Rappaport and the Alan Bates Archive, Christine Earle, Kari Stuart, Adam Walderman, Alain Silver, James Ursini, Jon Kaplan, Glenn Lovell, Pete Hamill, J.D. Zeik, Katie Oliveri, Jane and Jay Hudiburg, and Mimi and Dean Armstrong.

Contents

Introduction:
Reconsidering Frankenheimer

John Frankenheimer (1930–2002) began his career as a film director in 1951, shooting documentaries and training materials for the United States Air Force. He remained active behind the camera over the next five decades, amassing a body of work that includes more than 150 live television show credits, 35 feature-length films and several commercials. Despite this achievement, Frankenheimer's name today is not well known and the majority of his pictures, with the exception of *The Manchurian Candidate* (1962) and *Seconds* (1966), have been consistently ignored by contemporary critics.

This was not always the case. In the early Sixties, the director enjoyed a great deal of attention and acclaim in both the popular press and the trades thanks to movies like *Bird Man of Alcatraz* (1962), *All Fall Down* (1962), *The Manchurian Candidate*, *Seven Days in May* (1964) and *The Train* (1965). *Variety*, for instance, described *Bird Man* as "the finest 'prison' movie ever made.... [I]t achieves a human dimension way beyond its predecessors."[1] The same publication's review of *The Manchurian Candidate* was just as complimentary, declaring that the picture "'works' in all departments with story, production and performance so well blended that the end effect is one of nearly complete satisfaction."[2] And as the Sixties progressed, Frankenheimer began to draw the interest of upscale film journals, too. In 1965, for example, John Thomas surveyed the director's output in *Film Quarterly*, and in 1968, Charles Higham published a flattering profile in *Sight & Sound*, writing:

> One is aware constantly of his determination — in an increasingly impersonal Hollywood — to hold out for a personal statement, for a humanitarian ideal. He has sympathetically understood the agonies of growing up (*The Young Stranger, All Fall Down*), the dangers of extreme politics (*The Manchurian Candidate, Seven Days in May*), the necessity for personal honesty and avoidance of escapism (*Seconds*).[3]

Then in 1969, Gerald Pratley published *The Cinema of John Frankenheimer*, the first book-length analysis of the still young director's oeuvre. In it, the author described Frankenheimer as a master craftsman, whose

> body of work has been personal and consistently excellent, with variable structures, imaginative techniques, a documentary realism brought to life with the drama and conflict of human participation, and with extreme formal and thematic continuity.[4]

Critical acceptance of Frankenheimer was not universal at this time, though. The technical and thematic aspects of his work which so pleased Higham and Pratley managed to irritate Andrew Sarris and Pauline Kael, two of the era's most influential critics. In *The American Cinema*, published in 1968, Sarris wrote:

> A director of parts at the expense of the whole, Frankenheimer betrays his television origins by pumping synthetic technique into penultimate scenes as if he had to grab the audience before the commercial break. The selective eclecticism of his first film [*The Young Stranger*] ... has degenerated into an all-embracing academicism, a veritable glossary of film techniques. A director capable of alternating shock cuts and slow dissolves is obviously sweating over his technique. Instead of building sequences, [he] explodes them prematurely, preventing his films from coming together coherently.[5]

And Kael, writing about *The Fixer* for *The New Yorker* in 1968, used her review to malign the director's interest in hard, often unpleasant topics:

> Competent, professional American directors are generally at their worst when they become serious and ambitious; when they reach for mighty themes, they fall for banalities. They become clods who think they can turn into important artists by the simple expedient of not being entertaining.[6]

Kael may have been overly dismissive, but her observations were somewhat astute. By 1968, some of the levity and hopefulness that had permeated Frankenheimer's earlier TV and film projects had vanished, and *The Fixer*, a bleak adaptation of a bleak Bernard Malamud novel, was the first in a series of dark dramas he would direct over the next five years, including *The Gypsy Moths* (1969), *I Walk the Line* (1970) and *The Iceman Cometh* (1973). And though he returned his attention to action movies and thrillers in the mid–Seventies with *99 and 44/100% Dead!* (1974), *French Connection II* (1975) and *Black Sunday* (1977), these films, like their predecessors, were hardly optimistic, and their fatalism put off several critics. Vincent Canby, writing in *The New York Times*, for instance, blamed *Black Sunday* for being "a superior example of a kind of contemporary filmmaking that has become much less involving and fun as its subjects have become more serious."[7]

With the exception of *Prophecy* (1979), all of Frankenheimer's films from the Seventies were commercial disappointments. This lack of success weakened him professionally and he would spend much of the next decade cobbling out under-funded, and ultimately unwatched, pictures like *The Challenge* (1981), *The Holcroft Covenant* (1985) and *52 Pick-Up* (1986). And though he still found favor with many newspaper critics, interest from film journals during the Eighties was almost nonexistent, and the citations which appeared in film encyclopedias and reference books published during this time often characterized him as a creative washout and a hack, echoing the venomous judgments Kael and Sarris had delivered two decades earlier. A typical expression of this critical disdain can be found in Quinlan's *The Illustrated Guide to Film Directors*, which appeared in 1983: "One could forgive a director of almost anything after *The Young Savages*, *The Manchurian Candidate* and *Bird Man of Alcatraz*, although in truth there has been rather a lot to forgive since this American director's heyday."[8]

Frankenheimer in France on the set of *The Train* (United Artists, 1965).

Ironically, the warm reception *The Manchurian Candidate* received upon its re-release in 1988 damaged his reputation further. Though the picture, which had been out of general circulation for more than two decades, "won the admiration of millions of viewers," its critical and commercial success added weight to the now standard opinion that the director's career had fizzled after its brilliant start.[9] Canby, for instance, used the older film to cudgel *Dead Bang*, a police drama released in 1989: "John Frankenheimer, the director of one of the wittiest conspiracy films ever made, *The Manchurian Candidate*, is now responsible for one of the more trivial."[10]

That same year, Frankenheimer gave an interview to the *Los Angeles Times* and speculated that a return to grace was possible, but unlikely, as long as the has-been label persisted. He explained:

> [It's] really a struggle to get pictures made and to get the right material. What you don't want to do is just continually get material with fingerprints all over it. You've got

to get yourself in a position where material is being submitted to you before it's being submitted to anybody else.[11]

Several years would pass, however, before the director was able to reestablish himself. And this turn came about largely because of the success of four historical dramas he made for cable television, *Against the Wall* (1994), *The Burning Season* (1994), *Andersonville* (1996) and *George Wallace* (1997), all of which enjoyed high ratings and good reviews. In its appraisal of *Against the Wall*, *Variety* exclaimed, "Frankenheimer has triumphantly returned to the medium that catapulted his career 40 years ago with a simmering, seething retelling of the 1971 Attica rebellion." Just as important, all four pictures won best directing Emmys for Frankenheimer.[12] The director's triumph in cable television also contributed to a revival of critical interest in his career. In 1995, the American Film Institute published *John Frankenheimer: A Conversation with Charles Champlin*, a series of recorded talks between the director and the famous *Los Angeles Times* movie critic. Two years later, the American Film Institute released a flattering portrait of Frankenheimer for its *Directors* documentary series. And then in 1998, an expanded version of Pratley's book appeared, retitled *The Films of Frankenheimer: Forty Years in Film*.[13]

The major studios showed new interest during this period, as well, and Frankenheimer was offered several mainline, high-budget projects. Though *The Island of Dr. Moreau* (1996), the first of these, was received with contempt by many critics, the director's next feature, *Ronin* (1998), drew wide acclaim. Janet Maslin at *The New York Times*, for example, wrote,

> Directing like a world-weary Hitchcock with a taste for the breathtaking car chase, Frankenheimer propels this tale of intrigue through its tightly plotted paces with such conviction that he even makes an action hero out of Robert DeNiro [sic].[14]

Reindeer Games (2000), the director's last theatrical picture, also won admirers, drawing bemused responses, for instance, from critics like *The Washington Post*'s Stephen Hunter, who called this neo-*noir* comedy "a zesty ride the whole way. It's major fun for bad boys and girls; it should guide your sleigh tonight."[15]

Frankenheimer's comeback ended in the summer of 2002, however, when a stroke, triggered in part by back surgery, killed him. And though the obituaries that cropped up afterward were filled with praise, they invariably reinforced the idea that he had failed to live up to the promise of his early work. Sadly, the majority of the film journals ignored his passing; and the only lengthy commemorative piece devoted to his feature film work—a eulogy written by Richard Combs for *Film Comment*—painted Frankenheimer as a something of a neurotic, a depressive who never rebounded from the 1968 murder of his friend Robert F. Kennedy. Combs also used the occasion to denigrate Frankenheimer's work, attacking it with reductive evaluations like: "Once [his] cinema is confident of itself, from about the mid–Sixties on, the films begin to lose their grip."[16]

Such an assessment is hard to accept, given the technical and thematic strengths of such later films as *The Challenge, 52 Pick-Up* and *Ronin*, nor is it shared by everyone, and reappraisals of the director's career have begun to surface, although infrequently, in the years since his death. A citation which appeared in the 2002 edition of the Wallflower Critical Guide's *Contemporary North American Directors*, for instance, praised the director "for capturing the complicating nature of social situations while still delving into the psychology of his characters ... a rare and unique skill."[17] And in 2003, following a commemorative retrospective organized by Film Forum in New York City, which featured several of the director's films from the late Sixties and early Seventies, the *Village Voice*'s Elliott Stein noted the constancy of Frankenheimer's point of view, his persistent interest in existential scenarios and the ambiguity of morality in the modern world. Stein also heaped praise on the director's abilities as a craftsman and a storyteller. Of *French Connection II*, for example, he wrote that it "not only surpasses the original — a case could be made for it as Frankenheimer's most impressive film."[18]

But critics, by and large, continue to ignore the director, and for his admirers, this phenomenon is mystifying and frustrating. To be fair, some of his pictures *are* disappointing. With their sluggish plots and the overheated performances of their actors, *The Horsemen* (1971), *Year of the Gun* (1991) and *The Island of Dr. Moreau* leave much to be desired. But the charge that the quality of Frankenheimer's output plummeted, that he lost his grip after a grand start, is certainly overstated. Comparable statements, we must remember, were made about Fritz Lang and Orson Welles; and as the years have passed, the reputations of these directors have been rehabilitated by critics who recognized the almost impossible balance of style, form and content that distinguishes so much of their later work. *Pictures About Extremes: The Films of John Frankenheimer* is guided by the idea that Frankenheimer deserves similar consideration, that the merits of his movies surpass his reputation.

A Note on the Structure of This Book

A traditional auteurist survey, *Pictures About Extremes: The Films of John Frankenheimer* scrutinizes the director's cinematic output closely, assessing the thematic and stylistic aspects of individual films. It begins with a comprehensive overview of the director's career, looking at each movie's production history, as well as drawing attention to the events which contributed to Frankenheimer's development as an artist, including his experiences in live television, his friendship with Robert F. Kennedy, the difficulties he had with alcoholism and his subsequent recovery. While the pictures are presented chronologically in this biographical section, they are grouped in the subsequent section of analysis, the bulk of the book, by genre and theme. As few readers have had the opportunity to watch all of Frankenheimer's films, plot synopses appear with these critiques, and, when pertinent, additional information about each film's production history. The book takes its title, by the way, from remarks the director made in an interview he gave to *American Film* in 1989: "I love pictures about extremes.... [I]t's extremes. I seem to deal in extremes.[19]

Chronology

1930: John Michael Frankenheimer born to Walter and Helen Frankenheimer on February 19 in Queens, New York.

1947: After graduating from LaSalle Military Academy, enrolls in Williams College. Decides to become an actor, appearing in several college productions. Gains experience directing for stage. Takes up amateur automobile racing.

1951–1952: Graduates from Williams, marries Joanne Evans and enters United States Air Force. Assigned to Air Force's Motion Picture Squadron and moves to California. Gains experience directing documentaries and training films. Also shoots promotional television programs for a cattle breeder in Hollywood.

1953–1956: Encouraged by John Ford, decides to pursue television as a career. Following his discharge moves to New York, where he and Joanne decide to divorce. Hired by CBS as an associate director. Eventually promoted to director. Shoots programs for *You Are There, Climax!* and *Danger.* Marries second wife, Carolyn Miller.

1956: Films his first feature, *The Young Stranger,* for RKO Radio Pictures. Same year, *Playhouse 90* begins. Directs inaugural program, "The Forbidden Area," starring Charlton Heston.

1957: *The Young Stranger* released.

1958: CBS relocates *Playhouse 90* to New York.

1960: Shoots his last live television program, "Journey to the Day," for *Playhouse 90.* Signed by Harold Hecht to direct *The Young Savages:* first of five collaborations with Burt Lancaster.

1961: *The Young Savages* released. Upon advice of John Houseman purchases home in Malibu Colony.

1962:   Releases of *All Fall Down, Bird Man of Alcatraz, The Manchurian Candidate*. Divorces Carolyn.

1963:   John F. Kennedy killed. *The Manchurian Candidate* pulled from circulation. Frankenheimer marries Evans Evans in France during production of *The Train*.

1964:   *Seven Days in May* released. After completing *The Train*, John and Evans move into a Paris flat. Become acquaintances of the French director Jean-Pierre Melville.

1966:   *Seconds. Grand Prix.*

1967:   Signs multi-picture contract with MGM. Films *The Extraordinary Seaman* in Mexico.

1968–1969:   Hired to shoot promotional material for Robert F. Kennedy's presidential campaign. Present at the Ambassador Hotel in Los Angeles night candidate is slain. Incident precipitates a long depression. John and Evans return to Paris, begin intensive language instruction. Releases of *The Fixer, The Extraordinary Seaman, The Gypsy Moths*.

1970:   *I Walk the Line.*

1971:   Edits *The Horsemen* in Paris. At night attends cooking classes at Le Cordon Bleu.

1972:   *Impossible Object* screened at Cannes.

1973:   Returns to Los Angeles to film *The Iceman Cometh*. Purchases another home in Malibu Colony.

1974:   *99 and 44/100% Dead!*

1975:   *French Connection II.*

1977:   *Black Sunday.*

1979:   *Prophecy.*

1981:   *The Challenge.* Begins treatment for alcoholism.

1982:   HBO broadcasts *The Rainmaker.*

1985:   *The Holcroft Covenant.*

1986:   *52 Pick-Up.*

1987:   ABC broadcasts pilot for *Riviera*. Series not picked up. New York Film Festival screens *The Manchurian Candidate*.

1988:   UA re-releases *The Manchurian Candidate.*

1989:   *Dead Bang.*

1990:   *The Fourth War.*

1992:   HBO broadcasts "Maniac at Large."

1994–1996: Broadcasts of *Against the Wall, The Burning Season, Andersonville*. Frankenheimer wins a best directing Emmy for each. Receives 1996 Filmmaker of the Year award from American Cinema Editors.

1997: *The Island of Dr. Moreau*. Broadcast of *George Wallace*. The Museum of Television & Radio mounts a series of screenings commemorating Frankenheimer's career.

1998: Wins best directing Emmy for *George Wallace*. *Ronin* released. Appears in Simon West's *The General's Daughter*.

2000: *Reindeer Games*.

2001: "Ambush."

2002: HBO broadcasts *Path to War*. Damage to spine caused by lung cancer leads to back surgery in May. Following a second operation, Frankenheimer suffers a stroke and dies at Cedars-Sinai Medical Center in Los Angeles on July 6. That fall, receives posthumous Emmy for *Path to War*, also inducted into Television Hall of Fame.

CHAPTER ONE

A Biography

John Michael Frankenheimer was born in New York City on February 19, 1930, the son of a German-Jewish stockbroker and his Irish-Catholic wife.[1] The oldest of three children, he enjoyed a privileged childhood, despite growing up during the Great Depression.[2] "I came from a well-to-do family, never rich, not poor either," he once told the critic Charles Higham.[3] He attended private schools on Long Island from an early age and after graduating valedictorian from LaSalle Military Academy in 1947, enrolled in Williams College, an elite liberal arts school located in Williamstown, Massachusetts. Frankenheimer did not enjoy the experience, however, and though he played tennis on the college team and joined a fraternity, "I just couldn't seem to adapt to the place."[4]

During this period of anxiety and restlessness, Frankenheimer began to pursue new interests. He quit tennis and took up amateur automobile racing. He also joined the college's theater company, with hopes of becoming a professional actor, a decision that upset his parents, particularly his father. "It was the last thing in the world he wanted his son to be. Because not only was everybody in that line of work a homosexual, they made no money, which was even worse, if possible."[5] Despite being, by his own estimate, "stiff and nervous," Frankenheimer pursued acting with the same "fanatic drive to excel" that had characterized his experience as a tennis player; and before he graduated, he'd performed in several plays, often cast in lead roles.[6] More importantly, at the age of 20, he directed his first production, a Noel Coward play titled *Design for Living*. But, as he explained to C. Robert Jennings, "It was an appalling fiasco—the leading actor tripped over a couch, fell flat on his rear end, and everybody forgot his lines."[7]

As Williams did not offer a theater major, Frankenheimer graduated, in 1951, with a B.A. in English. Prior to graduation, however, the Korean War had begun; and to avoid the draft, he joined the school's ROTC program, which enabled him to secure a commission in the Air Force. During this time,

Frankenheimer also married his first wife, Joanne Evans. "Quite frankly, the only reason we got married was that we were living together and I had no money, and when I was called into the Air Force, the only way I could take her with me was to marry her so that the government would pay for it."[8]

That summer, he and Joanne moved to Washington, D.C. Assigned to the Aeronautical Chart and Information Service, Frankenheimer worked in the Pentagon's mailroom, which, he told Higham, "is a horrible, horrible place to be." At night, though, he continued his acting studies, taking courses at American University, while he spent his days sorting military mail, which proved to be crushingly dull:

> The boredom was so great that I read almost everything that came through there, and I read a directive that said they were forming a motion-picture squadron in Burbank, California, and you did not have to go through channels to apply to join it, which is really quite way out for the American military. So I immediately applied, and lied my tail off about how experienced I was with cameras and so on, and mentioned I had acting experience, and kind of *elaborated* my career generally. Before I knew it, I was assigned.

In 1952, the 21-year-old lieutenant and his wife moved to southern California. The idea of working on films frightened Frankenheimer, however, as much as it excited him. "When I got to Burbank, I went clear out of my mind. I had never *seen* a movie camera." He soon discovered that the other men in the Motion Picture Squadron were inexperienced, too. "I found that everybody *had* lied, none of the assignees knew *anything* about movies whatsoever." The majority of the 400 men who made up the unit, moreover, were not particularly interested in filmmaking. Keen on giving the men something to do, the squadron's commanding officer told Frankenheimer to get started on a project immediately. "[S]o my first job was taking this group of derelict air force men out to do the film and the only thing that was close enough was an asphalt plant. My first production was on how to make asphalt."[9]

Frankenheimer on the set of *Ronin* (MGM, 1998).

More short documentaries of this sort followed over the next several months and the work stimulated Frankenheimer's interest in filmmaking. On the weekends, he brought the squadron's two cameras home.

> I'd go out and shoot all manner of stuff. I shot a whole short subject about my auto-
> mobile. I guess that was the forerunner of *Grand Prix*. I tied the camera on to it and
> tried all kinds of angles. I started to read a lot. I read about Eisenstein's work and all
> the basic how-to-do-it books.[10]

Eventually, he was asked by his commanding officer to make an informational film about a local cattle breeder. The experience proved to be pivotal. "The guy had a weekly television show in Los Angeles, which he called the *Harvey Howard Western Roundup*, which was really Harvey Howard trying to sell people into buying his cattle."[11] One afternoon while Frankenheimer and his crew were shooting their film, Howard fired the men who wrote the scripts for his show. He then approached the lieutenant and invited him to write the introductions for the country and western music acts that appeared on the program. Though he had little experience as a writer and minimal knowledge of cows, Franken-heimer accepted the offer. He prepared for the task by reading about cattle in the Beverly Hills Public Library. Then he crafted the scripts and dropped them off at the television studio in Hollywood where the show was shot. Howard liked them and retained Frankenheimer. Then, a few weeks later, the cattleman fired the *Western Roundup*'s director and invited the lieutenant to take his place, which he declined at first, intimidated by his lack of experience. But he changed his mind after Howard told him that the work was relatively simple: "'There are two cameras,' the cattle breeder said, 'and you've got two choices: point them at me or at the cows.'"[12] Despite the primitive—and bizarre—nature of the show, Frankenheimer's interest in and commitment to filmmaking continued to increase. As he told Charles Champlin,

> I owe this guy, Harvey Howard, a tremendous debt, because the experience really con-
> vinced me that directing was what I wanted to do. I didn't want to be an actor any-
> more. I wanted to direct.

Before his discharge in June 1953, Frankenheimer worked on other projects for the Motion Picture Squadron, including training films which he shot for Gen. Curtis LeMay, the Air Force hawk who would serve as one of the models for the Gen. Scott character in *Seven Days in May* a decade later. On one occasion, as well, he flew with Chuck Yeager, the famous test pilot, while preparing a film about aerial gunnery.[13] He also continued to experiment at home with the squadron's equipment.

> I would take the camera and I would go out on weekends and shoot the hell out of
> stuff. I did films on everything—the desert, the freeway. I'd stand out there at rush
> hour and shoot the horrible congestion and accidents, and over them I'd have a sweet,
> dulcet voice reading the California Chamber of Commerce's spiel about how great the
> freeway system is.[14]

Frankenheimer considered staying in the Air Force, but chronic sinus problems prevented him from becoming a pilot, and his opportunities for promotion were restricted. So he set out to find work in Hollywood and was hired to assist John Ford on the West Point drama *The Long Gray Line*. But the project was postponed when Ford went into the hospital for cataract surgery, and Frankenheimer returned to New York with his wife after his discharge.[15]

The couple soon decided to separate, however. "When we got back to New York, Joanne and I realized that we [didn't] want to be married anymore, and we started proceedings to dissolve the marriage."[16] Frankenheimer took a cheap apartment in midtown Manhattan and continued his search for work. Several acquaintances from Williams had moved to the city themselves and had show business jobs, but none of them were willing to help. "[T]hey were all terribly glad to see me until they knew what I was there for.... I got the nicest turn downs you ever saw."[17] As the weeks passed and his resources dwindled, Frankenheimer grew increasingly desperate; and one afternoon, he showed up at the office of Dick Stanley, an executive at CBS television, and told the receptionist there that he wanted a job as an assistant director.

> [She] laughed at me and [Stanley] said, "Well, send that man back here," and I came and he said, "I just wanted to see what somebody looked like who was such a damned fool as to come up here and ask for a job.... You're even in the wrong damned building. But you sound like you've got a lot of guts to even try it."

Through Stanley, Frankenheimer met a producer named Hal Meier two days later in Grand Central Station. The meeting was successful, thanks, in part, to a coincidence: "[Meier] had also been in the Air Force during the Second World War and he'd been in the photographic squadron. We talked a lot and we got along very well."[18] Three weeks after this, he was offered a temporary position as an assistant director. "That was in 1953, and it all worked beautifully from there."[19]

During the early years of television, when most shows were broadcast live from New York, an assistant director was responsible for timing shots, positioning lights and cameras and staging actors, duties which Frankenheimer handled with ease; and because the equipment in the studio was somewhat comparable to the sort he'd used on *Harvey Howard's Western Roundup*, his familiarity with it enabled him to excel, and within a few weeks he rose up from news and weather programs to comedy series like *Mama* and *The Gary Moore Show*. Better assignments followed quickly. Frankenheimer moved over to *Person to Person*, for instance, an interview program hosted by Edward R. Murrow, where his duties included setting up remote cameras in the homes of the program's "guests," allowing them to be interviewed by Murrow from his desk in Manhattan.[20] He also worked on *You Are There*, one of the network's most popular shows. Hosted by Walter Cronkite, "it was a dramaticization [sic] of historical events with CBS newscasters actually 'interviewing' the people of the past — Washington, Napoleon, and so on." One of the directors he worked with on *You Are There* was none other than Sydney Lumet.[21]

Frankenheimer thrived as an A.D. and had little interest in becoming a director himself.

[I]n those days perhaps the most precarious profession in the world was being a television director.... [T]here were only three places to go, CBS, NBC, and ABC. ABC was not much then, so it was only CBS and NBC. You ran out of networks very quickly and one was not about to hire you if you'd been fired by the other.[22]

In the spring of 1954, however, he was offered a promotion, which he eventually accepted. This developed after an event that occurred on the set of *Danger*, a dramatic series that produced melodramas and action stories. In the middle of the broadcast of an episode titled "Escape Route," the program's director experienced an anxiety attack and ran off the set, forcing Frankenheimer to take up the reins and salvage the show. The next day he was contacted by Hubbell Robinson, one of CBS's vice presidents. Lumet was leaving *You Are There* to make movies in Los Angeles and Robinson wanted Frankenheimer to replace the departing director. The 24-year-old accepted with conditions: "I'll make a deal with you, and that is if I screw up I get my job back as an A.D."[23]

He never screwed up and kept his job as a television director for the next six years, despite the often chaotic conditions which characterized live TV production. The first show he directed, "The Plot Against King Solomon," was made for *You Are There*. Broadcast in November 1954, the episode featured a reenactment of Solomon's famous encounter with two women who claim the same baby as their own. The script, incidentally, was penned by Walter Bernstein (as Kate Nickerson), who later worked on *The Train*.[24] Frankenheimer did not stay long with *You Are There*, though, moving back to *Danger* in December; and over the next three months, he directed half-a-dozen programs, along the way meeting several people he would later work with again in his movies, including James Gregory, who would play Senator Iselin in *The Manchurian Candidate*, and Rod Serling, who would script *Seven Days in May*. Then in February 1955, he was asked by Martin Manulis, one of live television's most powerful producers, to work on *Climax!* in Los Angeles. Frankenheimer had married again and he and his new wife Carolyn relocated to California immediately.[25] For the next year and a half, he stayed with the program; and during this period, he adopted many of the techniques that would characterize his shooting style in the years to come, including the use of long takes, deep focus shots and fluid cameras. He also began to experiment, introducing expressive camera angles and symbolic lighting, which helped elevate the programs' pulpy plots into what Tise Vahimagi has described as "intense psychological character studies that go beyond traditional realism."[26]

One of the episodes Frankenheimer shot for *Climax!*, a program titled "Deal a Blow," led to the production of his first theatrical picture. Originally broadcast in August 1955, the drama featured James MacArthur as a teenager whose inability to cope with conservative social mores leads to trouble at home. The show had been written by Robert Dozier, whose father, William Dozier, became the president of RKO Radio Pictures in 1956. Sensing that the hour-long program would make a good film, Dozier secured the rights to the property and subsequently offered the project to Frankenheimer to direct.

Renamed *The Young Stranger*, the film was shot at RKO's studios in the summer of 1956, with MacArthur again cast as the unhappy son. Robert Dozier returned, as well, to re-work his original script.[27] But although he'd been hand-picked to make *The Young Stranger*, Frankenheimer nonetheless encountered many obstacles with his crew once shooting started.

> A great deal went wrong with the film. First, I was a new director and the production department tried to intimidate me by saying, "You have only twenty-five days." I had a producer [Stuart Miller] who wanted to be a director, and we didn't get along at all. I had a cameraman [Robert Planck] who had been under contract to Metro-Goldwyn-Mayer for twenty-five years, so that everything I wanted to do he said you couldn't do it.... The crew I had was just awful ... couldn't have cared less. They gave me open hostility. At a quarter of six you'd hear, "Fight night, tonight," that kind of thing, and you'd be trying to get a scene![28]

In spite of this, Frankenheimer still managed to create a coherent, frequently emotive portrait of family life in middle-class America. And though this account of a troubled teen was just one of many similarly-themed films Hollywood produced in the late Fifties, the director's realistic and non-exploitative treatment of his characters and their problems won favor from critics upon the movie's release in December 1956. *The Washington Post*'s Richard Coe, for example, wrote, "The season has brought many teenage tales, but this by far, is the most likely and best of the lot," while *Variety*, with somewhat less enthusiasm, remarked:

> A story of conflict between youth and parents, the plot indulges in "one note" dramatics that provide very little shading between the black and white of the problem, yet which are effective with the entertainment aim.... Debuting as a theatrical film director is John Frankenheimer, from TV, and he handles the switch neatly.[29]

The experience of making *The Young Stranger* proved to be so unpleasant for the young director, however, that he decided to return to live television once the production ended.[30]

By the mid–Fifties, the popularity of single-episode television dramas of the sort Frankenheimer had been directing was beginning to fade. But rather than abandoning the format, the networks introduced various changes, hoping to revive their audiences' interest. Episodes were now occasionally broadcast in color and new shows with 90-minute running times were developed in order to target middle class viewers who had the time and leisure to watch feature-length programs.[31] The first and best of these programs was *Playhouse 90*, the brainchild of Martin Manulis, Frankenheimer's supervisor on *Climax!*

Produced for CBS by Screen Gems, the program enjoyed a generous budget, allowing Manulis to draft many of the entertainment industry's most talented actors, writers and directors, and for the premier episode—"The Forbidden Area"— he tapped Frankenheimer, who would eventually shoot 28 episodes for the program over the next three and a half years.[32]

Just before its third season was to begin, however, Manulis would leave *Playhouse 90* and the Broadway producer Fred Coe stepped in to take over, precipitating two important changes. Pre-recorded segments were now introduced into the broadcasts with increasing frequency, a development which annoyed Frankenheimer. "[W]hen I found that television was turning into a purely tape and film medium, I started thinking about leaving."[33] And Coe also moved production from Los Angeles to New York, forcing Frankenheimer to depart from California, leaving behind his wife and their two infant daughters, Kristi and Elise. The separation from Carolyn was not entirely undesirable, however, as she and Frankenheimer were no longer on good terms.[34]

Though the move and his personal problems were distressing, Frankenheimer nevertheless continued to thrive professionally. In addition to *Playhouse 90*, he shot episodes for *The Dupont Show of the Month*, *Ford Startime* and *Sunday Showcase*. He also directed a series of programs based on stories written by Ernest Hemingway: "For Whom the Bell Tolls," "The Fifth Column" and "The Snows of Kilimanjaro." The latter featured Robert Ryan as an American hunter who dies from gangrene, but not before remembering moments from the past which have given his life value. This combination of fatalism and existentialism would surface often in Frankenheimer's subsequent work, in pictures as various as *Grand Prix*, *The Gypsy Moths* and *French Connection II*, where extreme circumstances coupled with physical suffering change the films' main characters, enabling them to find meaning and live with purpose in a brutal and absurd world.[35]

In less than a decade, Frankenheimer had transformed himself from a mediocre stage actor into one of live television's most important directors; but as the Fifties came to a close, the networks' increased use of pre-recorded material left him "feeling kind of like the village blacksmith after the invention of the automobile" and he decided to put the memories of *The Young Stranger* aside and look for work as a feature film director.[36] It was not a decision he made with pleasure. As he explained in a 1979 interview he gave to *Films and Filming*, "[H]onest to God, if live television hadn't ended, I'd still be doing it today."[37] The transition from television to features was hardly smooth. Frankenheimer was fired from his first effort, an adaptation of Truman Capote's 1958 novella *Breakfast at Tiffany's*, which had been brought to him by the writer George Axelrod. His removal from the project, after three months of work, came about when the picture's producer Martin Jurow signed Audrey Hepburn to play the film's lead. Hepburn and her husband Mel Ferrer "'Never heard of me,'" Frankenheimer recollected, "and they insisted that I be paid off and they hired another director, Blake Edwards."[38]

Frankenheimer managed to turn this disappointment into an opportunity, however. As he explained to Chris Chase at the *Los Angeles Times*: "I accused my agents, who were also Blake Edwards' agents, of conflict of interest, to put it mildly. And I said, 'You get me something, because here I am, and I've quit everything to do this.'"[39] Frankenheimer's agents came through a short time later and the disgruntled director was contacted by the producer Harold Hecht, who asked him to helm an adaptation of an Evan Hunter legal thriller titled *A Matter of Conviction*. Frankenheimer liked the story, which Hunter had based upon "newspaper accounts of gang feuds in East Harlem between entrenched Italians and Puerto Rican newcomers," and accepted the offer.[40]

The experience proved to be a tumultuous one, however, as the film's star Burt Lancaster was unhappy over the idea of working with a "television" director, and he attacked Frankenheimer on the set frequently. At one point, according to Lancaster's biographer Kate Buford, the actor even "lifted the tall director, acknowledged to be a master of the camera, and plonked him where he, the star, thought the camera should go."[41] Lancaster treated members of the film's cast poorly, too. On the last day of shooting, a violent argument erupted between him and his co-star (and former lover) Shelley Winters. "We got into the scene," the actress recalled, "and suddenly we weren't acting any more. We both began to break from the dialogue and call each other terrible names. The language was appalling on both our parts."[42] The actors were so loud, in fact, that a studio guard rushed onto the set and separated them.[43] In spite of Lancaster's behavior, Frankenheimer enjoyed himself making *The Young Savages*, as the film came to be titled. In an interview he gave to the *Los Angeles Times* during production he said, "I'm excited about this picture, and I'm doing it as honestly and realistically and as well as I can."[44] He was far less enthusiastic about his personal life during this period, however, as his marriage to Carolyn had now collapsed, and after cutting the film, he returned to New York City to distance himself from her.[45]

In New York, Frankenheimer continued to pursue his new career as a feature film director, meeting with friends he'd come to know during his days in television. One of these people was George Axelrod, whom he'd worked with briefly on *Breakfast at Tiffany's*. Axelrod was interested in making a movie out of Richard Condon's best selling political thriller *The Manchurian Candidate* and he wanted Frankenheimer to help him do it. The director liked the idea of working again with the writer, but he was unfamiliar with the novel. Axelrod, in response, asked Frankenheimer to meet him at a bookstore in Manhattan, and there the two spent an afternoon together, reading Condon's flamboyant novel. The story — which centers around a Communist plot to topple the United States government with the help of a brainwashed assassin — intrigued Frankenheimer and after finishing it, he told Axelrod that he would like to go in with him on the adaptation. The two then got on the phone and called the writer's agent. "It was three hours earlier in Hollywood," Frankenheimer said, "and by

Frank Sinatra and Laurence Harvey, the stars of *The Manchurian Candidate* (MGM, 1962), enjoy a break.

the end of the afternoon in California and the early evening in New York, [we] owned the rights."[46] The property proved to be comparatively inexpensive, as the novel "had been turned down by every studio in town.... [And] [i]t had been optioned and re-optioned and dropped and never been able to be made," a consequence of its lurid content and its sharp, satirical swipes at American political culture.[47] Axelrod and Frankenheimer then had the luck of attracting Frank Sinatra to the project, getting him to agree to play one of the leads and double as a producer, a development which landed them a financing deal. As Frankenheimer told Champlin: "[O]nce Sinatra said he wanted to do it ... United Artists backed it."[48]

Axelrod would devote his attention to the creation of a script after he and Frankenheimer solidified their arrangement with UA, and while the writer toiled on the adaptation, the director pursued other projects, the first being a screen adaptation of J.P. Miller's "The Days of Wine and Roses." Frankenheimer had shot a version of Miller's drama for *Playhouse 90* in 1958, but he was nevertheless released from the project when executives at Warner Bros. decided he did not have "a big enough name" to direct a production as prestigious and as expensive as the one they were planning.[49] Ironically, the picture (which was produced by Frankenheimer's one time mentor Martin Manulis) was given to Blake Edwards, the same person who'd replaced him on *Breakfast at Tiffany's*. "I've since gotten to like [Edwards] very much; he's a lovely guy," Frankenheimer told Champlin, looking back on the incident 30 years later. "But I wasn't president of his fan club back then."[50]

In November 1960, a few weeks after losing this assignment, Frankenheimer was again contacted by Harold Hecht, who wanted him this time to take over the direction of *Bird Man of Alcatraz*, a biopic about Robert Stroud, a convicted murderer who'd become an expert on bird diseases. The producer was unwilling to talk about the project over the phone, though, and since Frankenheimer was concerned about exposing himself to his wife Carolyn (and her lawyers) in Los Angeles, Hecht had to trick him into returning to the West Coast. The director recalled:

> I got a call from Hecht saying, "Look, we've got a problem with *Young Savages*. You've got to come out and work on it." And I said, "Harold, there's nothing wrong with that picture. Just don't f—k around with it, and get it out." He said, "You've got to come out." I knew something strange was up because Lancaster was at the airport to meet me.

The actor then explained that he wanted Frankenheimer to take over the direction of the Stroud project, as he had just fired the picture's director original Charles Crichton. "'[E]ven though we didn't get along,' Lancaster said, '...I loved the movie *Young Savages*, and I really want you to do [this].'" Frankenheimer took the job, and the film quickly resumed production.[51]

The director and the actor got along together on *Bird Man of Alcatraz* much better than they did on *The Young Savages*, but making the picture proved to be challenging anyway, as the unpredictable behavior of the film's animal actors made things on the set hectic, stretching out the picture's shooting schedule into February 1961. "Working with the birds was very, very tough.... [T]here's no such thing as a trained bird, only a hungry bird. And we just had to wait, and wait, and wait," Frankenheimer told Champlin.[52] Nor were the filmmakers helped very much by the bird handler they'd hired, a man named Canard, who was unable, or unwilling, to control the creatures.[53] Canard, moreover, was cruel, often treating the animals in a deplorable manner, something Lancaster recalled when he introduced the film at a Los Angeles retrospective hosted by the American Cinematheque in 1989. As Bill Higgins, who covered the event, wrote:

> During the repartee before the screening, Lancaster drew a gasp from the audience by revealing that, unbeknown to Frankenheimer or himself, a handler had prepared the birds in *Birdman* [sic] for scenes in which they grew ill and fell from their perches by pouring lighter fluid down their throats.[54]

Fortunately, Hecht and Lancaster eventually replaced Canard with "a wonderful guy named Ray Berwick, who really was able to train the birds to some extent and we re-did a lot of stuff we'd already done."[55] Berwick, incidentally, provided his services to Alfred Hitchcock on _The Birds_ (1963), as well. More complications emerged during post-production, however, when Frankenheimer, after putting together an early cut of the picture, came to the conclusion that the narrative was too long and too complicated; and to correct this, he felt that large sections of the picture had to be cut and new, more compelling material had to be introduced. Lancaster agreed with him on this and the two worked closely for several weeks, writing new scenes together, which they filmed that spring.[56]

Once this new footage was shot, Frankenheimer moved on to his next film, _All Fall Down_, an adaptation of a novel by James Leo Herlihy. His involvement with the production had actually begun several months earlier when the producer John Houseman approached him after his return to Los Angeles from New York City. Having signed a production deal with MGM, Houseman wanted to bring Herlihy's novel to the screen and he hoped Frankenheimer would lead the effort. A fan of the book and an admirer of the playwright William Inge, who'd been hired by Houseman to write the film's script, he "immediately agreed" to make the movie. Then while Frankenheimer worked on _Bird Man_, the producer went about finding the film's actors, giving roles to established players like Eva Marie Saint, Brandon De Wilde and Angela Lansbury, as well as the rising star Warren Beatty, who'd just completed work on Elia Kazan's _Splendor in the Grass_ for Warner Bros.[57]

Because of his friendship with Houseman, Frankenheimer enjoyed great latitude as he made _All Fall Down_, allowing him to create a high personal, highly stylized melodrama which drew favor from many critics. _Variety_ noted:

> Cinematically, _All Fall Down_ is virtually an art film. There are some masterful strokes in John Frankenheimer's design, notably the slow, poetic three-ply dissolves he has accomplished with editor Fredric Steinkamp, and the sensitive and painstaking photographic qualities, texture and composition he has executed.[58]

But despite the leeway Houseman gave Frankenheimer, some obstacles did materialize during production. The director had hoped to film _All Fall Down_ on location in Cleveland, where much of this story about a handsome adventurer and his spinster lover takes place, but MGM refused.[59] Beatty proved to be difficult on the set, too. Houseman in his memoir _Final Dress_ recalled:

> From the start, our most serious problem was young Mr. Beatty. With his angelic arrogance, his determination to emulate Marlon Brando and Jimmy Dean, and his half-baked, overzealous notions of "Method" acting, he succeeded in perplexing and antagonizing not only his fellow actors but our entire crew.

The filmmakers were nevertheless pleased with the film they made, confident that it would enjoy success at the box office, in spite of its art house trappings. Their hopes were smashed, however, by the manner in which the picture's release was handled. Houseman explained:

All Fall Down was [first] booked into the Plaza Theatre in New York and into a handful of similarly prestigious small houses in major cities. The wisdom of this strategy was confirmed by the news that the film had been chosen, not once but twice, as the U.S. entry at the Cannes Film Festival: first by the American Motion Picture Producers' Association and then again by members of the festival's own selection committee. Then, overnight, all our well-laid plans were blown sky-high.

MGM's most ambitious picture of the year was ... *Four Horsemen of the Apocalypse*.... Booked with considerable hoopla into flagship theaters all over the country, it turned out to be the year's major critical and popular disaster.

Desperately casting about for an instant substitute for its faltering monster, MGM discovered that it had only one film available, *All Fall Down*—a small, black-and-white program picture with no major stars. Prints were rushed through the labs, and within a few days, with no time for publicity or preparation, our sophisticated, neurotic little film was thrown into dozens of oversized movie palaces that habitually house major spectacles and musicals in color. Inevitably it withered and died.[60]

After completing *All Fall Down*, Frankenheimer spent the summer of 1961 preparing *The Manchurian Candidate*, polishing the script with Axelrod and casting the picture's remaining parts, giving roles to several actors he'd worked with before, including James Gregory, Whit Bissell and Madame Spivy.[61] He again hired Lionel Lindon to supervise the photography and David Amram, his composer on *The Young Savages*, to write the score. Frankenheimer had never worked with Sinatra, however, and the thought intimidated him. "I was scared of it. I had heard he was very difficult. I had heard that he treated directors badly, all those things."[62] But problems with the star never really materialized, short of a minor squabble over who should play Mrs. Iselin, the mother of the film's brainwashed assassin character. While Frankenheimer wanted Angela Lansbury, who'd starred in *All Fall Down*, to have the part, Sinatra insisted upon his friend Lucille Ball. The director then had Sinatra watch a screening copy of *All Fall Down*, after which the actor, struck by Lansbury's over-the-top turn as Warren Beatty's possessive mother, told him: "That's the lady."[63]

Frankenheimer had high hopes for *The Manchurian Candidate*, but the picture's performance was less than spectacular during its first theatrical run late in 1962.[64] This failure is perhaps hard to understand as critics by and large responded to the movie positively—*Film Daily* named it "Best Motion Picture" of 1962. Moreover, its cast featured not only one of the era's most popular stars, Frank Sinatra, but glamorous personalities like Laurence Harvey and Janet Leigh, too. And with its absurdist portrait of Cold War tensions, it was also funny, anticipating Kubrick's similarly themed, and commercially successful, *Dr. Strangelove* by two years.[65]

In the decades since its release, of course, *The Manchurian Candidate* has become one of the most famous movies produced in Hollywood in the Sixties. Much of its fame, no doubt, is a result of its prophetic storyline—its depiction of a sniper who not only shoots his mother to death, but her husband, a U.S. senator, as well, much as Lee Harvey Oswald would fire upon and kill President Kennedy a little more than a year after the film's premier. The parallels

A scene from *All Fall Down* (UA, 1962). Seated on the left is Brandon De Wilde.
The woman to the right is Madame Spivy, who also appears in *The Manchurian
Candidate*. In the center sits Frankenheimer's future wife Evans Evans.

between art and life, in fact, aroused a groundswell of interest in the picture
after the president's death, and United Artists briefly entertained the idea of
re-releasing it, a move, however, which was blocked by the film's producers,
Frankenheimer, Axelrod and Sinatra. As Axelrod explained to *The Washington
Post* in 1988, "The climate of the times was such that having an assassination
picture floating around seemed to be in grotesque bad taste."[66] The film was
then withdrawn from circulation, and subsequently slipped into obscurity, only
showing up on television a couple of times over the next two decades. But then,
in 1987, *The Manchurian Candidate* was given a special screening at the New
York Film Festival, an occasion which sparked a renewal of critical interest and
eventually prompted UA to give the picture a second theatrical release. Now
though, Sinatra not only supported the effort, he led it, and in 1988 the picture
opened again nationally, this time enjoying commercial success.[67] "The twenty-
six-year old film," wrote Lansbury's biographers Rob Edelman and Audrey
Kupferberg, "ended up earning raves, and box-office profits, and was as entertaining and riveting as any new film to hit movie screens that year."[68]

   Frankenheimer found himself without a new feature to engage his attention after he wrapped up *The Manchurian Candidate*. But thanks to the four

pictures he'd just directed, he was now financially secure, leaving him free to pursue non-commercial projects. And during this time, he agreed to shoot a promotional television program for the American Civil Liberties Union, a venture which had been spearheaded in part by the actor Kirk Douglas. The project never bore fruit, but it did introduce Frankenheimer to Edward Lewis, a producer who worked for Brynna, Douglas' production company after the project's cancellation, Lewis asked Frankenheimer if he'd like to make *Seven Days in May*, an adaptation of a best selling political thriller written by Fletcher Nebel and Charles Bailey II.[69] Like Condon's *The Manchurian Candidate*, Nebel and Bailey's 1962 novel focuses on a group of plotters who hope to overthrow the U.S. government. But while the conspiracy Condon invented is initiated and orchestrated by foreign, Communist ideologues, the threat which appears in *Seven Days in May* arises from within as a network of anti–Communist politicians, journalists and military leaders plot to abduct and eliminate a sitting president. A liberal democrat, Frankenheimer took the job because he was concerned over what he regarded as a blossoming of extremist sentiments in the United States, with anti–Communist groups like the John Birch Society "springing up all over the place"; and the idea of making a movie that offered harsh critiques of such organizations, and the hawkish politicians they supported, appealed to him.[70]

Frankenheimer and Lewis spent a year preparing *Seven Days in May*, hiring Rod Serling to write the script, Ellsworth Fredericks to direct the photography and Edward Boyle to design the film's sets. The filmmakers managed to sign several popular actors, too, including Frederic March, Edmond O'Brien, Ava Gardner, Kirk Douglas and, once again, Burt Lancaster. And when the film began shooting, the production proceeded with few difficulties, although Frankenheimer again found himself at odds with one of his actors. This time, however, problems were caused not by Lancaster, but, rather, by Douglas, who had become chagrined with the role he was playing — a Marine officer who betrays his supervisor at the Pentagon, a character played by Lancaster. As Frankenheimer explained to Higham:

> Kirk Douglas was very jealous of Lancaster; he felt he was playing a secondary role to Lancaster, which indeed he was.... He wanted to be Burt Lancaster. He's wanted to be Burt Lancaster all his life. In the end it came to sitting down with Douglas and saying, "Look, you punk, if you don't like it, get the hell out."[71]

Frankenheimer faced an additional problem when he learned from government officials that he would not be allowed to shoot footage at the Pentagon, where so much of the film's action takes place. The director got around this, though, by using hidden cameras, a tactic he would return to again when he made *Seconds, French Connection II* and *The Challenge*. Douglas, in his memoir *The Ragman's Son*, recalled:

> We needed just one crucial shot of the Pentagon to make it authentic. No filming allowed there. We had to get it. No way. So we stole the shot. We concealed the camera

in a van, parked on the street opposite the Pentagon. I strode up to the entrance, dressed in my marine colonel's uniform. The guard on duty saluted me. I saluted back. I walked into the Pentagon, waited a bit, then walked out. The guard looked at me a little strangely, but he was well trained, and not about to question a superior officer.[72]

In the summer of 1963, just as he was finishing *Seven Days in May*, Frankenheimer was contacted by Burt Lancaster, who'd gone to France to shoot another picture for United Artists, a World War II–era adventure called *The Train*. Once again, the actor had fired his director — this time it was Arthur Penn — and he needed Frankenheimer to step in and take over. The idea of making an action movie did not especially appeal to the director, but, as he explained to Tony Macklin, he took the job anyway, a decision which was to a certain extent forced upon him.

I only went to do the picture because Burt Lancaster asked me to do it and because private detectives were chasing me all over Southern California because of my ex-wife [Carolyn].... I had to get the hell out of there.[73]

Frankenheimer enjoyed living and working in France and in the spring of 1964, after he finished work on the picture, he and the actress Evans Evans, whom he'd married the previous December, took an apartment on the Iles St. Louis in Paris.[74] But as Frankenheimer had agreed to make another film — a science fiction feature called *Seconds*— with Edward Lewis before he left for France, the newlyweds were not allowed to stay long in their adopted country, and they soon returned to Los Angeles.

Shot for Joel Productions (another company owned by Kirk Douglas), *Seconds* is an adaptation of a 1963 novel by David Ely, which tells the story of a wealthy banking executive who undergoes radical plastic surgery in order to adopt a new life.[75] As he had on *The Manchurian Candidate*, Frankenheimer not only directed the picture, but co-produced it, too, enjoying great control over its development. He worked closely on the script with scenarist Lewis Carlino, for example, supervised the design and construction of the sets with art director Ted Haworth and discussed at length the look he wanted the film to have with his cinematographer James Wong Howe. He was not entirely successful, however, in persuading Paramount, the studio which financed the movie, to furnish him with the cast he wanted. Originally, he intended to give the film's main part to Laurence Olivier, but Paramount balked at the idea, worried that the aging British actor would not be able to draw large audiences. The part was then offered to Marlon Brando, who turned it down, then to Rock Hudson, who at that time was one of Hollywood's most popular stars. Hudson was worried, though, that he lacked the ability to play the part of the frustrated banker who trades his old identity for a new one. "I'm not that good an actor to be able to make the transformation," he told Frankenheimer. Undaunted, the director then decided that the film might be helped if he cast a second actor to play the banker *before* he undergoes the identity-changing operation. "I suddenly realized that this was the way to do the movie, that the same actor couldn't play both roles anyway." And for the part, he decided to use an old friend named John Randolph, an actor who'd been blacklisted in Hollywood since the McCarthy era.[76] A number of other blacklisted figures were also given parts in the picture, including Jeff Corey and Will Geer, who'd both refused to cooperate with the federal government when they were called up and asked to testify before the House Un-American Activities Committee in the early Fifties.

Frankenheimer felt great confidence about *Seconds* and he persuaded Paramount to premier the film at Cannes in May 1966. But to his dismay, the movie was received with boos and jeers as the audience recoiled from its avant-garde visuals and its bleak point of view — its suggestion that happiness is not attainable for some people.[77] As a consequence, Paramount put little effort into promoting the picture for its release in the States later that fall, and because of this the film vanished quickly, a disappointment which forced the director to re-evaluate his approaches to filmmaking. He explained to *American Film*:

> For me, *Seconds* was a terrible failure. It was a commercial disaster. And that's with the biggest star in the business at the time, Rock Hudson, in it. And I just ... it really shook me. I just said, hey, wait a minute. If I want to stay as a viable, mainline movie director in this business, I've gotta do something that's not a collector's item. After *Seconds* came out and didn't work, I said, I've gotta do more stuff like *The Train*. And that's when *Grand Prix* happened.[78]

Filmed during the spring and summer of 1966, *Grand Prix* was a labor of love for Frankenheimer, an opportunity for him to make a picture about one of his favorite diversions, Formula One auto racing. The idea for the movie had actually come to him two years earlier, shortly after he'd arrived in France to work on *The Train*. He told Champlin:

> I started going to a lot of races.... When I went to 24 Hours of Le Mans, and a lot of Formula One races and saw those crowds of two hundred, three hundred thousand people, that really triggered it.[79]

Frankenheimer was able to convince MGM that a film about the world's most expensive sport would find receptive audiences on this side of the Atlantic, and he and the producer Edward Lewis subsequently spent several months securing shooting locations in Europe and the United States, working closely with the *Fédération Internationale de l'Automobile*, the organization that oversees Grand Prix racing. A great deal of time was spent, too, putting the cast together and developing the film's script, for which they hired the television writer Robert Aurthur and then William Hanley, who would again work with Frankenheimer on *The Gypsy Moths*.[80]

In spite of the great efforts that went into preparing *Grand Prix*, making the picture proved to be exceptionally demanding as Frankenheimer led a 200-person crew around Europe, shooting scripted material as well as footage of actual Formula One races in France, England, Belgium, Italy and Holland.[81] The production was not without dangerous moments, as well. While the film was being shot in Monte Carlo, for example, Yves Montand, one of its stars, almost died. As Frankenheimer explained to *Road and Track* in 1992:

> Montand had a terrible crash.... And luckily, he got out of the car. He was covered with gasoline; he started to light a cigarette and just before he got the cigarette into his mouth, I knocked the lighter out of his hand. Otherwise he would have killed himself. That was horrendous.[82]

Post-production proved to be taxing, too. Originally, MGM had planned to release the picture in the summer of 1967, but the chiefs at the studio changed their minds, deciding instead to release it in December 1966 in order to tap Christmas audiences, and Frankenheimer, along with a team of six editors, had to rush to put a copy of the film together. But although this experience was stressful and exhausting, he felt afterward that the haste with which the movie was cut did not hurt the final product. As he told the *Los Angeles Times*: "I don't think ... that the film would be significantly different or better if I'd worked on it for another six months."[83]

Grand Prix did fairly well at the box office and with critics, and its success solidified Frankenheimer's standing with MGM, prompting the studio to reward him and Lewis with a new, and rather expansive, contract. As the *Los Angeles Times* reported in January 1967, five weeks after the film's premier: "Metro-Goldwyn-Mayer has signed a four picture deal with the respective production companies of director John Frankenheimer and producer Edward Lewis." Given a suite at the studio, the filmmakers proceeded to quickly develop the pictures they'd agreed to make. The first, a World War II farce called *The Extraordinary Seaman*, was filmed that summer in Veracruz, Mexico. The second, an adaptation of Bernard Malamud's novel *The Fixer*, was shot in the winter of 1967-1968 in Hungary. And the third, a skydiving adventure film called *The Gypsy Moths* was shot in the fall of 1968 in rural Kansas. Unfortunately, these pictures all failed at the box office and Frankenheimer and Lewis' relationship with the studio ended with *The Gypsy Moths*. The fourth film they were expected to make, "an original western musical" called *Lady Gay*, was never realized.[84]

While the arrangement with MGM kept Frankenheimer busy, it did not prevent him from pursuing other projects. In March 1968, for example, he was recruited by an advertising agency named Papert, Koenig, Lois, Inc. to shoot promotional material for Robert F. Kennedy shortly after the New York senator announced his decision to run for president.[85] Frankenheimer took the job, he said, because he disliked President Johnson and supported Kennedy's opposition to the United States' involvement in Vietnam. And though he and RFK only worked together for three months, they nevertheless developed a close relationship. As Frankenheimer explained to Champlin: "I did all the television, all the ads.... We became very good friends."[86] The director actually drove Kennedy to the Ambassador Hotel in downtown Los Angeles from his home in Malibu Colony the night the candidate was murdered. And though he didn't witness the shooting, he was standing nearby when it happened. As Nina Easton wrote in her profile of Frankenheimer:

> On the night of the 1968 California primary ... Kennedy was scheduled to return to Frankenheimer's Malibu home. While waiting for Kennedy at the entrance to the ballroom, Frankenheimer felt a person brush by; to this day, he's certain it was Sirhan Sirhan. Late that night, after the gunshots and the commotion, when at last it became clear that Kennedy had been critically wounded, Frankenheimer returned home alone — where six rented TV sets that Kennedy had requested sat eerily in the living room.[87]

The murder would leave a scar on Frankenheimer. As he told Macklin, he fell into "a very deeply depressed mood" after the killing, which he "didn't come out of ... for several years."[88] And to Rita Kempley at *The Washington Post*, he explained:

> I had a severe case of burnout after Bobby Kennedy's death.... I was 38 years old and my world was over as I know it. For the first time in my life during the campaign I really felt I was part of something that mattered, that wasn't just something on a page. I went into a decline and I didn't want to go on.[89]

Frankenheimer did not abandon his career at this point, but he did separate himself from Hollywood, moving back to Paris, where he and Evans began to take French lessons together. And although the geographical distance between them was now great, he continued to collaborate with Lewis, and together the partners worked on an adaptation of *The Horsemen*— a 1967 novel by the French writer Joseph Kessel about buzkashi, an "everyman-for-himself form of polo" played in Afghanistan.[90] The director and producer spent much of 1969 developing this project, with the understanding that Columbia, the studio which was financing the production, wanted a three-hour "road-show" epic, much in the vein of Lean's *Lawrence of Arabia* (1962) and *Dr. Zhivago* (1965). A scheduling conflict with the film's star Omar Sharif (who'd appeared in both *Lawrence* and *Zhivago*), however, postponed shooting until 1970, and this left Frankenheimer open to work on other projects. He explained to Pratley:

> Sharif [was] unavailable because of a prior commitment he had to James Clavell, and I was off for ten months with nothing to do, which didn't bother me, except that I was being paid by Columbia and the studio asked me if I would direct [another] film.[91]

The project which the studio offered him, an adaptation of a 1967 novel by Madison Jones called *An Exile*, did not really interest Frankenheimer, but he took the job. Almost immediately, he came to regret his decision, after finding himself at odds with the chiefs at Columbia, who refused his request to have Gene Hackman play the film's central character — a Tennessee sheriff who ruins his career and his home life after he falls in love with a moonshiner's teenaged daughter.[92] Instead, the lead was given to Gregory Peck, who was hoping at that point in his career to get away from the likeable hero roles he'd been playing for decades.

Frankenheimer came back to the U.S. to make *I Walk the Line*, filming it in the fall of 1969 in Tennessee and northern California, and once the picture was in the can, he returned his attention to *The Horsemen*, heading back to Europe for the film's primary shooting with leading man Sharif and supporting actors Leigh Taylor-Young and Jack Palance.[93] The production was burdened with numerous problems, though. A week into filming, Frankenheimer's cinematographer James Wong Howe had to step down because of illness. Fortunately, the director was able to replace him with another great technician, Claude Renoir, the nephew of Jean Renoir. But the production received another blow several weeks later when Columbia changed its mind about the type of movie it wanted. As Frankenheimer explained to Champlin, he was shooting in Spain when

> the powers that be ... came to the location to see me. They stood around in their dark suits and said "We've decided ... we don't want any more road-show movies. We're going to release this one just like any other, and what we want is a movie that runs two hours and not three and a quarter. There are going to have to be some cuts."[94]

Not wanting to lose the project, Frankenheimer agreed to the studio's demands, at first trimming the shooting script and then discarding large sections of the narrative months later in Paris, where he and editor Harold Kress cut the picture.[95] And although these measures ensured the movie's release, they damaged it, too, leaving *The Horsemen* disjointed, erratically paced and, in its final moments, difficult to follow, factors which contributed to its mediocre performance in the U.S. after its premier in the summer of 1971. Nor was the picture helped by the critics, many of whom were put off not only by the movie's continuity problems, but the florid manner in which the characters speak and the film's relentless violence, a trait which prompted Vincent Canby to remark:

> Here is fiction designed to glorify machismo of the most ignorant, savage sort, the cult of manliness that has, I suspect, its closest civilized equivalent in the totalitarian political movements of the 1930's, which put so much stress on style and very little on content.[96]

In Europe, though, the film enjoyed good reviews and strong sales; it also won a *Prix de Triomphe*, France's equivalent to the Academy Award.[97]

The Horsemen would be the last collaboration between Frankenheimer and Lewis, but neither of them realized this at the time; and after he finished *The Horsemen*, the director headed out to India to scout locations for *The Devil Drives*, a film about a nineteenth century explorer named Sir Richard Burton, which the partners had successfully pitched to Columbia. But although a script for the film was written (by John Richard Hopkins), *The Devil Drives* never went into production and Frankenheimer returned to Paris.[98] Freed momentarily from professional obligations, he used this time to pursue his newest passion, cooking; and for several months, he worked in restaurants throughout Europe.[99]

Frankenheimer's ability to speak and read the language of his adopted country helped him considerably when he began his next film, an adaptation of Nicholas Mosley's 1968 novel *Impossible Object*, much of which was shot in Paris. The project was the brainchild of a producer named Jud Kinberg, who'd obtained the rights to Mosley's book and secured financing for the film from a businessman named Robert Bradford. In 1972, Kinberg offered the picture to Frankenheimer, and because the director enjoyed Mosley's book, he came onto the project.[100] But working with Mosley, who Kinberg and Bradford had retained to write the film's script, proved to be difficult, as the novelist frequently challenged Frankenheimer's efforts to simplify his story's structure, and for this he was eventually fired.[101] The director was able, though, to recruit several people he enjoyed working with, including his wife Evans, the British actor Alan Bates, who'd starred in *The Fixer*, and Claude Renoir, who'd lensed *The Horsemen*.

Nonetheless, making *Impossible Object* turned out to be very difficult as Bradford failed to raise enough money for the production, and midway through filming, Frankenheimer was forced to use his own credit cards to meet expenses.[102] Bradford also mismanaged the picture's premier, rushing it off to Cannes before Frankenheimer had edited it to his satisfaction.[103] The film was received with much less hostility than *Seconds*, however, the last film which Frankenheimer had screened at the famous festival. The reviewer at *Variety*, for example, responded with this optimistic (if hastily written) assessment:

> The delicacy of the love tale, the tasteful nudity and the serio-comic love tangles are handled with fine visual aplomb by Frankenheimer helped by a good cast. Perhaps a little pruning of some of the sidebar wish-fulfillment segs of a sort of Fellinian party and love scene might be pruned a bit. Otherwise this looks good for European chances and should find its way stateside in urban centers with playoff indicated on its exploitable theme and treatment with some tightening a help.[104]

Unfortunately, Bradford was unable to land a distribution deal for the film in the U.S., a failure which pushed the production further into bankruptcy and prevented him from paying off the costs he had incurred; as a result of this, his creditors seized the film and "locked [it] in the vaults of [a] Paris bank"; and though Frankenheimer managed to secure a copy of the picture for himself — which he was able to screen at the Atlanta Film Festival in 1973 — *Impossible Object* would never receive a theatrical release on this side of the Atlantic.[105]

The director came back again to the States for his next movie, an exhausting interpretation of *The Iceman Cometh*, Eugene O'Neill's 1940 play about a group of daydreaming alcoholics and the problems they meet when they are forced to face reality. His involvement on the project began when he was still in Paris, months before he started shooting *Impossible Object*. Frankenheimer had been reluctant at first to take the job when it was offered to him by the producer Ely Landau, who as head of a production company called the American Film Theatre, wanted "to bring noted twentieth-century plays from Broadway and the West End" to movie audiences throughout the U.S.[106] But he changed

Hickey (Lee Marvin, leaning on bar) shares a moment with his friends in *The Iceman Cometh* (American Film Theatre, 1973). The blonde-haired woman in the foreground is Frankenheimer's wife, Evans Evans. The others pictured, from left to right, are Nancy Juno Hawkins, Hildy Brooks and Stephen Pearlman.

his mind when, as he explained to Champlin: "My ego kind of got in there and I said, 'If I don't do this someone else will and they're liable to screw it up. You better do this.'"[107] Frankenheimer then hired Thomas Quinn Curtiss, a film critic at the Paris-based *International Herald Tribune* (who'd been one of O'Neill acquaintances), to tailor the notoriously lengthy play for the screen, asking him to trim scenes and eliminate characters, while at the same time preserving the original's structural and thematic integrity. During rehearsal for the production in Los Angeles in late 1972, though, Frankenheimer and the ensemble cast he'd put together (which included old friends like Robert Ryan, Frederic March and Lee Marvin, as well as his wife Evans) discovered that O'Neill's story no longer made as much sense as it had before Curtiss' emendations, and to correct this, "we replaced at least half of the lines we had taken out" and decided eventually "to make the film as long as it had to be."[108]

With a running time of 239 minutes, *The Iceman Cometh* is Frankenheimer's longest feature. It is also one of the few films he made which was met with almost universal acclaim when it was released, as critics fawned over the performances of its cast, Jack Smith's realistic set design and cinematographer Ralph Woolsey's dexterous camerawork. The review which appeared in *Variety*, for instance, declared:

> The excellence of the cast alone, and the fame of the work and its author make this staged play worth the ticket.... It requires stamina, of course, to sit through four hours, but the experience is special.[109]

The Iceman Cometh was filmed on a sound stage which Landau had leased from 20th Century–Fox, and during production, Frankenheimer was approached by executives from the studio who asked him if he'd like to direct the sequel to *The French Connection*, William Friedkin's tremendously successful 1971 police drama about a pair of cops who pursue a French drug dealer in New York City. Frankenheimer was offered the job, he said, because the studio wanted to set the sequel in Marseilles and they needed a director who spoke French. Because he liked the idea of returning to France, he agreed to make the film, but he could not begin the picture immediately because the sequel's writer Robert Dillon had not yet completed the script.[110] However, another screenplay by Dillon, a comedy about gangsters called *99 and 44/100% Dead!* was ready, and the studio offered it to Frankenheimer, as well, and he accepted.

A futuristic adventure story about a hit man who finds himself caught between a pair of rival gangs, *99 and 44/100% Dead!* was shot in Los Angeles and Seattle during the fall of 1973, with Ralph Woolsey again serving as director of photography. Unfortunately, the production did not go smoothly, as Frankenheimer found himself frequently at odds with the film's leading man Richard Harris over the way in which the actor should interpret his part. As he told Pratley: "I argued with [him] continually telling him to stop playing up the comedy and humor of the situation and trying to be bigger than life ... to be cute.... I wanted him to be real." And the strain between them, Frankenheimer felt, damaged the quality of the picture. "He and I did not get along through the first two-thirds of the movie, and I think that hurt us."[111] Moreover, this self-consciously kitschy film, despite being filled with gun play, car chases and sex, failed at the box office and with the critics, yielding for Frankenheimer some of the worst reviews of his career. In his write-up for *Time*, for instance, Richard Schickel sneered, "Call it *100% Dead* and be done with it," while Gary Arnold at *The Washington Post* complained:

> *99 and 44/100% Dead!* ... is an unsavory blend of the vicious and the facetious. About three parts of the former to one of the latter. The intention was evidently an elaborate deadpan spoof convention gangster movies, but the effects are not amusing.[112]

Frankenheimer's work on *French Connection II* proved to be far more successful. As serious as *99 and 44/100% Dead!* is comic, this character-driven thriller marked a return to form for the director, much of its strength arising from Claude Renoir's camerawork and Gene Hackman's performance as the film's ornery, but somewhat endearing protagonist Eddie "Popeye" Doyle. The

Edmond O'Brien, John Frankenheimer and Katherine Baumann at the cast party for *99 and 44/100% Dead!* (20th Century–Fox, 1974).

film also featured an especially engaging narrative, the result of Frankenheimer's decision to take the script from Robert Dillon and pass it on to two experienced "police" movie writers, Alex Jacobs (*The Seven Ups*) and Pete Hamill (*Badge 373*). In 2006, Hamill — who'd known Eddie Egan, the New York City police detective upon whom Hackman's character Popeye Doyle was based — recalled his involvement in the project:

> [Frankenheimer] called me from Marseilles, asking me to help [and] I said I would try to get there within two days. "Why not one?" he said, and laughed nervously. I never asked why he called me. Someone hand-delivered a script to my place in New York and I read it on the plane.
>
> John, at that time, had a major problem. He had already shot nine days of the existing script. He had developed a reputation for going over budget, so had no flexibility. He couldn't re-shoot what was already in the can.
>
> That gave me a problem too, since I had to write around the existing pieces, which, as always, had been shot out of order. It was like working on a jigsaw puzzle. The basic problem was that Hackman, a great movie actor, had nothing to act. And the reason for that was that Roy Scheider [Hackman's co-star in *The French Connection*] was not in the sequel, and Hackman had nobody to bounce his lines off. He would never talk to a French cop the way he talked to Scheider in the Billy Friedkin original.
>
> ...My first work was on the following day's pages, trying to make the character sound

like Popeye Doyle.... Within a day-and-a-half (with naps in between) I had written enough for them to keep shooting for six or seven days.... Hackman was ecstatic. He had something to act! .... At any rate, I was in Marseilles for nine days and fixed the dialogue throughout.[113]

Regrettably, *French Connection II* failed to become a breakaway hit, though the film was received well by reviewers, winning praise even from Vincent Canby, one of the director's least forgiving critics:

> The concerns of "French Connection II" are not much different from those of old Saturday-afternoon movie serials that used to place their supermen in jeopardy and then figure ways of getting them out. The difference is in the quality of the supermen and in their predicaments.
> Popeye is a colorful and interesting—though hardly noble—character, and when the Marseilles drug people kidnap him, forcibly create a heroin habit in him, and then release him, you have a very special kind of jeopardy that the film and Mr. Hackman exploit most effectively. The perverse intensity and the anguish in these sequences recall some of Mr. Frankenheimer's best work in "The Manchurian Candidate" and "Seconds."[114]

French Connection II may not have given Frankenheimer the popular exposure he'd wanted, but it did help him land his next picture, *Black Sunday*, a high-budget "disaster" spectacular about a pack of terrorists who attack the Super Bowl with a blimp. As Champlin explained in a profile of the picture he wrote for the *Los Angeles Times*: "Paramount, looking for someone to do 'Black Sunday,' sent one of its executives to the first press screening of 'French Connection II' at the Egyptian in Hollywood, and it won [him] the assignment."[115] Frankenheimer would spend much of 1975 back in the States, developing *Black Sunday*, casting actors, scouting locations, and overseeing the creation of the script with writers Ernest Lehman, Kenneth Ross and Ivan Moffat. Because of his desire for verisimilitude, he also set out to get footage of real football games and real blimps, an objective which required him to work closely with organizations like the National Football League and the Goodyear Tire & Rubber Company.[116] Robert Evans—who produced the picture along with Robert L. Rosen — remembered in his memoir *The Kid Stays in the Picture*:

> John Frankenheimer ... possibly more than any other director I've worked with, knew how to execute an almost impossible logistic feat. First he got permission from the NFL; then the Orange Bowl in Miami, where the Super Bowl was taking place; then shooting the actual Super Bowl (Pittsburgh vs. Dallas). He then [convinced] Goodyear into allowing us to use their blimp as the "heavy" in the picture.

The scale of the production was indeed great, requiring the director to shoot on location in Miami, Washington, D.C., Los Angeles and Morocco, with "a cast of thousands upon thousands."[117] And in the fall of 1976, once primary shooting was completed, he was sure that he'd met the task of making a film which was at once realistic and exciting, and expected the picture to do well at the box office. The chiefs at Paramount were confident, too, and after watching an early cut of the picture, they offered Frankenheimer "two million dollars worth of new commitments."[118] *Sunday*'s release was postponed several months, however, when problems with the lab which was preparing the special effects for the film's climactic sequence materialized. In an interview he gave to *Films and Filming*, the director explained:

> [W]e had a terrible time getting the blimp into the stadium. We could have released the picture six months earlier if we had been able to solve that, because we were waiting for the optical people. The first opticals we had were lousy; second ones were lousy. We had to do the whole thing three times.[119]

When the picture premiered in April 1977, sadly, it failed to draw the numbers the filmmakers had expected, a disappointment Frankenheimer attributed to its belated release, arguing that when the movie arrived in theaters the public's appetite for disaster movies had largely disappeared. "We just came out at the wrong time," he told Glenn Lovell at *The San Jose Mercury News*. He believed, as well, that some of the film's novelty was spoiled by Universal's release of *Two Minute Warning* (a similarly themed thriller in which a sniper terrorizes a crowd at a football stadium) in the fall of 1976.[120]

Frankenheimer fell into a funk and began to drink heavily after the release of *Black Sunday*. "When [the movie] ... didn't go through the roof, as everyone [said] it would," he told *The Houston Chronicle*, "I used that as an excuse to go over the edge. I'd always been a heavy drinker. It got out of control."[121] He continued to work during this time, though, spending much of 1977 pursuing projects at Paramount, including an adaptation of a war novel by William D. Blankenship called *Tiger Ten*, which was never realized, and *Players*, a film about tennis, which eventually went to British director Anthony Harvey. He also worked briefly on *The Brinks Job* with the independent producer Dino De Laurentiis, but creative differences arose between the two and the picture was subsequently given to William Friedkin. As Frankenheimer explained to *Films and Filming*:

> I wanted to make one movie, and Dino wanted to make another; and he didn't really like my script, and I really didn't agree with him about the direction he wanted the picture to go. And we parted as friends.

Then, late that year, Michael Eisner, the head of Paramount, came to Frankenheimer and asked him if he'd like to shoot a horror film, which the director considered and agreed to do.[122]

Collaborating again with the producer Robert L. Rosen, whom he'd worked with on *French Connection II* and *Black Sunday*, Frankenheimer invited David Seltzer, who'd penned the 1976 hit *The Omen*, to write the film's screenplay, having him develop the plot around a giant, mercury-poisoned bear that attacks human beings in the Maine woods. Certain that the story would lure audiences into the theater, Frankenheimer went to great lengths to keep the details of the

Resistance and protest surface often in Frankenheimer's films. Here a Native American activist named Hawks (Armand Assante), flanked by supporters (actors John A. Sheymayne and Steve Sheymayne; it is unknown which is John or Steve), takes a stand against a logging company in *Prophecy* (Paramount, 1979).

script a secret. He explained to Roderick Mann at the *Los Angeles Times*, right before shooting began:

> We've got a subject which could easily be ripped off by TV, or by some quickie film producer. Both Bob Rosen ... and I have seen how easily this can happen, and since we've got a subject which is quite extraordinary, we're not going to take any chances. So we've hired our own security force, headed by this former CIA man. And the whole crew has been required to sign a loyalty oath.... [N]o scripts have been allowed out of this office. Both the leading man and the leading lady were required to read the script right here. Other players read only their own roles.

Frankenheimer was guarded about the film's title, too, telling the press that the picture would be called *The Windsor Project*, when it was actually *Prophecy*. The "Windsor" in the bogus title, by the way, "was taken from the name of one of the Paramount Studio gates."[123]

Although Eisner budgeted $7 million for the movie, much of *Prophecy* was shot in British Columbia, rather than in the U.S., in order to keep costs low.[124] (Frankenheimer and Rosen would again return to Canada for similar reasons when they made *Dead Bang* and *The Fourth War*.) The interiors, on the other hand, were filmed in Los Angeles, where Frankenheimer used a series of puppets designed by Robert Dawson for the film's monsters. He did this, he explained, because of what had happened with *Black Sunday*. Instead of having the film's special effects produced in the lab, he wanted to

> have every element of the movie there [on the set]. In other words, we did have a twelve and a half foot creature on the set that we used for the tie-in shots, and we used other creatures, too. We had about three beasts for the big one. That whole set was also built in two-thirds scale. And we had a beast that was only seven feet tall, with a dancer, a mime, who controlled it. We needed that so the beast could move freely going forward.... And we had a full functional head that was separate from the body.... We were not at the mercy of the optical department in this picture.[125]

And these measures proved to be successful as *Prophecy* arrived in theaters without delay and performed well, turning a profit. The reviews it received, however, were generally poor, as many critics charged the film with being unoriginal and didactic.[126] The write-up in *Variety* was especially disparaging:

> *Prophecy* is the picture that had an ex–CIA agent in charge of security so the plot wouldn't be ripped off by television. Well, he must have slipped up because the same film, or variations of it, have been on after midnight for 30 years or more. Quite simply, director John Frankenheimer has made a frightening monster movie that people could laugh at for generations to come.[127]

The response from *Time* was just as scathing: "*Prophecy* is silly, overproduced and boring; there isn't a single scary moment. When the audience shrieks, it is only because the characters are too stupid to get out of harm's painfully obvious way."[128] Even Frankenheimer's frequent advocate Charles Champlin regarded the movie with scorn: "When mutation horror misses, it strikes camp ... evoking Godzilla rather than some god-awful truth, and thus it is in *Prophecy*."[129]

In spite of the commercial success that came with *Prophecy*, Frankenheimer's spirits remained low and he continued to drink heavily. He nevertheless continued to work, spending much of 1979 and 1980 pursuing new assignments, though he was unable to see any of them through to completion. These projects included a political thriller set in Cuba called *Destinies*, which never made it past pre-production, as well as *First Blood, An Officer and a Gentleman* and *The Pursuit of D.B. Cooper*, which were subsequently passed on to other directors.[130] Eventually, however, he secured a deal with CBS Theatrical Films — a semi-independent studio created by the CBS Broadcast Group — to make *The Equals*, an action movie about two Japanese brothers who feud over a pair of ancient swords. Frankenheimer took the assignment because the film's subject matter appealed to him. "I liked that it was a modern samurai movie with a sword fight," he told *The New York Times*, "because, God, I loved all those Kurosawa movies."[131] Featuring Toshiro Mifune, Atsuo Nakamura and the American actor Scott Glenn, the picture was shot on location in and around Kyoto, Japan during the spring and summer of 1981. (Mifune, of course, had made his name appearing in several "samurai" movies—many of which Kurosawa directed—like: *The Seven Samurai* (1954), *Yojimbo* (1961) and *Sanjuro* (1962).) The production was not without problems, however, as Frankenheimer was not always able to make his ideas clear to his "cameraman and crew [who] were mostly Japanese." But thanks to Mifune, who spoke English, and who also allowed the director to shoot the film's interiors in the studio he owned, the production was completed in a timely fashion.

Frankenheimer enjoyed himself a great deal during his time in Japan. Working with Mifune, one of his stars from *Grand Prix*, was in itself agreeable. He also became acquainted with the island nation's delicious cuisine. As he explained to Roderick Mann in Los Angeles after he'd completed primary shooting on the picture: "I had the best steak I've ever eaten in my life in Kyoto. I've eaten all over the world and never tasted anything like it. It was so good I haven't been able to look at a steak since I got back."[132] Frankenheimer may have enjoyed himself a bit too much in Japan, however, for after his return to the United States, he came to the realization that he had to do something about his drinking. "What happened to me was that my claim that I never drank while I worked went out the window because on *The Challenge* [as *The Equals* came to be titled] I drank while I worked." He then checked into a treatment program at St. John's Hospital in Santa Monica, and following his release, he joined a recovery program.[133] "I straightened out in 1981," he told Bernard Weinraub in 1994, "and from that day on I haven't had a drink."[134]

But while the quality of Frankenheimer's personal life began to improve, his career continued to experience obstacles and frustrations. In the spring of 1982, for instance, three months before the release of *The Challenge*, CBS decided to "shrink the scope of its film operation," and instead of releasing the picture itself, it contracted Embassy Pictures to handle distribution, an arrangement which, in Frankenheimer's words, "didn't work."[135] The picture was further hurt by the poor reviews it received, as many critics dismissed it for being too violent. Kevin Thomas at the *Los Angeles Times*, however, found much in it to admire:

> *The Challenge* ... is surely the best American-made martial arts movie yet. Beyond that, it is one of the extremely few successful attempts by Americans to explore on the screen certain aspects of Japanese culture.
>
> It accomplishes this by never losing sight that it is first and foremost a genre piece, an adventure fantasy made real by gritty, perceptive characterization and a terse style.[136]

The director then spent the next two-and-a-half years after *The Challenge* on projects that failed to move out of pre-production, including a racing movie called *Speed* and a crime thriller titled *Wilderness*.[137] He did manage, however, to successfully shoot an adaptation of N. Richard Nash's play *The Rainmaker* for HBO during the summer of 1982, his first television production after a 22-year break.[138] Then in January 1984, he was contacted by the producer Ely

HE HAS TRAINED EVERY THOUGHT, EVERY MUSCLE, EVERY NERVE, FOR THIS MOMENT OF TRUTH.

THE CHALLENGE

One American against all odds.

Master of the Martial Arts: Toshiro Mifune stars in Frankenheimer's homage to "samurai" cinema, *The Challenge* (CBS Theatrical Films, 1982).

Landau, for whom he'd made *The Iceman Cometh* a decade earlier. Landau had purchased the rights to *The Holcroft Covenant*—Robert Ludlum's best selling novel about a secret network of neo–Nazis and their desire to plunge the world into anarchy—and he wanted to know if Frankenheimer was interested in bringing it to the screen.[139] A fan of the American author's books, he accepted the offer. But once he'd committed himself, the director came to realize that the screenplay Landau wanted him to shoot was inadequate, and to correct this, he hired his old friend George Axelrod to do a rewrite.

The reunion between the director and writer did not turn out as well as each hoped, though. Before shooting began, Landau suffered a stroke, forcing his wife Edie, whose experience as a producer was limited, to take up the production's reins, a development which put a great strain on the cast and crew.[140] And Axelrod, struggling with the convoluted structure of Ludlum's novel, failed to complete the rewrite before shooting was scheduled to start, prompting James Caan, the movie's original lead, to quit.[141] This, in turn, compelled Frankenheimer to find a replacement as fast as possible. Luckily, he was able to draw Michael Caine, who rushed to the set in Germany, where shooting had

The Film of
ROBERT LUDLUM'S
suspense-packed bestseller
The Holcroft Covenant
Distributed by THORN EMI Screen Entertainment.

THORN EMI
Screen
Entertainment

A scene from *The Holcroft Covenant* (Thorn EMI, 1985). When Frankenheimer found people he liked, he worked with them again when he could. Michael Lonsdale, the actor on the left, appeared in *Riviera* and *Ronin*. The man on the right, André Penvern, also played a bartender in *French Connection II*.

already begun. As the British actor recalled in his autobiography *What's It All About?*: "I didn't even have time for a wardrobe fitting and [so] wore my own clothes in the movie."[142] Despite these troubles, Frankenheimer managed to cobble together a memorable, if not entirely coherent, thriller, though a bungled deal with the film's distributors prevented it from getting a wide release and the picture flopped when it arrived in theaters in the fall of 1985.[143]

After *The Holcroft Covenant*, Frankenheimer was approached by MTM Enterprises, Mary Tyler Moore's production company, which offered him the chance to shoot a feature-length pilot for a television series the company was planning, a program called *Riviera*, which would follow the adventures of an American secret agent who lives in the South of France. After accepting the project, the director left for Nice to begin shooting; and working with ace cameraman Henri Decaë (*Bob le flambeur*, *The 400 Blows*) he managed to craft an exciting story which he loaded with exquisite footage of the ancient city and the rough hills and bright beaches that line the Cote D'Azur. But the executives at MTM were not happy with the product Frankenheimer delivered to them. Fearing the picture was too sophisticated for general audiences, they insisted upon re-editing it and introducing new footage, which Frankenheimer did not direct. Unable to stop the changes, and disgusted by their impact upon his work, he responded by petitioning the Directors Guild of America, asking the organization to remove his name from the program. His efforts were successful and when ABC broadcast the pilot on May 31, 1987, the pseudonymous Alan Smithee, rather than John Frankenheimer, was listed in the credits as the director.[144]

Frankenheimer followed the shooting of *Riviera* with another action film, an adaptation of Elmore Leonard's 1974 crime novel *52 Pick-Up*, which tells the story of a "tough guy" businessman who stands up to a gang of blackmailers. The project was initiated by Frankenheimer after he read Leonard's novel on a flight to England. Seeing a movie in the book, he set out to find who owned the rights, and learned they belonged to Cannon Films, an independent outfit headed by Menahem Golen and Yoram Globus. Cannon had already produced an adaptation of the novel, though, a 1984 thriller starring Rock Hudson and Robert Mitchum titled *The Ambassador*, which moved the story's original setting from Detroit to Israel. Golen and Globus nevertheless responded favorably to the idea of having someone of Frankenheimer's stature working for them, and green-lighted the production, giving the director enough of a budget to cast stars like Roy Scheider and Ann-Margret to play the film's male and female leads. The chiefs were not willing, however, to spend much on the movie's pre-release publicity, a decision which Frankenheimer felt was responsible for its inability to find audiences when it opened in theaters in the fall of 1986.[145] (The director, of course, blamed incompetent marketing and distribution for the commercial failure of *All Fall Down*, *The Gypsy Moths*, *I Walk the Line*, *The Horsemen*, *The Iceman Cometh*, *French Connection II*, *The Challenge* and *The Holcroft Covenant*, as well.) Bad reviews, however, may have also hindered the film's performance, as several mainstream critics censured the picture for its lurid subject matter, while others, somewhat surprisingly, found it a bit boring. For example, Patrick Goldstein at the *Los Angeles Times* wrote:

> Veteran director John Frankenheimer also commits the unpardonable sin of dragging out virtually every scene, draining the film of any jagged edges it might have originally had. At nearly two hours, the movie is a bloated mess.[146]

More than a year would pass before Frankenheimer started work on his next feature, a police thriller titled *Dead Bang*, but his involvement with the project dated back to his time at Paramount, when he'd hired scenarist Robert Foster to develop a narrative around the real life exploits of a Los Angeles County Sheriff's Department detective named Jerry Beck, who'd stumbled upon and subdued a ring of neo–Nazi terrorists.[147] Paramount had ultimately passed

on the picture, but Frankenheimer had held onto the script, eventually securing a production deal with the Lorimar film company. But while Lorimar lent
its support to the picture, it charged the director with giving the lead role to
the television actor Don Johnson; and the star and the director did not get along
together well, as Johnson — much like Lancaster on the sets of *The Young Savages* and *Bird Man of Alcatraz*— insisted upon controlling the production, making demands about the cast, the script and so forth. Wanting to see the project
through, Frankenheimer tolerated Johnson's poor conduct; but he did not look
back on the production or his leading man with any sort of fondness in subsequent years. As he recalled:

> Once a movie starts and you find yourself in a situation where you have a very difficult
> star, it's like you're a hostage. There's nothing you can do. You've got to get through it.
> [As the director], you can say, "I'm not going to continue here, find someone else." But
> that's tough to do if you've created the project and worked with the writer on it from
> the beginning.[148]

While he was finishing *Dead Bang*, Frankenheimer was asked by Wolf
Schmidt, the president of Kodiak Films, to direct *The Fourth War*, a military
thriller about a pair of colonels— one American, one Russian — who "fight a
private battle that threatens to upset the peace between the United States and
Soviet Union."[149] Featuring Frankenheimer's friend Roy Scheider, German actor
Jürgen Prochnow and Tim Reid, who'd also appeared in *Dead Bang*, the film
was shot in the winter and spring of 1989 in Calgary; and after its completion,
Frankenheimer was once again confident that he'd created a film which was
commercial and exciting. But once again his hopes were thwarted when the picture failed to attract audiences. This time bad timing, not poor marketing, hurt
the picture at the box office. Between the completion of the film and its release
in the spring of 1990, that is, tensions eased between the U.S. and the U.S.S.R.
with the dismantling of the Berlin Wall, an event which heralded the end of
the Cold War and robbed *The Fourth War* of its timeliness.[150] The film nevertheless mustered a high number of friendly reviews. Desmond Ryan at *The
Philadelphia Inquirer*, for example, wrote: "*The Fourth War* is Frankenheimer
at his most engaged — a film that melds action and tension with strong and
urgent issues."[151] Jonathan Rosenbaum compared the picture favorably "to the
lean, purposeful work [Frankenheimer] used to do for such 50s TV shows as
Studio One and *Playhouse 90*."[152] And Janet Maslin used much of her review to
commend the way in which Frankenheimer directed his actors, heaping praise,
in particular, upon Scheider: "Mr. Scheider and Mr. Frankenheimer," she wrote,
"work well together."[153]

The director launched into his next project in the summer of 1989, a series
of commercials which he filmed for AT&T in Paris. The job paid well, but, as
he explained to *Back Stage*, he didn't take it for mercenary reasons.

> It's not easy finding film projects that creatively justify taking a year-and-a-half of my
> life. Yet the only way a director can keep his skills sharpened is to keep working.

The director works with Lara Harris in *The Fourth War* (Kodiak, 1990).

Shooting commercials is not only an excellent way to stay active, it's a very exciting medium. Some of the best visual techniques used in motion pictures today have come from commercials.[154]

He worked in Europe, as well, on his next picture *Year of the Gun*, the story of an American writer who arouses the wrath of a group of Italian terrorists when he writes a novel about them. In an interview he gave to *The New York Times*, Frankenheimer said that he decided to make the movie because he liked its Hitchcockian plot, which rests upon the terrorists' misapprehension of reality and the drastic consequences that follow.

I love movies where an innocent man is involved in some conspiracy that he knows nothing about.... That's what this is. And I love movies where somebody does something for a very valid reason, and it turns out to be all the wrong things, which in this case is what happens.... I like the fact that nobody is who he seems to be.

The production was hampered, however, by financing problems, which postponed shooting until the fall of 1990, forcing Frankenheimer to film much of the picture in gray, wintry conditions, though the story takes place during spring. Edward Pressman, the film's producer, was unable to raise sufficient funds for the film's pre-release build up, as well, and when the picture arrived in theaters it did little business.[155]

The string of flops that followed *Prophecy* significantly weakened Frankenheimer's standing in Hollywood, but he remained hopeful that his career would eventually recover.[156] And while no new feature projects materialized after *Year of the Gun,* in 1992 he was approached by HBO to direct a show for its popular horror series *Tales from the Crypt.* Wanting to work, Frankenheimer took the job and shot the program — which tells the serio-comic story of a serial killer who works (and attacks her victims) in a library — over four days in Los Angeles.[157] The decision proved to be an important one, as four months later, the cable network, pleased with the job he'd done, came back to Frankenheimer and asked him to direct a TV feature, a dramatization of the tragic prison uprising which took place in Attica, New York in 1971.

Impressed with the script he was given, Frankenheimer took this job, as well. He then proceeded to find locations for filming, settling eventually on the Tennessee State Penitentiary in Nashville, a massive, Victorian-era facility which had ceased operation in 1992.[158] To increase the docudrama's believability, he also cast former inmates who had been present during the uprising as extras. In addition, Michael Smith, the film's technical consultant (and the model upon whom the film's main character is based) had been one of the guards at Attica who'd been taken hostage by the inmates and later injured when the New York State Police and the National Guard retook the prison. Frankenheimer shot *Against the Wall,* as the picture was eventually titled, in the spring of 1993, and a year later, when the film had its television premier, it drew almost unanimous acclaim from critics, the best response the director's work had received in many years. For instance, Jon Matsumoto at the *Los Angeles Times,* wrote, "Intensely involving and socially trenchant, HBO's *Against the Wall* is the rare TV movie that contains the force and complexity of a quality feature film."[159] And *Variety*'s Ray Loynd exclaimed, "John Frankenheimer has triumphantly returned to the medium that catapulted his career 40 years ago with a simmering, seething retelling of the ... Attica rebellion."[160] HBO was pleased by Frankenheimer's effort, too, and it offered him a follow-up project, a biopic about the environmental activist Chico Mendes and his efforts to save the Brazilian rainforest from reckless land developers. Once again impressed with the script, the director accepted the job and flew down to Mexico to shoot the picture in the spring of 1994.

Against the Wall and *The Burning Season,* the title HBO gave to the Mendes film, would both win best directing Emmys for Frankenheimer, as would his next production, *Andersonville,* a film about a Civil War–era prison camp, which he shot in 1995 for the TNT cable network. And these successes not only lifted the director's spirits, but gave his career new momentum, providing him with opportunities to again work on high profile productions. As he noted in an interview he gave to Glenn Whipp:

> [The TV work] changed my life. What it did ... is it altered my perception of myself and the town's perception of me. I woke up and realized I had a lot more work in me. I remembered why I got in this business to begin with — to do the work, to create something that's good. And people around here saw I wasn't some old fart who couldn't handle the job anymore.[161]

Evidence of this renewed interest in Frankenheimer surfaced in the spring of 1996, when he was asked by New Line Cinema to take over the reins of *The Island of Dr. Moreau*, a $35 million adaptation of H.G. Wells' 1896 novel about a scientist who tries to turn animals into human beings. The studio had fired the picture's original director Richard Stanley four days into shooting and it hoped Frankenheimer could rescue the production, much as he had when he was asked to helm *Bird Man of Alcatraz* and *The Train* in the early Sixties. Wanting to work with Marlon Brando, the film's leading man, Frankenheimer took the assignment enthusiastically and departed for North Queensland, Australia, where the production was located. But when he arrived, he shut down the film for a week-and-a-half because he was unhappy with the screenplay the studio had given him (which Stanley had written), and he had it re-crafted by Ron Hutchinson, who'd written *Against the Wall* and *The Burning Season*, and the veteran script doctor Walon Green.[162]

During shooting, unfortunately, other crises developed. A security detail had to be hired after the filmmakers heard that Stanley, angered by his dismissal, planned to sabotage the film's sets.[163] Moreover, the actor Val Kilmer, one of the movie's other stars, often challenged Frankenheimer, showing up on the set late and refusing to listen to the director's requests and suggestions. The experience was so unpleasant that Frankenheimer afterwards told Rita Kempley:

> It was dreadful working with Val Kilmer. They don't come any worse. It's a shocking travesty that anybody ever hires him.... Will Rogers never met a man he didn't like. Well, Will Rogers never met Val Kilmer.... You have to work hard to find enough bad things to say about him, let me tell you.[164]

He was still able to look back on the production with a degree of fondness and pride. As he told Eleanor Ringel at *The Austin American-Statesman* in 1998:

> Frankly, I think there's some good stuff there. But the experience of making it was hellacious. Actually, the result was better than anybody had any right to expect. But I couldn't write that chapter in my autobiography. Not until a couple of people are dead. But what's the saying? Whatever doesn't kill you makes you stronger. Whatever happens to me from now on has got to be easy compared to that.[165]

When it was released in September 1996, however, few critics found much to like about *The Island of Dr. Moreau*, deriding it for being overblown and didactic, the same charges which had been hurled at his last "monster movie" *Prophecy*. The film recouped New Line's investment, though, even turning a profit eventually. And this success further strengthened the 66-year old director's standing in the industry. As Gary Arnold in *The Washington Times* remarked:

> Quite a few reviewers sneered at the finished product, despite or because of outrageously amusing performances by Marlon Brando and Val Kilmer as depraved despots. Nevertheless, Mr. Frankenheimer had reaffirmed his reputation within the business as a trouble-shooter.[166]

Frankenheimer spent the remainder of the Nineties developing projects for both the big and small screen, and the first picture he completed after *The Island of Dr. Moreau* was a biopic about George Wallace, the segregationist governor from Alabama. Like Frankenheimer's friend Robert Kennedy, Wallace was shot by an assassin on the presidential campaign trail. He survived the attack, though, and gradually came to regret — and recant — the racist views which had helped to make him a national political figure. It was this unlikely change of heart which interested Frankenheimer and contributed to his decision to shoot the picture when it was offered to him by TNT; but finding someone suitable to play the part of the governor proved to be elusive, and Frankenheimer eventually set the project aside in order to pursue others. It was during this time, in fact, that he made *The Island of Dr. Moreau*. Once he was done with *Moreau*, however, he did not return immediately to the Wallace feature, but, instead, started work on a Depression-era crime film for Universal called *The Long Rains*, in which the actor Gary Sinise had agreed to star. The film was never realized, but during its development, Frankenheimer and Sinise became friends, and later, when the director re-commenced with the George Wallace project, he offered the lead to Sinise. The actor was at first reluctant to take the part, though, as he felt great revulsion for Wallace. But he agreed to read the script and decided afterward that he would take the part, impressed, just as Frankenheimer had been, by Wallace's change of heart and the efforts he took to make amends to the people he'd hurt with his racist policies.[167]

When TNT premiered *George Wallace* in August 1997, the feature generally won praise from critics, many of whom were impressed by its realism, its reenactments of actual events and Gary Sinise's canny imitation of the governor. The film's claims to authenticity are debatable, however, as its writers Paul Monash and Marshall Frady felt free to sensationalize parts of their narrative in order to amplify its impact. And these departures — which include a fictional suicide attempt — riled Governor Wallace's family members, prompting them to threaten a lawsuit before shooting began on the grounds that the changes were "not only inaccurate but meanspirited."[168] The project aroused the anger of the Alabama government, too, and the state's Film Office refused to allow Frankenheimer and his crew to shoot at the capitol in Montgomery.[169] Undiscouraged, the director decided instead to shoot the picture in Sacramento — the home of California's state house — and Los Angeles.

After finishing the *Wallace* picture, Frankenheimer moved on to a $60 million feature for MGM called *Ronin* — which follows the exploits of a CIA agent who "leads a pack of leaderless mercenaries on a cat-and-mouse hunt through the narrow streets of southern France."[170] Written by J.D. Zeik and then re-worked in part by David Mamet (using the pseudonym Richard Weisz), the film's title was taken

from the name given in ancient Japanese legends to the warrior class of samurai who worked as freelance hired guns after their masters were killed. The [movie's] present-day "ronins" are those members of the intelligence community who find themselves looking for new employers as the Cold War thaws.[171]

Frankenheimer made the picture, he said, because:

It seemed like a good thing to work on.... I liked the characters, I liked the idea there were these professional people without real attachments anymore. I liked the fact that the action scenes came out of what the characters did, rather than just one of these arbitrary things that you see all the time. And I loved that it took place in France.[172]

After spending much of the fall of 1997 planning the film, Frankenheimer and his crew started shooting in November, using locations in Paris, Arles and Nice; and as always, he insisted upon achieving authenticity and realism whenever he could. His director of photography Robert Fraisse told *American Cinematographer*: "John wanted this movie to appear onscreen almost like reportage, as if we had shot things that were really happening."[173] And to create this effect, he refused to use "blue screens ... [and] computers" for the film's spectacular chase sequences, shooting instead on location with real cars and drivers.[174] Frankenheimer also insisted upon putting his actors in the cars which were used in these scenes. He explained:

We had great drivers, and we did some shots with the actors in the real cars during the scenes.... I got the English right-hand-drive versions of the cars we were going to shoot. That way, we could have the stunt driver on the right, driving the car, and a phony steering wheel on the left for the actors, so we could photograph the actors "driving" the cars.[175]

Despite its scale, the production was beset with few difficulties, although a scandal involving the film's leading man Robert De Niro materialized just before primary shooting ended in February 1998. As *The New York Times* reported, the police led the actor away from his Paris hotel room one morning and interrogated him for 10 hours in an effort to find out what he knew about a local prostitution ring. No charges were preferred, however, and De Niro subsequently claimed that he was innocent, that "he had been a victim of abuse of power by the investigating judge."[176]

In September 1998, when MGM released *Ronin*, the reviews which came out were generally strong. *Time*'s Richard Schickel, for example, praised the film's "sheer stylishness," which

derives from the counterpoint between Mamet's verbal manner — weary, knowing, elliptical — and director John Frankenheimer's bold visual manner. Frankenheimer has always liked to hold a large number of people at different depths in his frames, and that serves well the tense interplay of the actors when they're plotting and scheming. It also provides a nice contrast to the car chases that are another Frankenheimer specialty. (Remember *Grand Prix*?) He loves sending his vehicles screeching through narrow European streets, and he apparently loves trying to top himself, because there are three such sequences here. They are done the old-fashioned way, by stunt drivers, which gives these thrill sequences immediacy, a nervy élan that special-effects techies can't quite generate on a computer screen.[177]

The director chats with his stars Ben Affleck and Charlize Theron on the set of *Reindeer Games* (Dimension, 2000).

The film failed to become a blockbuster, but the excellence of its craftsmanship nevertheless made a strong impression on industry people, leading to more offers. For a short time, for example, the director talked with 20th Century–Fox about the possibility of shooting an adaptation of *Dirty White Boys*, a bestselling adventure novel by film critic Stephen Hunter.[178] He was also approached by Harvey and Bob Weinstein, the heads of Miramax and Dimension Films, who asked him if he'd like to make a $40 million crime thriller about a casino heist called *Reindeer Games*. Frankenheimer then agreed to read the film's screenplay, and took the job, telling *Variety*: "This is one of the best-written scripts I've read in a long time."[179]

For *Reindeer Games'* cast, the director landed two of Hollywood's hottest stars, Ben Affleck and Charlize Theron; he also signed several actors he'd worked with on other projects over the years—Lonny Chapman, Clarence Williams III and Gary Sinise. Shooting commenced in March 1999, but because the film's story was set in winter, Frankenheimer took his cast and his crew up to subarctic Calgary to take advantage of the region's snow. The shooting went well, in spite of the extreme conditions, and when the Weinsteins watched an early cut of the movie in the summer of 1999, they were so pleased that they signed Frankenheimer to a non-exclusive four-picture deal.[180] But after preview audiences responded negatively to the movie's extremely violent content, the Weinsteins asked Frankenheimer to re-shoot and re-edit portions of the picture, a development that delayed the project's completion and postponed its release date two months, forcing it to miss the Christmas Day premier which the producers originally planned.[181]

Reindeer Games performed sluggishly at the box office, a consequence, perhaps, of its out-of-season arrival. The poor reviews which met the picture may have hurt it, as well, as many critics responded with distaste to its improbable plot. A few were appreciative though, drawing comparisons between it and Quentin Tarantino's *Pulp Fiction* (1994), while others compared the picture to director's own earlier work. Rex Reed, for example, wrote:

> Mr. Frankenheimer can still establish characters, set up complex situations and remove the safety caps on life's wilder fantasies with nimble feet and technical dexterity. Rarely has a Christmas Eve setting looked so terrifying.[182]

The movie's disappointing yield did not impede Frankenheimer's comeback, however, and he spent much of 2000 developing projects for the Weinsteins and TNT, including an adaptation of Hemingway's final novel *Across The River and Into The Trees* and a biopic about his friend Robert Kennedy.[183]

That year, he also directed a short promotional film for the BMW automobile company. The director then moved on to another feature for HBO, an historical reenactment of Lyndon Johnson's management of the crisis in Vietnam called *Path to War*. The foundation for the film, which would turn out to be Frankenheimer's last completed work, was laid almost ten years earlier in 1991, after *The New Yorker* published a series of excerpts from *Counsel to the President*, Clark Clifford's memoir about the roles he played in Lyndon Johnson's administration during the late Sixties. Inspired by Clifford's recollections, a young writer named Daniel Giat decided to write a dramatic script about the Vietnam era and its impact upon American history and culture; but instead of focusing on battlefields in southeast Asia, he wanted to narrow in on the conversations and meetings which took place in the White House and the Pentagon as LBJ and his men tried to devise a plan to neutralize Ho Chi Minh and his army.[184] Giat then spent five years on the project, making extensive use of the Johnson Library in Austin, Texas and reviewing hundreds of hours of conversations the

Frankenheimer, 2002.

president recorded during his stay in the White House, before he managed to land a deal with HBO Pictures, the cable network's film production company.

Several years would pass before Giat's script went into production, as the project's producers struggled to find someone to direct it. Early on, Frankenheimer was offered the job, but because of his distaste for Johnson and his policies, he declined. The producers then signed Barry Levinson to make the movie, but after two years, he was fired for failing to get the film off the ground.[185] The producers then went back to Frankenheimer, and were pleased to learn that in the years since they had first approached him, the director had adopted an interest in the nation's thirty-sixth president, a shift which came about after reading Robert Caro's best-selling biographical analyses of Johnson's career, *The Path to Power* (1983) and *Means of Ascent* (1990).[186] He explained:

> I became more and more sympathetic to [him]. I realized that this is a man who really — in spite of all his flaws — wanted to do the right thing. He wanted greatness and in pursuit of that greatness, he brought himself down.[187]

After Frankenheimer took the job, he went to work quickly, compressing and tightening up Giat's sprawling script, having it vetted for accuracy by Michael Beschloss and Howard Dratch, two experts on the Johnson administration; and with casting director Mindy Marin, he selected his principals, eventually giving the lead role to Irish stage actor Michael Gambon after failing to sign his first choice Gene Hackman.[188] With a budget upwards of $17 million, Frankenheimer and his crew started filming in the fall of 2001, just weeks after the September 11 bombing of the Pentagon; and because of heightened security in the nation's capital, the filmmakers were obliged to shoot the bulk of this film about Washington politics in Sacramento, Pasadena and Los Angeles.

HBO vigorously promoted *Path to War* in the weeks leading up to its May 2002 premier, and the film received a great deal of notice in several large papers, with reviews and features appearing in *The New York Times*, *The San Francisco Chronicle* and the *Los Angeles Times*, as well as several smaller papers, including many in Texas, Johnson's home state. For the most part, the write-ups were positive. Tom Shales at *The Washington Post*, for instance, wrote:

> The film ... is remarkably and unrelentingly compelling, a major accomplishment for the filmmakers when one considers that it's to a large degree a dramatized debate among governmental figures.[189]

And the few objections which materialized were directed not at the film's craftsmanship, its themes or its structure, but, rather, at its leading man. Jeff Guinn at the *Fort Worth Star-Telegram* complained:

> This film exemplifies how getting little things wrong can torpedo the best-intentioned production. The problem is mostly with Gambon.... [W]hoever tutored him in the vagaries of a Texas accent failed miserably. Instead of LBJ's Lone Star twang, Gambon delivers an unintentionally humorous pastiche of mush-mouthed drawl. It's so ridiculous that it detracts from every scene.[190]

Gambon's performance was nevertheless nominated for an Emmy.

Path to War would be Frankenheimer's final film, and it would yield him his fifth Emmy for directing, too, though it was awarded posthumously in Sept. 2002. But before he died, he began work on *Exorcist: The Beginning*—a prequel to the popular 1973 horror film directed by William Friedkin—for a group called Morgan Creek Productions. Preparation for the movie had actually begun several years before Frankenheimer accepted the offer. As Laura M. Holson explained in *The New York Times*, the films' producer James G. Robinson originally hired scenarist William Wisher to craft the picture's screenplay in 1997. But Wisher's story, which focuses on a "young priest [who] travels to post–World War II Africa, where the devil confronts him and makes him question his faith," disappointed Robinson, who felt that it "lacked the psychological terror of the original film." The producer then "hired Caleb Carr, the New York author of the best-selling novel *The Alienist*, for a rewrite." Carr's celebrity, in turn, "attracted the attention of John Frankenheimer ... who signed on to the film in August of 2001."

Frankenheimer spent several months planning *Exorcist: The Beginning*, finding locations in Spain and Britain and assembling his cast, giving the film's central part to another Irish actor, Liam Neeson.[191] In May 2002, however, two months before filming was scheduled to start, Frankenheimer went into the hospital for reconstructive back surgery. For years, the director had been suffering from lung cancer and the metastatic growths caused by the disease had damaged his spinal chord and vertebrae, leaving him in chronic pain. And though his prognosis was good following the operation, and he planned to return to the production, he was forced to return to the hospital to undergo further surgery in June. But this time when he came home, he decided to quit the movie, and two weeks later on July 6 he died, the victim of a stroke. He was 72.[192]

CHAPTER TWO

Problems at Home

Although he is best known for his political thrillers and action films, Franken-heimer directed several features which explore the conflicts that can arise in families—between siblings, parents, husbands and wives. These movies might be regarded as an extension of the psychological dramas he shot for television in the Fifties. *The Young Stranger*, in fact, was adapted from a show he origi-nally directed for the *Climax!* series. At the same time, *The Young Stranger*, as well as *All Fall Down, Impossible Object* and *The Iceman Cometh*, all share much in common with the director's other films, as each narrows its attention on a single male character, a Promethean non-conformist who pays a dear price for being unable to adhere to the rigid standards of the status quo.

The Young Stranger (1957)

Frankenheimer's first feature takes place over the space of a few days, a trait it shares with *The Extraordinary Seaman, The Gypsy Moths, Prophecy, Against the Wall* and *Reindeer Games*. The picture's action revolves around Hal Ditmar (James MacArthur), a 16-year-old high school student who lives in Beverly Hills with his mother Helen (Kim Hunter) and his father Tom (James Daly), a powerful Hollywood producer. Shortly after the film opens, Hal and his friend Jerry (Jeff Silver) go to the movies, where Hal arouses the anger of a customer (Eddie Ryder) by propping his feet up on one of the seats in the the-ater. When the dispute escalates, thanks to Hal's sarcasm, the establishment's manager Mr. Grubbs (Whit Bissell) arrives and orders the boys to leave. They comply, but before they can get out of the building, the autocratic manager approaches them:

GRUBBS: Hey, wait a minute, you two. I told you two to wait.
HAL: We get our money back?

GRUBBS: Get into my office.

HAL: Why? Is that where you keep the money?

GRUBBS: I said, get into my office.

HAL: Why?

GRUBBS: Never mind that now. Just get in there.

The boys refuse to heed Grubbos, however, and start for the exit. But once they step outside, a doorman tackles Hal and drags him back into the theater, where he is grabbed and pushed by Grubbs until he strikes back, slugging him on the chin. A short time later, a detective from the Juvenile Bureau named Shipley (James Gregory) arrives, listens to the theater manager's skewed account of the scuffle and takes Hal to the police station, holding him there until the boy's father comes to get him. Unfortunately for Hal, his father, just like the policeman, refuses to accept his claim that he acted in self-defense. Nevertheless Ditmar uses the power of his position as an industry player to persuade Grubbs to drop his complaint against the boy. Far from winning Hal's gratitude, however, the gesture contributes to the riff which has developed between them. And at the dinner table, a few nights after the trouble in the theater, the father and son begin to argue:

DITMAR: Listen, you. You don't know how lucky you are to be getting off so easily. You think I enjoy having to ask my friends to get my son out of trouble with the police?

HAL: I didn't ask you to call.

DITMAR: You would rather have gone to jail, I suppose?

HAL: I was innocent.

DITMAR: You said that before and I didn't notice it having any profound effect on anyone.

HAL: Doesn't it strike you as just little bit dishonest?

DITMAR: What?

HAL: Well, if you think I'm so guilty, then pulling strings to get me out of it is dishonest, isn't it?

The intensity of the conversation rises quickly and Hal storms off. But then, rather surprisingly, he pays a visit to Grubbs (in his office, we should note) to apologize for having hit him. But once he does this, he asks the manager to come clean about what actually happened when the two came to blows. Instead of agreeing to this, Grubbs grabs the boy, much as he did before; and much as he did before, Hal slugs him. He winds up in the police station again, as well. But this time, as Shipley listens to the boy's account of the fight, he concludes that Hal is telling the truth; and he calls Grubbs, as well as Ditmar, into the station, where the manager eventually admits to having lied. The news humbles Ditmar and he goes to Hal, apologizes and jokingly says, "I'm glad it's Grubbs you hit and not me. That's some shiner you gave him." The boy's anger vanishes when he hears this and he allows Ditmar to put his arm around his shoulder. Then the pair leaves the station and head for home.

The angry theater manager Mr. Grubbs (Whit Bissell, with flashlight) approaches Hal (James MacCarthur, far left) and his friend Jerry (Jeffrey Silver) in *The Young Stranger* (RKO, 1957).

With its upper middle-class teenaged hero who finds himself at odds with the rules and mores of mainstream society, *The Young Stranger* somewhat resembles Nicholas Ray's *Rebel Without a Cause* (1955), which premiered in theaters less than a year before this film went into production. (The composer Leonard Rosenman, incidentally, scored both films.) However, the self-loathing Jim Stark, the character James Dean portrays in the earlier picture, is far more alienated and damaged than Hal. In many ways, in fact, Frankenheimer's strong-willed protagonist actually seems to be quite comfortable in the bourgeois world in which he lives. When the picture begins, for instance, we watch him flirt with female students at school. When school lets out, he pals around with his best friend Jerry. And when he reaches home, he jokes with his mother, who clearly adores him. The case might even be made that the healthiness of Hal's self-esteem, his belief in his own worth, precipitates the problems and unhappiness which arise around him later. We see evidence of this, for example, in the movie theater, when Hal rests on his feet on the seatback. After the patron asks him to move his feet in a civil and respectful manner, he is cooperative; but when, a moment later, the man insults him, Hal returns his feet, letting the customer know how little he thinks of him. This gesture, in turn, prompts the offended man to fetch Grubbs.

Arguably, Hal's pride and ego foster his dispute with Grubbs in the theater lobby, too, for although the boy later claims that he punched the manager in order to protect himself, it's debatable as to whether or not Grubbs ever poses a real threat to his safety. After all, Grubbs, with his head of gray hair, is a slight person, who lacks Hal's height and muscle. Moreover, he doesn't actually try to hurt the boy; he tries to grab his sleeves, to get him into the theater's office, in order to prevent other customers from watching this embarrassing incident. And while it's certainly possible that Hal is frightened by this treatment and that he feels the need to strike the little man, at the same time, it seems to be possible that he hits him in order to compensate for the humiliating treatment he received from the doorman just a few moments before. We can't tell.

It seems unlikely, however, that Hal slugs Grubbs because he has deep psychological problems, a claim we cannot make about James Dean's Jim Stark. But like Jim, and a spate of other "teen drama" heroes from the era, Hal is unhappy at home, and his dissatisfaction seems to develop largely in response to his father's aloof personality, his tendency to devote more attention to his job than his family, as well as his habit of criticizing the boy, of putting him down with joking remarks. We see an instance of this unpleasant sarcasm early in the film when Hal, tired of his clunker of a car, asks if he might be able to borrow Ditmar's.

> HAL: I just thought if you didn't need your car tonight, well, it'd save us pushing mine after the show.
>
> DITMAR: Oh, I don't think one more night of pushing is likely to inflict any lasting damage on your physique. Do you?
>
> HAL: I suppose not.
>
> DITMAR: Then there would seem to be an outside possibility of your being able to get along without my car.

And after the fight in the theater, the relationship between the two worsens, especially when Ditmar refuses to listen to his son's claims that Grubbs attacked him. In fact, whenever Hal attempts to persuade him to think differently, Ditmar grows more rigid, using threats of punishment to lend strength to his arguments, showing the same intolerance and desire for control which mark the customer in the theater, Grubbs, and the police detective Shipley (who, at one point, actually tells Hal that he would like to beat him up).

The defects in Ditmar's personality impair his relationship with his wife Helen, too. Late at night, for instance, following one of his fights with Hal, she approaches her husband in their bedroom, where he is reading a script for a movie he is making, and tells him that she fears their marriage is exhausted and suggests they might be happier with a divorce:

> All this constant tension, all this silence. I've been afraid you might just ask me to leave some day. I'm afraid you might not want to ask me because it would embarrass you, or interfere with your work. Trying to please you. Apologizing for not being able to please you. Afraid of not being good enough, not keeping up with you. I'm tired of living with that fear.

Frankenheimer did not get along well with his crew as he made *The Young Stranger*, and he later regarded the film as a failure. But the picture is still very much a part of his oeuvre. The injured marriage motif for example surfaces in *All Fall Down*, *Seconds*, *Grand Prix*, *I Walk the Line*, *Impossible Object* and *Prophecy*. Depictions of strained relationships between parents and children appear in pictures like *Bird Man of Alcatraz*, *The Manchurian Candidate*, *The Horsemen* and *The Fourth War*. And the film's brave, but occasionally insufferable protagonist anticipates later characters like *The Train*'s Lebiche, *French Connection II*'s Popeye Doyle and *Reindeer Games*' Rudy, who, just like Hal, arouse our admiration and confound our sympathies simultaneously.

Frankenheimer managed to leave his stylistic stamp on the picture, too, imbuing it with the same "realist" pictorial qualities he achieved in his live television productions with the frequent use of deep focus compositions and long takes. We see a good example of this late in the film at the police station when Ditmar approaches Hal, after listening to Grubbs' admission. As the conversation transpires, the humbled father stands in the background of the shot, small and in shadows, while the bright white face of his son, situated in the foreground, looms across the screen. A division, both literal and figurative, exists between the two figures, the shot indicates, while at the same time, the similarly sad expressions that fall on their faces suggest that these two people, these tired opponents, are suffering in much the same way.

All Fall Down (1962)

Late in 1960, John Houseman asked Frankenheimer if he'd like to direct *All Fall Down*, an adaptation of a novel by James Leo Herlihy. The young director took the job, he explained to Higham, because he liked the novel "very much."[1] He was also interested in working with William Inge, the Pulitzer Prize winning dramatist Houseman commissioned to write the script. Frankenheimer could not commit himself fully to *All Fall Down* until the summer of 1961, because he had to finish *Bird Man of Alcatraz* with Burt Lancaster, and when he was able to join the production, he found that Houseman had already cast some of the film's most important parts, picking Warren Beatty to play the production's ne'er-do-well protagonist Berry-Berry and Angela Lansbury as his mother. Frankenheimer was still able to cast several actors himself, however, including Karl Malden, who'd played Burt Lancaster's prison official nemesis in *Bird Man*.[2]

Like Elia Kazan's *Splendor in the Grass* (1961), which Inge also scripted, and in which Beatty also starred, *All Fall Down* tells the story of a love affair which exists between a pair of beautiful neurotics. And just as it is for the star crossed couple in the earlier picture, the union between these two comes undone in a spectacularly painful manner. But while *Splendor in the Grass* focuses primarily on the fallout caused by the break-up of its characters' love affair, *All Fall Down* spends the majority of its time building up to the tragic split, introducing us to the lovers long before they meet one another.

The film opens in the Florida Keys, where a young teenager named Clinton Willart (Brandon De Wilde) searches for his older brother Berry-Berry (Beatty), having ridden down from Cleveland to Florida on a bus.[3] He's arrived with $200 in his wallet, hoping to help his brother buy a shrimping boat. But Berry-Berry, guilty of beating up a girlfriend (Evans Evans), is in jail, and Clinton has to use his money to bail him out. Berry-Berry, we soon learn, is little more than an adventurer, whose good looks allow him to exploit women for money and sex. And he soon separates from Clinton, hired by a rich dowager to act as a steward on her yacht. The teen then returns to his nagging mother Annabelle (Lansbury) and his alcoholic father Ralph (Malden) in Ohio. He is troubled, too, it turns out, a high-school dropout, who spends his days in a sweet shop, writing in a notebook. But then, when a pretty 30-year-old spinster named Echo (Eva Marie Saint) visits the Willarts, the boy's outlook changes. He becomes happier, more sociable, and more engaged with his world, even taking a job as a car wash attendant, earning money for Christmas presents. In contrast, the gigolo Berry-Berry is miserable. After his stint on the yacht, he rides with a woman up to Louisville, where, in a drunken fit, he destroys a storefront crèche scene with a street sign and then slugs his female companion in a bar, for which he again winds up in jail—on Christmas Eve. This time, though, his father, amused rather than angry, bails him out.

The film then leaps several months ahead to spring. Once again Echo is in Cleveland, staying with the Willarts. Berry-Berry has come back, as well. But he has not contacted the family, choosing instead to live and work in secret on an apple orchard outside the city. But then the prodigal son contacts his parents, eventually joining them one morning for breakfast. And when Echo descends into the kitchen that same morning, still wearing her nightgown, he falls in love instantly—and moves back into the house a short time later, an answer to his mother's prayers. As the summer passes, Echo and Berry-Berry spend a lot of time together, attending concerts, visiting museums, eventually consummating their relationship. But when Echo becomes pregnant, Berry-Berry repudiates her. Stricken, the woman decides to leave the Willart house immediately, heading out in a terrible rain, and 20 miles from town, she loses control of her car and speeds off of an embankment, killing herself. It is not clear whether or not her death is a suicide, but Clinton is sure his brother is to blame, and after heading out to the orchard, he hides in Berry-Berry's bedroom

A young teacher (Barbara Baxley) asks the drifter Berry-Berry (Warren Beatty) to drive her to Louisville in *All Fall Down* (UA, 1962).

with a gun, prepared to shoot him. But when his brother enters the room and begins to weep, having learned about Echo's death, Clinton is moved by his suffering and changes his mind. The affection and admiration he once felt for his brother has disappeared, however, and he tells him about this change. Then he walks off, leaving the older boy to think about what he's lost and destroyed.

All Fall Down fared poorly at the box office when it arrived in theaters in the spring of 1962, a development which Frankenheimer and Houseman attributed to MGM, blaming the studio for inadequately promoting the picture. And although some of the reviews it received were favorable, many were not. Philip K. Scheuer, for example, labeled the project as "second-rate Inge" and attacked Beatty, charging him with overacting and with making the Berry-Berry character "plain ridiculous."[4] Bosley Crowther maligned the film for similar reasons, arguing that Berry-Berry is too unlikable, too repellant to woo so many women so easily, a factor which degrades the picture's believability. He wrote:

> It is the essential arrangement that everyone in the story is madly in love with a disgusting young man who is virtually a cretin.... This persistent assumption that everybody ... would be so blindly devoted to this persistently noxious young brute provokes a reasonable spectator to give up finally in disgust. They all must be crazy in this picture.[5]

Far from the charming, but cowardly Bud Stamper we find in *Splendor in the Grass*, Berry-Berry *is* a lout, who treats the people who love him callously. He's also a violent person and a thief, fond of hitting his benefactors with his fists and robbing precious items from their jewelry boxes, including a ring which he gives to Echo at one point, making her more receptive to his advances.

The movie never lets us know why Berry-Berry behaves in this manner or why, as he tells Clinton, he hates life. He just does. And we might argue that Frankenheimer and Inge's failure to be explicit about the source of this anguish hurts the picture, as it stops us from understanding, identifying with and developing sympathy for the character, which is what seems to have happened with Scheuer and Crowther. But Ellis Amburn, in his biography of Beatty, has suggested that Berry-Berry's personality and his actions are understandable if we read the character as a repressed homosexual, mutilated by the prejudices and pressures of the heterosexual status quo, which both his family and the women he sleeps with epitomize. "Warren's role," he wrote, "was another typical product of the mid-twentieth-century gay sensibility represented by *A Streetcar Named Desire*, *Picnic*, and *Cat on a Hot Tin Roof*, rather transparent homoerotic fantasies about wayward, usually misogynistic hunks."[6] Incidentally, both Inge and Herlihy—whose best known novel *Midnight Cowboy* is the story of a male hustler—were homosexuals. (Unhappily, each committed suicide, too.)

Amburn's hypothesis is, of course, open to debate. If the Berry-Berry we see on the screen is so gay, then why does he fall so hard for Echo? Moreover, the character's alienation and his hatred of women might just as likely stem from his strange relationship with his mother, whose attraction for him appears to be less than healthy. Throughout the film, that is, Frankenheimer provides us with clues that Annabelle Willart's affection is almost sexual. The night he returns home, for instance, she rushes through the house to kiss him. And while this is a normal thing for a mother to do, Frankenheimer and his director of photography Lionel Lindon shoot the woman's face in soft focus, lending her a look which is undeniably carnal. Annabelle is apparently unconscious of her desire for her son, though, but it seems to permeate her thinking nonetheless, revealing itself often when she speaks. After he begins to go with Echo, for example, she wonders aloud to Ralph: "It hurts me to realize Berry-Berry is in love. Why should it make me so sad? ... It's just that it hurts, when the boy you love loves somebody else." And when the others in the family reject Berry-Berry, smashing his framed photograph on the floor, Annabelle screams: "I love him! I don't care what he's done! I'll love him always! Forever!" Her remarks, by the way, echo those of the stripper Clinton meets in Florida, the one Berry-Berry beat up, who says to him: "I'm not really sore. He can come back.... I want him back."

The film only offers us hints that Annabelle's love is incestuous: we can't be absolutely sure that she feels this way. At the same time, we can't overlook the fact that her personality is offensive to Berry-Berry, contributing to his restlessness and anger. As he tells Clinton: "I guess you know I hate her guts. That's why I stay away." And perhaps his hatred of the woman also plays a role in his decision to abandon Echo: he may not leave her because of the potential burden a baby presents, but because pregnancy will eventually transform her into a mother, making her like Annabelle.

Because of Houseman's friendship and support, Frankenheimer was given great latitude as he made *All Fall Down*, and this freedom enabled him to create a film which, despite its backing from mainstream MGM, portrays contemporary American culture in an extremely unflattering light. Of course the film's unhappy plot, its examination of the breakdown of a family, plays a large role in establishing the movie's pessimistic tone. But the manner in which the filmmakers constructed the picture plays an important part in this, too. Frankenheimer fills the screen often with harsh, violent, even sleazy images, such as the dancers and call girls who occupy the strip joint in Florida, a milieu the director would later return to in both *The Gypsy Moths* and *52 Pick-Up*. The film's mood is also darkened and enriched by Lindon's expressive camerawork and the picture's frequent use of symbolism. Berry-Berry, for example, is almost always filmed in some sort of confined place, such as the jail cell in Key Bonita, or the tiny room he lives in at the orchard, or the cage-like rocker he sits in on his parents' patio, a technique which reminds us constantly that despite his claims to the contrary, he is a prisoner, a trapped Narcissus, forced forever to contemplate himself and his anguish. And just like the mythological Narcissus, whose handsome face had the ability to arouse love instantly, Berry-Berry is adored by a creature named Echo, who, like her namesake, dies after her sweetheart scorns her.[7]

Impossible Object (1973)

Impossible Object primarily follows a British writer named Harry (Alan Bates), who lives in rural France with his American wife Elizabeth (Evans Evans) and their three sons. On a visit to an art museum in Paris one day, Harry meets and falls in love with a married French woman named Natalie (Dominique Sanda). Eventually, Harry decides to leave his family and move to Paris, doing this, he says, in order to complete the book of short stories he is writing. Of course, being in Paris allows him to meet Natalie often. But this arrangement is hardly a happy one, as he experiences painful, conflicting emotions, which he describes in one of the stories he writes during this period, a portion of which he reads aloud.

> The person with whom I was in love came to be with me each morning. She would cross the square leading to the house, unlock the door and climb the stairs to my room with footsteps I longed for and at the same time hoped would not come. I tried to tell myself that love is like this.... You want what you haven't got and when you've got it,

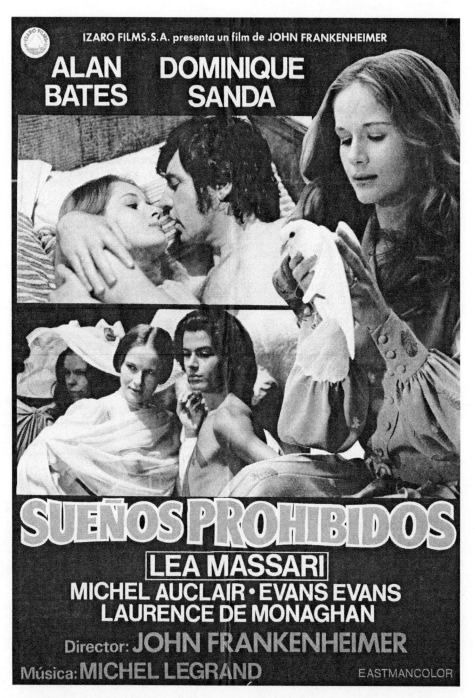

Harry (Alan Bates) makes love to Natalie (Dominique Sanda) in *Impossible Object* (Franco-London Film-Euro International/Izaro Films, 1972/1978). From the poster prepared for the film's 1978 release in Spain.

you don't want it as much. But I knew that if she didn't come each morning, I would be in despair.

Harry's anguish gradually becomes suicidal and he tries to kill himself, slashing his wrist with a rusty razor. He survives, however, when his wife and sons unexpectedly arrive at his flat, preventing him from finishing the effort, an oddly comic moment. Natalie then becomes pregnant, prompting her and Harry to leave for Morocco, where they have the baby. Following this, Harry's three sons pay him and Natalie a visit, convincing their dad to take them out on the ocean in an open boat. Natalie and the baby come along, too; but sadly, when they attempt to return to land, violent waves capsize the boat and wrest the infant from its mother's hands. The action then leaps ahead several years to a piazza in Rome, where by chance Harry and Natalie run into each other at a café, having grown estranged after their baby's death. The conversation becomes intimate quickly, however, as Harry pours himself a glass of wine, and suggests that their love affair has not yet reached its conclusion.

HARRY: Did you think that was the end?
NATALIE: Yes.
HARRY: Well, it isn't.
NATALIE: Why not?
HARRY: We're having lunch together, aren't we? You do see that, don't you?
NATALIE (smiling): Of course I see that.

Then the film ends, as the camera pulls away from the couple and pans across the piazza, which is filled with statues of ancient gods and goddesses, much like the museum where they first met.

With its poignancy and its sophisticated craftsmanship, *Impossible Object* may be the most interesting—and challenging—film Frankenheimer made in the early Seventies. And much of its charm results from its nonlinear narrative, which not only jumps back and forth in time, but between fantasy and reality, too. Early on, for example, we watch as Harry and his wife Elizabeth host a birthday party for their youngest son. After the meal, Harry takes his children and their friends into the family's cellar, where they play a game of hide and seek in the dark. Unfortunately, one of the players, a pretty teenaged girl named Cleo (Laurence De Monaghan), who is dating the oldest of Harry's sons, touches a live electrical wire and electrocutes herself in the middle of the game; and to save her, Harry has to perform mouth to mouth resuscitation, pressing his lips against hers, creating a qausi-erotic image which upsets both his son and his wife. Frankenheimer then cuts to the Paris café where Harry and Natalie often meet for drinks and conversation, and we learn that Harry has just told this story, about the game in the cellar and the injured girl, to Natalie, forcing her to wonder, much as we do, if what she has just heard has really happened or if he made up at the typewriter. "God, Harry," she says, "I never know what's true and what isn't with you."

As the film progresses, the lines between "what's true and what isn't" continue to blur. At one point, the writer visits a strange sex party where nude women walk around a pool with enormous hats and a vampish Italian woman rides about in a rickshaw which is pushed by two bodybuilders. On another occasion, Harry stands in a copse of trees which is flanked with rows of doors, and when he opens these doors, he is transported across time and space to places like Paris and Rome. Which scenes, we wonder, are records of Harry's experience and which ones are his artistic creations? We might be able to claim with some confidence that the sex party vignette is a fantasy, thanks to the outlandish clothing the people wear and the bizarre remarks they make. But the story of Cleo in the basement, presented in a comparatively sedate and realistic manner, is probably a fantasy, too. Is it thus possible that the story of the baby's drowning, which is shot in the same realist manner, is made up, also? For if the electrocuted girl is an illusion, how can we say the dead child isn't one, too? And what about the final dialogue between Natalie and Harry? Is it an event which actually happens?

Because of its perplexing structure, it seems unlikely *Impossible Object* will ever garner a wide audience, and people who only know the director by his thrillers may have difficulty finding similarities between them and this self-consciously artistic work. The film's singularity is further enhanced by its central character's penchant for speaking esoterically and his tendency to read from his writing, which recalls the work of writers like T.S. Eliot and Thomas Pynchon with its labyrinthine qualities. At one point, he speaks to us about the meaning of the film's title, but his explanation is strange, almost inscrutable.

> I wanted to write you something impossible, like a staircase climbing a spiral to come out where it started or a cube with a vertical line at the back overlapping a horizontal one in front. These cannot exist in three dimensions but can be drawn in two; by cutting out one dimension a fourth is created. The object is that life is impossible; one cuts out fabrication and reality. A mirror is held to the back of the head and one's hand has to move the opposite way from what was intended.

Life and art are no different from one other, evidently, as they are both creations of the mind.

Interestingly, Frankenheimer, in remarks he made to the press, offered a different interpretation of the film's title, arguing that it not only refers to "life," but to "living," or how to live one's life effectively. He told the *Los Angeles Times*: "The impossible object is to lead the life you visualize for yourself and to be able to compensate for that."[8] A person can never hope to achieve his goals completely and that failure must be accepted and handled well, he seems to suggest; and to a certain degree, Harry's behavior exemplifies this line of thinking. When, for instance, the baby is lost on the beach in Morocco, he doesn't cower under the weight of disappointment and panic, but, instead, reaches out to Natalie, to calm her and give her comfort.

This strength which Harry displays during an extreme moment, this "grace under pressure," is a trait that characterizes many of Frankenheimer's heroes, ranging from *Bird Man of Alcatraz*'s Robert Stroud, who responds stoically when he is forced to leave his birds behind in Leavenworth, to Sam in *Ronin*, who remains conscious, and keeps cool, when a bullet is removed from his body without anesthesia. Harry's magnanimity on the beach, his efforts to pacify the distraught woman, reveal to us, as well, that his personality is no longer so self-centered, that he now has the ability to care for others. It seems that the crisis in the ocean water — the emotional and physical duress it causes— has precipitated a positive change in his personality, much as the beating Hank Bell receives from the delinquents in *The Young Savages* awakens his heart and the torture Yakov Bok experiences in *The Fixer* stirs his conscience. *Impossible Object*, in short, is marked by the same thematic concerns which materialize elsewhere in the director's oeuvre. Moreover, outside of the picture's expressive editing and its occasionally surreal sets, it looks very much like a Frankenheimer film, displaying many of the director's favorite shooting techniques, such as single set-up takes, large depth of field compositions and natural lighting, as well the use of location sets and non-actors, like the Moroccan fishermen who rush to help Harry and Natalie find the dead child in the waves.

The Iceman Cometh (1973)

Frankenheimer followed *Impossible Object* with an adaptation of Eugene O'Neill's *The Iceman Cometh*, which he shot for the independent producer Ely Landau's American Film Theatre project in 1973. An admirer of O'Neill since his days in college, Frankenheimer enjoyed making the picture a great deal and later came to regard it as one of his favorites, in part because the opportunity to work with an ensemble cast reminded him of his days in live television, and because he liked many of the people he'd recruited for the production, including Frederic March, the star of *Seven Days in May*, and Robert Ryan and Lee Marvin, who'd both worked on programs he'd directed for CBS in the Fifties. In fact, many of the film's players— Bradford Dillman, George Voskovec, Evans Evans, Sorrell Brooke and Joe Pedi — were veterans of live television. Brooke and Pedi, moreover, had both appeared in a live television production of the play which Sydney Lumet — with Landau producing— directed in 1960.

Like the play, Frankenheimer's version of *Iceman* opens on an early morning in 1912, in Harry Hope's bar, a skid row dive in lower Manhattan where several drunks are sleeping, their heads on the tables in the barroom. These people, these bits of "human debris"— a pair of veterans from the Boer War, a couple of faded anarchists, a failed lawyer, a disgraced journalist and so forth — are awaiting the arrival of a man named Hickey (Marvin), a hardware salesman who visits the bar once each year to celebrate the birthday of Harry Hope (March) and to get drunk with the regulars, paying for everyone's booze.[9]

But when Hickey arrives that evening, he surprises the bar's clientele, telling them that he no longer has the urge to drink because he has abandoned all the pipe dreams he had, all the impossible longings for a better life which tortured him and made him want to drink in the first place. Convinced that he can help his friends find peace, the messianic Hickey "wheedles and argues to persuade them to [do the same] and to face reality by venturing forth from the saloon into the outside world."[10] To his disappointment, however, the plan yields mixed results. The drunks come to realize the futility of their dreams, but the discovery makes them miserable, rather than happy. It also destroys the camaraderie which has arisen between them over the years. And even worse, the liquor

Lee Marvin plays Hickey in *The Iceman Cometh* (American Film Theatre, 1973).

they drink—for escape and comfort—no longer seems to work. As Harry at one point exclaims: "What's wrong with this booze? There's no kick in it."

Hickey then makes one last attempt at winning the barflies to his way of thinking. He does this by letting them know how he got rid of his own pipe dreams, explaining to them that he grew tired of telling himself that he could be a good husband to his wife, which he'd never been able to do because of his fondness for womanizing and drinking. He tells them, as well, that he felt the need to free his wife from her pipe dreams, her fantasies that he would someday be a good husband. And to do this, he says, he killed her with a gun.

For Hickey, this crime seemed necessary at the time, an act of mercy to relieve his wife of her suffering; but as he tells the story, he begins to wonder if he might have been insane, a point the drunks latch on to, as it raises the possibility that the salesman's other ideas have been insane, too, including his theories about pipe dreams. Then, after the police arrive and take Hickey off to jail, Hope and his customers begin to return to their old ways, becoming friends again as they talk about their plans and dreams, and drink. But there are two people in the group who are unable to enjoy this forgetfulness the others find, an old political radical named Larry Slade (Ryan) and Don Parritt (Jeff Bridges), the son of Larry's former lover, who has betrayed his mother to the police. Hickey's efforts have stirred the young man's conscience to such a point that he tells Larry that he plans to kill himself and heads upstairs. The despondent Larry then stands by one of the bar's windows, waiting for the young man to throw himself off the roof, which he eventually does, just as Hope and his patrons begin to sing and dance, once again happy and once again drunk.

Running nearly four hours, *The Iceman Cometh* is Frankenheimer's longest theatrical feature. When the film premiered in the fall of 1973, incidentally, it was presented with not one, but two intermissions. And while the length of the original play put off many reviewers when it was first produced in 1946, the critics who watched the film in 1973 were more than willing to sit through O'Neill's dense tragedy and offer their praise. In his review for the *Los Angeles Times*, for example, Champlin wrote:

> In its length and in its intensity, *The Iceman Cometh* was a bold choice to lead off Ely Landau's American Film Theatre series. It is, on the other hand, so majestic and thrilling an achievement that the AFT could hardly have had a more auspicious start or a more persuasive proof of high purpose.[11]

Much of the picture's strength, of course, is drawn from O'Neill's bleak, but compelling analyses of human suffering, idealism and friendship. And though Frankenheimer was more or less prevented from reworking the play's structure and dialogue, his film still bears many of the stylistic and thematic markers which distinguish his other productions, including those in which he enjoyed complete control over the script's content. For instance, the filmmaker's fondness for *mise-en-scene* realism manifests itself in the picture's visuals, as once again he uses long takes frequently and carefully orchestrates the blocking of his actors as they move about the picture's single, claustrophobic set. But shooting the film in this manner proved to be challenging. The director explained in an essay he wrote for *Action* in 1973:

> [T]he problem was how to vary camera angles without making the camera obtrusive–to keep the audience orientated, and to never lose the actors.... I planned the entire film as a montage of shots, utilizing maximum depth of focus. The most common composition was a large head in the foreground with two or three other characters sharp in the background.[12]

The film's technical aspects were singled out in several reviews, by the way, when *The Iceman Cometh* was released. *Variety* noted that "Frankenheimer's direction, appropriate to a filmed play, is well-controlled, unobtrusive and smooth, there's so little interference by the camera it's almost unnoticeable." Champlin declared:

> The setting is no more than a stage's worth of bar and back room, but the visual interest, the feeling of moving and pausing like an invisible eavesdropper, is continuous yet never obtrusive or gadgety.

And in 2003, when Kino Video released the film on DVD, along with the other 13 films which were created for or distributed by the American Film Theatre, Richard Schickel, writing for *The New York Times*, exclaimed:

The set ... is long, narrow and dimly lit. It allows Frankenheimer wonderful camera placements—the people carrying whatever scene or moment he is emphasizing in the foreground, but with the ongoing life of the bar (and its barflies) constantly perceived in the background.[13]

But while this approach to shooting is typical of Frankenheimer, we should note that Lumet constructed his shots in quite the same way for his interpretation of the play in 1960. The earlier production, however, was filmed in black and white and made use of a simpler and much less naturalistic set than the one Jack Martin designed for Frankenheimer.

The tone of Frankenheimer's film is also harsher than Lumet's, thanks in part to Marvin's turn as Hickey, the tragic salesman. Cast against type, the actor creates a particularly disconcerting version of the character, playing him as a sort of swaggering bravado, a man who at once exudes conviviality, arrogance and menace, who fills each of the scenes in which he appears with a degree of tension and violence which the television production, which had the quieter and milder Jason Robard, Jr., playing Hickey, lacks. Several critics, however, found Marvin's "tough guy" Hickey to be more offensive than sympathetic. "A hole in the play," *Variety* claimed. "Instead of dazzling [the drunks in Hope's bar] ... his prods to action are more like a thug's threats." And unlike earlier (and subsequent) interpretations of the character, Marvin plays Hickey as though he is sane, a man who succumbs to mistaken convictions rather than madness. Frankenheimer explained in the article he wrote for *Action*:

> [I]t must be perfectly clear to an audience that Hickey is sane. It has been argued that Hickey is a madman—that when he admits his insanity near the end of the film that this has to be taken literally. I believe that Hickey was sane when he killed his wife and is sane when he comes to the bar.[14]

And because Hickey is responsible for his actions in this treatment of the story, the version of him we find here is not especially sympathetic, another reason why, perhaps, Martin's performance was dismissed by so many in the press.

The decision to portray the salesman as a sane individual, though, complicates and even enriches the play's themes. If Hickey is insane, then we can perhaps discount his claims about the need for destroying pipe dreams, much as the drunks in Hope's bar do. But if he is sane, then we cannot dismiss him and his ideas so easily. He may be a murderer, but he is still an advocate for accepting life as it is, a commendable point of view, which is also one of Frankenheimer's core themes. In other words, we cannot read this version of O'Neill's narrative as an argument for living in bad faith, for softening the sharp edges of reality with comforting daydreams and fantasies. As the director explained:

> When I studied O'Neill's *The Iceman Cometh* in college, my English professor dogmatically stated that this was a play about the necessity of guarding illusion in life—that O'Neill's message was: life without illusion is unlivable. To this day ... this is an opin-

ion still held by many. However, it is not mine and this is the main reason I chose to do the film. In my opinion, *Iceman* is far more complex. It is not a work about having to live with illusion but rather one that explores the necessity and the horrible pain of living without it.[15]

Chapter Three

The Physical Challenge

Recalling the novels and stories of Ernest Hemingway, many of Franken-heimer's films feature athletes and sportsmen who pursue physical challenges with intense enthusiasm. Arguably, these pursuits in themselves have little meaning. The drivers in *Grand Prix* hurl themselves over strips of asphalt at tremendous speeds, often crashing and killing themselves and others. The sky-divers in *The Gypsy Moths* leap out of planes and plunge to the earth. The rid-ers in *The Horsemen* strike at one another with whips and sticks as they vie for the possession of a headless calf stuffed with sand. The pursuit of these absurd and dangerous endeavors, however, paradoxically imbues the men's lives with meaning. Whenever a person risks his life in this manner, these films suggest, he comes to value it — if not understand it — more.

Grand Prix (1966)

Frankenheimer's interest in automobile racing developed in college when he would watch and occasionally participate in small races in western Massa-chusetts. And in subsequent years, it became an obsession, prompting him to attend a professional race car driving school, to become friends with celebrity drivers like Phil Hill and Jochen Rindt and to make a movie about the sport, *Grand Prix*.[1]

Based in part on the experiences of real drivers, the director's first color film opens in Monaco at the start of the 1966 racing season, with cars speed-ing along the famous city's winding streets.[2] Midway through the contest, Pete Aron (James Garner), an American driver, crashes into a car driven by Scott Stoddard (Brian Bedford), a Briton, nearly killing him. The film then shifts gears and Frankenheimer directs our attention to the lives Aron, Stoddard and two other drivers, an Italian named Nino Barlini (Antonio Sabato) and a Frenchman named Sarti (Yves Montand), lead off the track. Because of the accident, for instance, Aron is fired from the team for which he competes, and he takes work as sports reporter, covering races for TV. While recuperating in the hospital, Stoddard is confronted by his wife Pat (Jessica Walter), who tells him that she will no longer tolerate his dangerous existence, and leaves him. Sarti, in contrast, finds love after meeting an American woman named Louise (Eva Marie Saint), a fashion writer, and Nino becomes attached to a woman named Lisa (Françoise Hardy).

As the season progresses and the men move from one grand prix circuit to the next, their relationships with their lovers evolve, becoming increasingly complex. Sarti and Louise hope to marry one another, but they cannot, because Sarti's estranged, and unloving, wife (Genevieve Page) refuses to give him a divorce. Nino, enjoying the celebrity that comes with victory, begins to cheat behind his lover Lisa's back. And Pat Stoddard, still in love with Scott, asks for him to take her back — after having a brief affair with Aron. Rather appropriately, the film comes to its end with the final race of the season. Once again, the four central characters appear, but this time Sarti crashes — and is killed — and Aron, who has been hired to race for a Japanese automobile manufacturer named Yamura (Toshiro Mifune), crosses the finish line safely, winning the competition. The film then cuts ahead in time several hours to the race track's deserted starting line, where Aron stands alone, the sound of grinding engines filling the soundtrack, reminding us that although this season is over, another will follow, and with it more of the same glory, thrills and death which have characterized this one.

Grand Prix is significant because it is one of the first of Frankenheimer's features to espouse an idea he would return to regularly over the next four decades, the belief that one's existence is not so much defined by what one thinks, but by what one does. In this instance, it is automobile racing which instills meaning and purpose into the characters' lives, and it does so, we learn, because it exposes them to danger, to the awareness that life is fragile. As Aron explains to his employer, the Japanese automobile magnate Yamura:

> I don't think there's one of us who doesn't ask himself at least once in the middle of a race, "What the hell am I doing here?" Of course, when it's over, we conveniently forget that we asked ourselves that question.... Maybe to do something that brings you so close to the possibility of death and to survive it is to feel life and living so much more intensely.

MGM released *Grand Prix* as a "reserved seat" feature, requiring customers to pay an elevated admission price; and commercially it was very, if not exceptionally, successful.[3] And the reviews the movie received were for the most part favorable as many critics responded enthusiastically to its technical aspects, praising Frankenheimer and his director of photography Lionel Lindon for the sense of immediacy they were able to achieve with the material they shot. Bosley Crowther, for example, wrote:

Aron (James Garner) awaits rescue after his collision with Stoddard in *Grand Prix* (MGM, 1966).

> As it stands—or as it runs—this three-hour picture about the professional and romantic rivalries of four drivers making the grand-prix circuit in the season of 1966 is a smashing and thundering compilation of racing footage shot superbly at the scenes of the big meets around the circuit, jazzed up with some great photographic trickery.[4]

Grand Prix's visuals are indeed magnificent, as the director insisted upon shooting on location as much as he could, filming real cars driven by real Formula One drivers in real races, in lieu of dummy cars, miniatures and process shots. And to intensify the viewers' experience, to spare them the monotony of simply watching the automobiles speeding about the circuits, Frankenheimer and Lindon shot the races from a variety of angles and distances, using remote controlled cameras which they mounted to the fronts and mid-sections of the cars, as well as several aerial shots which they filmed with helicopters.[5] The picture was also lensed using the Super Panavision 70 camera system, allowing the director to compose his shots with a super-wide aspect ratio, enabling him to cram the screen with a great deal of images and actions at once. In addition, the graphic designer Saul Bass, who'd worked with the director on *The*

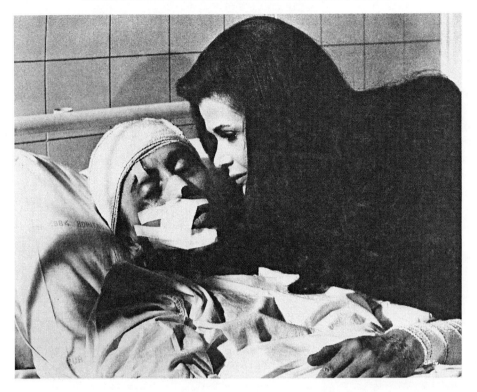

Pat Stoddard (Jessica Walter) tells her husband Scott (Brian Bedford) that she's leaving him in *Grand Prix* (MGM, 1966).

Young Stranger and *Seconds*, introduced several spectacular split-screen arrangements for the film's racing sequences, often lending them a quality which is at once kaleidoscopic and surreal.

The critics were much less appreciative of the story's other parts, the narrative strands that chronicle the protagonists' personal lives. Crowther decried the filmmakers' decision to give so much screen time to the men's love affairs. "The big trouble with this picture," he complained, "is that the characters and their romantic problems are stereotypes and clichés." Stephen Farber, writing for *Film Quarterly*, was similarly unimpressed and described these romantic scenes as "awfully boring."[6] *Variety*, however, argued that they played an essential part in the overall structure, blending into and complementing the film's other, less intimate segments:

> Frankenheimer has shrewdly varied the length and the importance of the races that figure in the film.... The director, moreover, frequently divides his outsized screen into sectional panels for a sort of montage interplay of reactions of the principals—a stream of consciousness commentary—that adroitly prevents the road running from overwhelming the personal drama.[7]

There is indeed much to admire in these scenes, especially the irony-laced conversations which transpire between Sarti and Louise; but Crowther's and Farber's criticism is nevertheless understandable and in many respects accurate, as the love scenes do move slowly and they lack the excitement and technical verve which we find in the race scenes. It may be surprising to learn that although this material was added to widen the picture's commercial reach, offering those who might care little for racing something else to watch and care about, it was actually Frankenheimer, and not the chiefs at MGM, who sought its inclusion. As the director explained to Betty Martin at the _Los Angeles Times_ in advance of the picture's release: "We hope the film will appeal to people who know nothing about cars." And he added that one of the models for _Grand Prix_—the inspiration for its ensemble cast and its tangled web of romantic sub-plots—was Goulding's _Grand Hotel_ (1932).[8] We can perhaps detect, as well, the influence of Lelouch's _A Man and a Woman_—the story of a race car driver who falls in love with a young widow—which had its premier at Cannes (and won the Palm d'Or) in May 1966, just as Frankenheimer's film began production.[9] But while the decision to focus so much attention on the characters' _affaires d'amours_ may not be particularly original, these stories, as derivative as they might be, still bear the mark of their maker, as each portrays love as a futile, and occasionally excruciating, endeavor, the same jaundiced point of view we find in _The Young Stranger, The Young Savages, All Fall Down, The Manchurian Candidate_ and _Seconds_. In fact, the only relationship that appears in the film which might be described as secure and stable and healthy is Sarti and Louise's—and it ends in flames and tears.

The Gypsy Moths (1969)

In 1964, Skylight Press published James Drought's _The Gypsy Moths_. Reminiscent of William Faulkner's _Pylon_ (1935), Drought's story about professional skydivers cultivated a small but enthusiastic following after its release, and this development encouraged the author's agent to shop the novel around Hollywood. Eventually a copy landed on the desk of the producer Edward Lewis, who liked it and passed it on to Frankenheimer, who liked it as well, and the partners purchased the property. The playwright William Hanley was then hired to write the script and several strong actors were cast, including Gene Hackman (fresh from _Bonnie and Clyde_), Deborah Kerr and Burt Lancaster.[10]

One of Frankenheimer's headier films, _The Gypsy Moths_ nevertheless features a fairly straightforward plot. Two days before the Fourth of July, a trio of skydivers—Rettig (Lancaster), Browdy (Hackman) and Malcolm (Scott Wilson)—arrives in a sleepy Kansas town called Bridgeville to perform a stunt

Rettig, Browdy and Malcolm perform high above the ground in *The Gypsy Moths* (MGM, 1969). The men in the photograph are not the film's stars, but members of a skydiving team Frankenheimer hired for the production.

show. After spending the afternoon preparing for the show and publicizing it, Retting and Browdy learn from Malcolm, the group's youngest member, that he lived in Bridgeville when he was a boy. The three then pay a visit to Malcolm's aunt and uncle, Elizabeth (Kerr) and Allen Brandon (William Windon), who still live in the town. Pleased to see her nephew, Elizabeth invites him and the others to stay at her home for the night. Then, following dinner, the three guests head into town and visit a strip joint called the Paradise, where Browdy strikes up a friendship with a dancer (Sheree North). Bored and restless, Retting and Malcolm leave the club, and as Malcolm checks out the town, Rettig heads back to the Brandons' house and begins to chat with Elizabeth. The two take a walk together, during which Elizabeth explains to him that she and Malcolm's father were once sweethearts; instead of marrying her, though, he married her sister and together they had Malcolm. When the couple died in a car accident a few years later, Elizabeth hoped to adopt the boy, but Brandon, the man she married, objected. Rettig and Elizabeth then return to the house and make love on the living room couch as Brandon lies awake upstairs, fully aware of what's happening.

The next day, Rettig asks the homemaker to leave with him, but she declines.

> ELIZABETH: The merciful stranger come to save me from the terrible boredom and love-lessness of my life. Is that what you think you are?
>
> RETTIG: I'm only offering you a way out.
>
> ELIZABETH: I don't want a way out!

He and the others then head out to an airfield on the outskirts of town and perform their show. But during the finale, Rettig, wearing a bizarre, moth-like costume, is killed when he fails to pull his parachute on a particularly dangerous jump called the "cape stunt." Deeply upset, Browdy convinces Malcolm that they should put on a second show in order to raise funds for the dead man's funeral. Malcolm agrees, but insists that they will only make one jump, the same one that killed their friend. The next day, Independence Day, Malcolm attempts the "cape" jump, and like Rettig, he is slow to pull the ripcord, though he does pull it. The experience transforms him, however, and when he lands, his interest in skydiving is gone. That night, Browdy drives Malcolm to the Bridgeville train station. After the men say goodbye to one another, a fireworks display begins and Malcolm boards his train.

The Gypsy Moths was met with little interest when MGM released it in the fall of 1969. Gary Arnold, for instance, complained: "The [characters'] speech is flat, the compositions are flat, the color is flat, and the pace — well, the pace is heroically, exaltingly, supernaturally flat" and Vincent Canby accused the director of stringing together a series of "dimly articulated emotional crises" instead of introducing action and danger the subject matter called for.[11] Roger Ebert, on the other hand, argued that the director weakened the film's character studies and the narrative's emotional impact by using too much stunt footage.[12]

The Gypsy Moths is a slow film, yet it bears well under repeated viewing, in part because of Frankenheimer's fondness for using symbols and metaphor, creating a *mise en scene* which is rich with inference. Frequently, the director uses visual cues to suggest that his protagonists resemble moths: for instance, the tailfins that poke up from the rear of the men's clunky, old car look like wings; when Rettig chats with Elizabeth in the playground, he wanders toward a streetlight, as if drawn by its glow; and in their rooms at the Brandon house, Browdy and Malcolm position themselves near lights. The film's title also links the three skydivers with moths—gypsy moths in particular. But why gypsy moths? In the Lepidoptera order, these creatures are unusual because they can lay their eggs anywhere, while other varieties can only lay their eggs on certain surfaces. Gypsy moths, in short, have more freedom than other moths. Similarly, the men in the film, unencumbered by marriages, mortgages and the like, freely rove about the landscape as they search for work and adventure. Their freedom is hardly absolute, however. They cannot work unless they find audiences who will pay to watch them jump, after all, and they cannot find these audiences unless they travel constantly.

But while Browdy, Malcolm and Rettig share the same appetite for danger, each of them is a loner ultimately, incapable of or uninterested in forming or maintaining lasting relationships. When Malcolm leaves Bridgeville at the end of the picture, for example, he also leaves behind the possibility of a love affair with Annie (Bonnie Bedelia), the Brandons' young boarder. Similarly, Browdy forgets about and moves on from the strip joint dancer, the one he sleeps with and jokes about marrying. And Rettig is so alienated that he kills himself — if we interpret his death as a suicide, as "a way out." At the same time, the argument might be made that Rettig, unlike his colleagues, craves love and commitment, and this is why he asks Elizabeth to run away with him. But although the woman, to a certain extent, is attracted to the ageing daredevil, the adventure and volatility he promises and the threat he poses to her middle-class comforts and habits overpowers her own desire for companionship. As she tells her husband, the man she stays with but doesn't love, "[Rettig] wanted me to go with him.... The thought terrified me."

Determining where Frankenheimer's sympathies lie in this argument between freedom and stability is difficult, as he focuses just as much attention on the merits and the shortcomings of the parachutists' lives as he does on the Brandons'. The neutrality of his position is further enhanced by the film's journalistic — almost sterile — tone, which results from the director's frequent use of documentary filmmaking techniques. There is the footage of the skydivers performing in the air, of course, which was shot by Carl Boenisch, who jumped with the men, a camera mounted to his crash helmet. And a great deal of screen time is given to informative content, to footage that enables viewers to see what professional skydivers do before and after they jump, such as checking their equipment, folding their parachutes and the like. The same analytical objectives characterize Frankenheimer's treatment of the film's dramatic sequences, the scenes in which the skydivers are not jumping, when they are interacting with the Brandons and the others. Keeping clear of the expressionist flourishes that mark pictures like *All Fall Down*, *The Manchurian Candidate* and *Seconds*, the director handles the camera in these scenes as objectively as possible, using it to establish setting, reveal character, move the plot and little more. And because of this, the film's action scenes and dramatic scenes flow into one another smoothly, avoiding the stylistic disjointedness that hurts *Grand Prix*.

The Horsemen (1971)

In 1968, Frankenheimer and his producing partner Edward Lewis secured a deal with Columbia Pictures to shoot an adaptation of French writer Joseph Kessel's *The Horsemen*, a sprawling novel about *buzkashi*, a ferocious game played in Afghanistan in which men on horseback fight for the possession of a headless, stuffed calf. For the script, Frankenheimer called upon Dalton Trumbo, who'd written *The Fixer* for him a few years earlier. Encouraged by the studio to adhere closely to Kessel's book, Trumbo produced a script for a three-hour film. The story's length became a problem during production, however, when Columbia told Frankenheimer it wanted him to make a much shorter film, prohibiting him from shooting several, critical expositional scenes, which, in turn, damaged the picture's continuity.[13]

Despite its structural flaws, *The Horsemen* has many merits, including the performances of the male leads Omar Sharif and Jack Palance, Georges Delerue's wistful score and Claude Renoir's often enthralling photography of the Spanish landscape, where much of the movie was shot. Renoir's footage of actual *buzkashi* matches is memorable, as well, and Frankenheimer weaves this material through the narrative just as he did with the racetrack footage in *Grand Prix* and the skydiving sequences in *The Gypsy Moths*. *The Horsemen* also resembles these earlier pictures with the emphasis it places upon the inner lives of its heroes, in particular Uraz (Sharif), a *buzkashi* athlete who ruins his leg during a match.

Set in contemporary Afghanistan, the film opens with a series of gliding aerial shots that lead the viewers' attention from the peaks of a jagged mountain range to the flat waste of the Asian steppe, where Tursen (Palance), an old man who raises horses for the king of Afghanistan, owns a farm. Crippled from his days as a *buzkashi* horseman, Tursen rises up from his bed, staggers outside and selects a team of riders, or *chopendoz* as they are called, to compete in a royal buzkashi tournament in faraway Kabul. One of those he selects is his son Uraz, a brazen character who envies his father's reputation as the greatest rider who ever lived in this part of the kingdom. Told by Tursen to win at all costs, Uraz heads out to the capital city on a magnificent stallion called Jahil, which his father has loaned to him. He performs well at the competition, but loses the match when he is thrown from his mount and dragged by the leg across the playing field, much like the stuffed calf for which he and the other *chopendoz* have been competing.

Hours later, the injured man wakes in the hospital with his leg bound in a cast. Shamed by his defeat, he tells his servant Mukhi (David De) to take him from Kabul immediately. He also has Mukhi remove the cast from his leg, convinced it will not heal if sunlight cannot reach it. As the two head out, Uraz then decides that he wants to take the shortest route home, a road called the "dead man's path" which will lead them through the snowy mountains. Mukhi refuses at first, but when his master promises to give him Jahil if he dies, he consents. Uraz's generous offer arouses Mukhi's greed rather than his loyalty, however, and once the men strike out into the frontier, he becomes increasingly treacherous as Uraz becomes increasingly ill — avarice and disease, the director seems to suggest, are correlative phenomena. Eventually, the sickness

Uraz (Omasr Sharif) and Mukhi (David De) begin their trip back to Tursen's ranch in *The Horsemen* (Columbia, 1971).

so overpowers Uraz that he loses consciousness, but a nomad woman named Zereh (Leigh Taylor-Young) saves him. When he recovers, though, he is disgusted that a person of such low birth has touched his body. Nonetheless, he allows the woman to join him and Mukhi as they cross the mountain pass, a bad decision, as she immediately begins to conspire with the servant to steal the horse from the weakened chopendoz.

When the group arrives upon a great bazaar, Uraz, a habitual gambler, wagers the stallion Jahil on a ram fight, which he wins. A short time later, Zereh and Mukhi try to steal the horseman's winnings, but he subdues them, threatening to toss the bills into the violent, snowy wind. The unhappy trio then resume their trek through the mountains, but stop when they encounter a shepherd, who tells Uraz in private that he must cut off the infected part of his leg with an axe if he hopes to live. The horseman agrees and afterward conceals the shortened leg with his boot. He then punishes Zereh and Mukhi for their earlier treachery by having the nomad woman throw the money he won at the ram fight into a fire.

Thanks to the demands the studio placed upon Frankenheimer and Trumbo's script, the movie begins to lose its coherence at this point. After the remarkable sequence with the money, the narrative abruptly jumps to Tursen's ranch, where Mukhi and Zereh are brought before the old man, who listens as Uraz describes their crimes. Both before and after their attempt on his life, Uraz has displayed little more than malice to these people, but when he is asked by his father to decide upon an appropriate punishment for them, he inexplicably replies that nothing should be done, that they should be freed. Why does he feel this way? Has he undergone a profound change since the incident with the money on the mountaintop? Has he become a merciful person? Or is he trying, perhaps, to confound his father? We can't tell. Tursen's behavior is similarly obtuse. After agreeing to free the disloyal servant and his lover, he gives Mukhi the horse Jahil. Is this done to punish Uraz for being so lenient in his judgment, or perhaps because Uraz lost the *buzkashi* in Kabul, or is it because Mukhi raised the animal? Again, we cannot tell because of the final act's fragmented condition.

The picture ends with a series of similarly perplexing scenes. While Uraz dresses in his tent, he is approached by Zereh, the nomad. Though she once disgusted him, now she awakens his desire and he makes loves to her. He also gives her a large sum of money. But immediately following this, he goes to his father and begs the old man to buy Jahil back from Mukhi because he hasn't got the money for it himself. Uraz then performs a series of stunts on the great horse at a feast, and afterward, no longer interested in concealing his secret injury, removes his boot and reveals his shortened leg to the crowd. The action then returns one final time to Tursen's farm, where Uraz explains to his father that in spite of the fact that he almost lost his life trying to get back to the old man's home, he will now return to the frontier.

The Horsemen may be disjointed, but it still bears the stamp of its creator with the appearance of motifs and themes we find elsewhere. Heroes with physical impairments and injuries, for instance, appear in *The Train*, *I Walk the Line*, *French Connection II*, *Black Sunday*, *Against the Wall*, *Andersonville*, *George Wallace* and *Ronin*. And variations of the strained parent-child relationship can be found in *The Young Stranger*, *All Fall Down*, *The Manchurian Candidate*, *The Fourth War* and *The Island of Dr. Moreau*. In addition, Uraz's insolent manner and his reckless, often violent behavior are traits he shares with *Bird Man of Alcatraz*'s Robert Stroud and *Dead Bang*'s Jerry Beck. And like the skydiver Rettig in *The Gypsy Moths*, Uraz seems to be half-in-love with the grave, something he also shares with his father Tursen, who tells him at one point that both men "pursue death as lesser men pursue women." Yet unlike Rettig, Uraz lives, triumphing over the dangers he sets before himself. And while it is his ability to outwit his enemies which plays a part in his survival, the help he receives from others—like Zareh at first and later the shepherd—is crucial, too, reminding us that no man is an island, not even a lordly *chopendoz* like Uraz.

In one of his interviews with Pratley, Frankenheimer compared *The Horsemen* to *Easy Rider* (1969), Dennis Hopper's famous motorcycle movie about a pair of bikers who, much like Uraz, travel a great distance through hostile country. The two films, he felt, were thematically linked, as both offer portraits of non-conformist characters who resist the dominant values and beliefs which circulate in their communities.[14] Uraz, for instance, expresses this disregard when he heads off into the wilderness in the film's final moments, defying and rejecting the prosperous, land owner existence his father represents. We should note, though, that Uraz is not the only protagonist in Frankenheimer's cinema who might be labeled "anti-establishment." Hank Bell defies his employers, the popular press and the will of the public, for example, when he sabotages the state's case against the teen killers in *The Young Savages*. The militant Hawks organizes an armed response to the corporate logging interests who pollute the environment in *Prophecy*. And Chico Mendes stands up to the Brazilian government, foreign businessmen and rich ranchers as he tries to protect the rubber tappers in *The Burning Season*.

The Challenge (1982)

Much like *French Connection II*, *The Holcroft Covenant* and *Year of the Gun*, *The Challenge* explores the problems an American character faces when he enters a foreign country. In this instance, a down-and-out boxer finds himself in Kyoto, Japan caught between a pair of feuding brothers.

The origins of this conflict, we learn from the film's opening sequence, date back to the final days of World War II, when an old man named Yoshida (Shog Shimanda), the elderly patriarch of an aristocratic clan, decides to pass on a pair of ancient sabers called "The Equals" to his eldest son Toru (Toshiro Mifune). The ceremony is disrupted, however, by Yoshida's youngest son Hideo (Atsuo Nakamura), who stages a violent attack and steals the swords.

The film then jumps to contemporary Los Angeles. After 37 years, Toru Yoshida has located one of the swords his brother took from him, and he has sent his paraplegic son Toshio (Sab Shimono) to collect it. To convey the weapon back to Japan safely, Toshio hires an ex-boxer named Rick Murphy (Scott Glenn), who agrees to fly to Kyoto with the sword, which he hides in a golf bag. But upon his arrival, the American is abducted by Ando (Calvin Jung), a thug who works for Hideo, who in the years since the war has become a powerful businessman. After determining that the weapon Rick has transported is a fake, Ando tracks down Toshio, who refuses to let on where the real sword is located. In one of the film's more grotesque scenes, Ando responds to Toshio's refusal by killing him, pushing him out of a moving truck, not realizing that the sword he wants is hidden in the paralyzed man's wheelchair.

Rick then escapes from Ando and finds refuge in Toru's *dojo*, an academy for the martial arts. An ungracious guest, he sneers at his hosts and their culture, even chiding the grieving Toru when Toshio's wheelchair — and the sword it concealed — are returned to the school. Then, once he is paid for his efforts,

Rick leaves the *dojo* and heads to a bar, where he is again confronted by Ando, who offers him a large sum if he will return to Toru as a student and steal the newly recovered sword.

The American agrees, but when he tries to leave the compound, his conscience rises up and prevents him from completing the job. He then confesses to Toru and as punishment the teacher has Rick bury himself up to his chin in dirt. The punishment proves to be a rite of passage for the ex-boxer and afterward he commits himself sincerely to his training, quickly mastering his teacher's fighting techniques. Toru's daughter Akiko (Donna Kei Benz) is then kidnapped by Hideo, and Rick, who is in love with her, follows Toru to Hideo's home, an enormous complex set in a mountain valley.[15] The men penetrate the building and wind up in Hideo's office, where the brothers fight one another with the ancient Equals. When Toru falls, though, Rick takes up his sword and attacks Hideo. The struggle which ensues is bloody, but Rick is the better fighter, and he kills the evil businessman. Then he takes the dead man's sword and sets it, along with the one he's been using, before the injured Toru.

Anticipating Quentin Tarantino's *Kill Bill* films, *The Challenge* borrows heavily from Asian genre cinema, especially the cycle of samurai (or *chambara*) films which flourished in Japan from the end of World War II up to the late Seventies. In particular, the movie is indebted to Kurosawa's *Yojimbo*, the story of an errant bodyguard (played by Toshiro Mifune) who, like Rick before his conscience awakens, positions himself between warring factions for self-gain. The two films are thematically linked, too, as each addresses what the British film critic Sarah Donaldson has described as "the displacement of Japan's feudal order by a corrupt business class." These likenesses, no doubt, can be attributed in part to John Sayles, one of the film's scenarists, who'd been an admirer of *Yojimbo* since his days as a college student.[16] We can also detect the influence of low budget, sensationalistic *chambara* on the picture, especially the *Sword of Vengeance* series from the mid–Seventies, in which an assassin named Lone Wolf and Cub conceals an arsenal of traditional samurai weapons in a baby carriage, much as Toshio Yoshida hides a dagger and a sword in his wheelchair. Again, this may be the influence of Sayles, who'd been writing scripts for Roger Corman at New World Pictures when the studio abridged and combined and then released the first two Lone Wolf and Cub movies as *Shogun Assassin* in 1980.

Throughout the picture, as well, the influence of Japanese gangster, or *yakuza*, movies reveals itself with the inclusion of smartly dressed characters like Ando and the others who carjack Toshio's truck early in the film.[17] The wealthy businessman Hideo, we learn, is also connected to the underworld, having amassed his fortune through crooked means, using hired men and murder to protect his interests. Frankenheimer borrows heavily from "chop socky" cinema, too, introducing several *karate* fights, where characters attack one another with their feet and their fists, rather than guns and swords. These hand-to-

Teacher and Pupil: To escape from Hideo, Rick (Scott Glenn) feigns an attack on Toru (Toshiro Mifune) in the woods outside Kyoto in *The Challenge* (CBS Theatrical Films, 1982).

hand combat scenes, by the way, were staged by the American action film hero Steven Segal.

But while *The Challenge* owes much to Asian cinema, it is still very much a Frankenheimer film, featuring several familiar themes. The picture draws attention to the importance of loyalty and friendship, a concern it shares with films like *The Train*, *99 and 44/100% Dead!* and *Ronin*. And like *Grand Prix* and *The Horsemen*, it focuses on the ways in which physical discipline and pain can bring about positive changes in a man's character. When the film opens, for example, Rick is an unattractive individual, prone to arrogance and selfishness. He insults Toshio and Akiko when they visit him in his slum apartment. Later, he picks fights with the other students at Toru's academy in Japan. He also sets out to deceive the old man, too, in order to steal his sword. But with exposure to Toru's teachings in the ways of *bushido*, the samurai code of ethics, he begins to change, becoming increasingly selfless and concerned about the welfare of those around him, like Akiko and the little boy Jiro (Kenta Fukasaku), who works at the *dojo*.[18] The extent of the change only becomes evident to him, though, when he violates this code and learns that his conscience will not let him steal his teacher's sword.

Frankenheimer's partiality for symbolic compositions surfaces frequently in *The Challenge*, too. In the picture's closing moments, for instance, a high angle shot of the Equals lying side by side before Toru appears on the screen. Frankenheimer follows this with a tracking shot that leads the viewer's attention away from the swords to an exterior view of Kyoto as the sun rises behind a nearby mountain. All is well in Japan, the sequence implies, now that Toru has his swords back. But the Equals are more than just precious heirlooms for the elderly patriarch; they also symbolize his family's honor, which Hideo sullied when he broke the traditional line of succession and stole the swords. Their recovery, in short, marks the recovery of the Yoshida clan's honor.

Rick, of course, plays an essential role in this process, first as the mercenary courier who helps Toshio bring the lost Equal back to Japan and then as the dutiful pupil who rises to aid his fallen teacher. The American's skill with the samurai sword and his willingness to adopt the principles of *bushido* suggest that the tensions and hostilities which can arise between people of different races, cultures and nationalities can be transcended by shared beliefs and conduct, an idea Frankenheimer also puts forth in *Grand Prix*, where drivers from around the world overcome cultural differences and become friends because of their shared interest in and experience with Formula One racing.

But although *The Challenge* may end with a shot of the sun rising, it is still a dark movie, preoccupied as it is with problems like murder, revenge and hate. And though Rick and Toru enjoy success in the film's final moments, their victory is invariably colored by the tremendous suffering and loss which Toru's obsessive pursuit of the swords has caused, including the death of his son, the injury of the little boy Jiro at the *dojo* and Akiko's kidnapping. For the most part bereft of humor and filled with grim images, the film also tends to emphasize mankind's underside, its penchant for meanness, a quality that not only afflicts the film's villains, but its heroes, too. We see an instance of this in the dinner that Toru hosts for Rick, where tiny eels swim about in glasses of sake and lobsters are cut in half and eaten alive. Why do the Yoshidas eat in this manner? "They taste best," Akiko explains to Rick, smiling broadly, "when they're fresh."

CHAPTER FOUR

Threats to Freedom

The freedom of thought and the freedom of expression are of paramount importance in Frankenheimer's films. And several of his narratives follow men who lose and then struggle to regain their capacity to think and to do as they wish. We see this scenario played out to great effect in *French Connection II* when Doyle buckles under the weight of heroin and becomes an addict, then weans himself from the mind-addling drug and then restores himself and his ability to pursue his enemy Charnier. Similarly in *The Manchurian Candidate*, Raymond Shaw regains the ability to make choices for himself once he breaks free of the mental shackles created for him by his Red Chinese and Soviet handlers. In turn, many of the antagonists in Frankenheimer's movies are those who try to wrest freedom from individuals, be it Charnier or the Old Man in *Seconds* or the blackmailers in *52 Pick-Up*. Arguably, the controlling mother figures we find in *All Fall Down*, *Bird Man of Alcatraz* and *The Manchurian Candidate* are also guilty of this behavior. In many of the films in which government and politics are the subject—films like *Black Sunday*, *The Holcroft Covenant*, *Year of the Gun* and again *The Manchurian Candidate*—the same theme materializes. But in these pictures we find that the heavies are not only opposed to individual freedoms and civil liberties, but to the democratic institutions which protect them, as well.

The Manchurian Candidate (1962)

Like *The Challenge* and *The Holcroft Covenant*, *The Manchurian Candidate* starts with a short prologue which is set during wartime. But while the other pictures open at the end of World War II, *The Manchurian Candidate* starts in 1952, right in the middle of the United States' three-year conflict with Soviet-supported North Korea. The sequence does not begin on the battlefield, however, but in a brothel, where a company of American soldiers are enjoying themselves. Their revelry ends abruptly, though, with the arrival of their N.C.O. Sgt. Raymond Shaw (Laurence Harvey), who tells the men it's time to leave. The soldiers, Shaw and an officer named Capt. Ben Marco (Frank Sinatra) then head out on a night patrol mission, during which they are attacked and captured by the enemy.

After this, the film leaps ahead several weeks, to an airfield in the United States, where Raymond is greeted by a crowd of patriotic well-wishers as the film's narrator lets us know that some time after the ambush in Korea, the sergeant conducted himself with great valor on the battlefield, and for this he's been decorated with the Congressional Medal of Honor. Wanting to exploit her son's celebrity, Raymond's mother (Angela Lansbury) appears a few moments after he steps off the plane, turning his arrival into a photo opportunity for her right-wing politician husband, Sen. John Iselin (James Gregory).[1] Disgusted by this, Raymond then explains that he has accepted a job at a newspaper in New York City, where he will work for a columnist who despises the Iselins and their politics.

But as the war hero optimistically begins his new life in New York, his friend Marco, a career officer, finds himself suffering horribly two hundred miles to the south. The film's narrator explains:

> The war in Korea was over. Captain, now Major, Bennett Marco had been reassigned to Army Intelligence in Washington. It was, by and large, a pleasant assignment, except for one thing. Night after night, the Major was plagued by the same recurring nightmare.

In this nightmare, which Frankenheimer dramatizes, Marco, Raymond and the others in the platoon sit in a stuporous state before a group of communist agents, spymasters and assassins, as a Red Chinese psychiatrist named Yen Loh (Khigh Dhiesh) prattles on about brainwashing and mind control. The doctor then proceeds to demonstrate the effectiveness of his ideas, commanding Raymond to strangle one of the other soldiers, which he does. Hoping to rid himself of the horrible dream, Marco heads up to New York to talk to Raymond. To his surprise and relief, the major learns from his friend that another soldier from their platoon has also been having the same "swinger of a nightmare." "Do you remember Al Melvin, the corporal in the patrol?" Raymond says. "Well, I had a letter from him a couple weeks ago.... He said he was going out of his mind.... He keeps dreaming that the patrol is all sitting together in this hotel lobby and there are a lot of Chinese brass and Russian generals.... Is it the same thing you've been dreaming?"

Following this, Marco returns to Washington, reports what he has discovered and upon receiving authorization from his superiors, begins an investigation, trying to find out what happened to him and the others in Korea, eventually learning that Raymond has been brainwashed by the Chinese and their Russian allies, programmed to do their bidding. Simultaneously, and com-

Prisoners of War: Marco (Frank Sinatra) and Raymond (Laurence Harvey) in one of the dream sequences Frankenheimer created for *The Manchurian Candidate* (MGM, 1962).

pletely unaware of his predicament, Raymond continues to pursue his career and his love life, reuniting with an old girlfriend, Jocie Jordan (Leslie Parrish), whom he marries. But tragedy quickly follows. Jocie's father (John McGiver), like Raymond's step-father, is a U.S. senator. Jordan regards the Iselins as dangerous reactionaries, and at a party, when Mrs. Iselin asks the senator if he will try to block her husband's efforts to run as the vice presidential candidate in a forthcoming national election, Jordan says that he will. Raymond's infuriated mother then summons her son and leads him into a hypnotic state, using a deck of cards and a series of verbal commands. Once again, the director has given us another counterfeit, another character who hides behind a false persona. Far from being an ardent anti-communist, the woman is a Red agent, collaborating with Yen Loh and the others on a secret scheme to overthrow the United States government, a plan which cannot work if her husband's bid is blocked. Raymond then proceeds to act upon his mother's orders, murdering Jordan. Unfortunately, he shoots his new wife Jocie, as well, when she walks in upon the killing.

After hearing about the deaths of the Jordans, Marco finds Raymond, who has no memory of the tragedy, in a New York City apartment. There, the major

The Iselins (Angela Lansbury, James Gregory) host a masquerade party in *The Manchurian Candidate* (MGM 1962).

hypnotizes his friend, trying to find out what he knows, what he's done and what he's been programmed to do.

> MARCO: All right, let's start unlocking a few doors. Let's begin with the patrol. You didn't save our lives and take out an enemy company or anything like that, did you, Raymond? Did you?

RAYMOND: No.

MARCO: What happened?

RAYMOND: The patrol was taken by a Russian Airborne Unit and flown by helicopter across the Manchurian border.... we were worked on for three days by a team of specialists from the Pavlov Institute in Moscow. They developed a technique for descent into the unconscious mind, part light-induced, part drug.

MARCO: Never mind all that. Not now. Tell me what else happened....

RAYMOND: We were drilled for three days. We were made to memorize the details of the imaginary action.

Marco also learns that something sinister has been planned for the upcoming political convention where Iselin will be nominated for vice president, but Raymond cannot give him specific details. Marco then attempts to re-program Raymond, to ruin Yen Loh's work:

The links, the beautifully-conditioned links are smashed. They're smashed as of now because we say so, because we say they ought to be smashed. We're bustin' up the joint, we're tearin' out all the wires, we're bustin' it up.... You don't work anymore. That's an order.

After this, rather optimistically, Marco allows Raymond to leave the apartment, to visit his mother, who once again leads her son into a hypnotic state, telling him:

You are to shoot the Presidential nominee through the head. And Johnny will rise gallantly to his feet and lift [the dead man's] body in his arms, stand in front of the microphones and begin to speak. The speech is short, but it's the most rousing speech I've ever read. It's been worked on here and in Russia on and off for over eight years. I shall force someone to take the body away from him. And Johnny will leave those microphones and those cameras with blood all over him, fighting off anyone who tries to help him, defending America even if it means his own death, rallying a nation of television-viewers into hysteria to sweep us up into the White House with powers that will make martial law seem like anarchy.

Frankenheimer then moves the action to a convention center, where Raymond, a "crack shot since childhood," finds a booth high above the floor and the stage where the candidates sit. Perched up there, he assembles his gun and trains the sights on his step-father's running mate, the presidential candidate, whose name is Ben Arthur (Robert Riordan). But before he pulls the trigger, Raymond shifts his aim, firing at Iselin instead, then his mother. Having spotted Raymond moments earlier, Marco rushes up to the booth, but arrives too late. "You couldn't have stopped them. The army couldn't have stopped them. So I had to stop them," Raymond says. Then he turns the gun on himself and commits suicide.

When it premiered in July 1962, *The Manchurian Candidate* generally drew strong reviews, though some critics, like the perennially fussy Bosley Crowther, complained that its

basic suppositions ... are extremely hard to take as here put forth. We are asked to believe that, in three days, a fellow could be brainwashed to the point that two years later, he would still be dutifully submissive to his brainwasher's spell. And the nature of the plot and its key figure here in this country [Raymond's incestuous mother], when finally revealed, are so fantastic that one is suspicious of the author's sincerity.[2]

Philip K. Scheuer, in contrast, argued that the plot's exaggerated aspects made it engaging: "*The Manchurian Candidate* is not only fascinating because it is so unpredictable as storytelling but also because it reverts to the kind of moviemaking that made cinema — sheer film — a joy and end in itself."[3]

In 1988, however, when the film was re-released theatrically, critics around the nation responded to it with unfettered praise. Roger Ebert exclaimed: "Frankenheimer's 1962 masterpiece re-emerges as one of the best and brightest of modern American films."[4] Janet Maslin described it as "arguably the most chilling piece of cold war paranoia ever committed to film."[5] And Richard Corliss wrote:

> Few movies attempt to anatomize a whole sick society, to dissect the mortal betrayals of country, friend, lover and family; fewer films achieve this goal with such energy and wit. Voters will make their own choices this year, but for moviegoers the election is over. This Candidate delivers.[6]

Indeed, *The Manchurian Candidate* is an unforgettable piece of work, a nightmarish rendering of modern America, which is at once funny and troubling. But while the film is unquestionably original, it has been frequently compared with some justification to the work of other directors. Jonathan Rosenbaum, for instance, has argued: "It's conceivably the only commercial American film that deserves to be linked with the French New Wave, full of visual and verbal wit that recalls Orson Welles."[7] And Greil Marcus, who wrote a monograph about the film for the British Film Institute, has described it as being "made up of bits of Hitchcock and Welles, of *Psycho* and *Citizen Kane* most obviously."[8] The links between *Kane* and *Candidate* are primarily stylistic, we should note, as the latter film makes frequent use, much as the earlier does, of deep focus photography, chiaroscuro lighting and subjective shots which approximate the points of view of the mentally disturbed protagonists who people its tortuous plot. And the director's debt to the *nouvelle vague* is largely stylistic, too. The "irrational," elliptical cutting which appears in the picture's celebrated dream sequences, for example, brings to mind similarly edited passages which we find in pictures like Resnais' *Hiroshima Mon Amour* (1959) and *Last Year at Marienbad* (1961) as well as Truffaut's *Shoot the Piano Player* (1960).[9] But Hitchcock's influence upon the film is felt more, on the other hand, in its thematic content and its structure. Like *Psycho*, the picture plays on false appearances and confused mental states; and like Hitchcock's protagonist Norman Bates, Raymond Shaw doesn't know that he is a killer, as he suffers from a type of amnesia which prevents him from remembering the murders he commits; and like the lonely motel clerk, he's been damaged by an imperious mother, leaving him frustrated and torn, hating and desiring her at once.

Other films by Hitchcock may come to mind, as well. An amnesiac killer shows up in his 1945 melodrama *Spellbound* as well as an elaborate and surreal dream sequence. And in both the 1934 and 1956 versions of *The Man Who Knew Too Much*, a sniper awaits amidst of crowd of people, prepared like Raymond to kill a political figure. Interestingly, the actor Reggie Nalder, who plays the assassin in the 1956 version of *The Man Who Knew Too Much*, shows up in this film, too, playing a Russian agent. And Janet Leigh, who plays Marco's love interest Rosie, was of course the leading lady in *Psycho*. Frankenheimer, by the way, was not embarrassed about his indebtedness to the Master of Suspense. As he explained on the film's DVD commentary, talking about Marco's efforts to locate Raymond in the convention hall:

> The trick here is how does Sinatra find Laurence Harvey? And we could never come up with it. And finally one day I said to George Axelrod, I said, "*Foreign Correspondent.*" And we both knew exactly what was meant by that. In other words, in *Foreign Correspondent* Joel McCrea finds where the Nazis are in this mass of windmills ... [A]ll the windmills are going in one direction except for the one where the spies' radio is, which is going the other direction because that's electrically powered. Today they call such a thing an homage, but in those days I think I would have called it a rip-off. Anyway I think I have to admit to the fact that I ripped off Hitchcock here because what happens here is all the lights dim except for one. Raymond Shaw's light [in the spotlight booth] does not dim. And that's how Sinatra finds out where he is.

But while the movie reveals the influence of other directors, it is still very much a Frankenheimer picture, exploring themes and tropes which had appeared in his earlier films and would continue to materialize regularly over the next 40 years. We can detect in Marco's relationship with Raymond, the director's predilection for portraying unlikely friendships, a motif he also visits in *Bird Man of Alcatraz*, *The Fixer*, *The Horsemen*, *French Connection II* and *Ronin*. His fondness for having his characters appear in costumes also shows up on a number of occasions. The featherbrain Iselin dresses as Abe Lincoln at a masquerade party, for example, while his wife wears a Little Bo Peep outfit, and Raymond, in the film's climactic sequence, disguises himself in priest's garb to avert attention as he slinks through the convention hall. The director's penchant for filling his shots with symbolic iconography surfaces, too. American flags dot the screen frequently as do painted portraits and sculptures of Lincoln, who, just like the Iselins, was slain by an assassin. The film closes, as well, with an image of a solitary figure reflecting upon the events which have just transpired, a composition Frankenheimer also uses to end *I Walk the Line*, *The Challenge*, *Dead Bang* and *George Wallace*; in this case, we find Marco staring out a window, muttering, "Hell.... hell," as he thinks about his lost friend.

The Train (1965)

During World War II, a woman named Rose Valland was the curator of the Musée du Jeu de Paume, a Paris gallery that housed a large collection of modern art. A member of the French Resistance, Valland used her position to protect the museum's paintings from the Germans throughout the war, and in 1961, she published a memoir about her experience titled *Le front de l'art*. The book was subsequently picked up for development by United Artists with Arthur Penn slated to direct. But in the summer of 1963, just after production began, the film's star Burt Lancaster fired Penn and contacted Frankenheimer, asking him to take over direction, just as he'd done on *Bird Man of Alcatraz*.

To help his friend, Frankenheimer accepted the job, though he insisted that a new script had to be written before filming could resume.

> [T]hey had been shooting for a week.... I went to France. I [hadn't] read the script. I was on the airplane and if hijacking had been in vogue then, the plane would have gone right back to Los Angeles because the goddam picture was *The Train*, and the train didn't leave the station until page one-hundred-eighty, which was when the picture was over.[10]

And upon his arrival in France, he asked the film's producer Jules Bricken to "shut the picture down for three weeks while I brought in some new writers [including Howard Dimsdale and the blacklisted scenarist Ned Young, who'd also worked on *Seven Days in May*, and who would subsequently make an appearance in *Seconds*], and we took a hotel room and rewrote the whole damn thing."[11] To make Valland's narrative more interesting, Frankenheimer asked his writers to invent several action scenes, having them build the film's plot around an uprising in which members of the French Underground use force to stop a train (which has been seized by a mad colonel played by Paul Scofield) from carrying off the Musee du Jeu de Paume's collection. Much of what appears on the screen in this film, that is, is fictitious. As we read in the liner notes MGM prepared for the film's DVD release:

> While *The Train* depicts the French Resistance thwarting the art theft through a combination of trickery, sabotage and death defying heroics, it was actually accomplished through bureaucratic red tape: the real-life art train, bogged down by an endless barrage of paperwork, made it no farther than a railroad yard a few miles outside Paris.

When shooting resumed in the fall of 1963, the script was not yet complete, however, but Frankenheimer proceeded anyway. And over the next several months, more challenges arose. A staged train crash went awry destroying equipment. The onslaught of cold weather "fogged up the cameras and ... made the ground too hard to safely detonate explosives" for many of the film's action sequences.[12] And the chilly air made the actors' breath steamy, a real problem given that the movie's action took place in late summer. As Frankenheimer recalled:

> [S]moke was coming out of everybody's mouth so that to get Scofield's stuff we had to use a big wind machine. And behind the wind machine we had these torches, flame throwers, and the wind was coming out hot, you see, onto Paul so that therefore there was no smoke coming out of his mouth.... So now we're ready to do the third take. I say, "OK, we'll do it again." I wasn't looking and the French cameraman comes up to me and he said, "We cannot do it again." I said, "Why can't we do it again? He said,

"Look at Mr. Scofield. He's cooked — he's cooked!" And he was absolutely beet red. We'd burned him with the flame. So we had to send him back to his hotel for two days.[13]

Eventually, the weather became so cold that UA was forced to shut the picture down until the spring of the following year.[14]

Set in Paris during the last weeks of the German Occupation, the picture opens at the Musee du Jeu de Paume, the gallery Valland described in her memoir. In order to raise funds for his army, a Nazi officer named von Waldheim (Paul Scofield) has decided to empty the museum of its priceless paintings, which he hopes to transport to Germany by train. The museum's curator Madame Villard (Suzanne Flon) responds to this by contacting Lebiche (Burt Lancaster), a railroad official who doubles as the head of a group of anti-German resistants. Lebiche considers the woman's request for help, but turns its down on the grounds that he will not risk the lives of men for works of art. Instead, he tells an old engineer named Boule (Michel Simon) to drive the "art train" into Germany. But although Boule is not a member of the Resistance, the idea of aiding the Germans troubles his conscience, and he sabotages the train.

When von Waldheim discovers the old man's treachery, he has him executed and orders Lebiche to drive the train himself. The murder upsets Lebiche and after he departs from the train yard, his assistants Didont (Albert Remy) and Pesquet (Charles Millon) persuade him to save the paintings, and instead of completing the run to Germany, he turns the train back for Paris, crashes it and flees. Von Waldheim answers this attack with more violence, ordering his soldiers to execute several railroad workers. He then forces a group of French citizens to board the train and he and his soldiers again head off for the German border, prompting Lebiche to come out of hiding and derail the train with explosives. The colonel then has the crated paintings unloaded and the hostages shot. Simultaneously, a column of retreating German troops materializes. Von Waldheim remains with the paintings, however, while his men set off. Moments later, Lebiche shows up, and when he finds the colonel, standing unarmed amidst the dead bodies and the paintings, he shoots him with a machine gun.

Like Pontecorvo's *The Battle of Algiers*, which was released two few years after Frankenheimer's film, *The Train* provides its viewers with a portrait of occupation and resistance, a record of oppressed people using cunning, sabotage and even terror to strike back at a foreign enemy. And like Pontecorvo's picture, *The Train* casts its protagonists in a sympathetic light.[15] It does this, primarily, by drawing attention constantly to the great danger that attends active resistance — Boule, Didont and Pesquet, after all, all die — as well as to the viciousness that characterizes men like von Waldheim, who kill innocent people so easily. We should mention, though, that this proud German officer, as cruel as he is, possesses some redeeming traits, too — at least when the film opens. Early in the film, for instance, when he wanders into Madame Villard's museum, the colonel stops before a painting for a moment, staring at it with

Lebiche (Burt Lancster) shares a moment with Christine (Jeanne Moreau) in *The Train* (UA, 1965).

a soft expression on his face. He then says to the curator after she approaches him:

VON WALDHEIM: Do you like it?

VILLARD: Need you ask?

VON WALDHEIM: This is degenerate art, you know. As a loyal officer of the Third Reich, I should detest it. I've often wondered at the curious conceit that would attempt to determine tastes and ideas by decree.

Von Waldheim, it seems, has the ability to love something. But as the film progresses, he loses this modicum of decency, becoming more interested — to the point of obsession — in exploiting the paintings' value than in staying true to his beliefs. As Frankenheimer told Macklin: "He really does love art. He's an educated man and he's a man who's frustrated. He becomes a maniac."[16]

But while the characters who belong to the French Resistance in this film, along with their friends and supporters, starkly contrast the venal likes of von Waldheim and his men, their personalities are hardly faultless. For instance, the hotel owner Christine (Jeanne Moreau), who takes in Lebiche after he crashes the train, is reluctant at first to provide him with help. Why? She fears

Lebiche (Burt Lancaster) dynamites the railroad in *The Train* (UA, 1965).

that the sort of insurgent activity he engages in can disrupt the economy of the town where she lives, and thus hurt her business, which is dependent upon German clientele.

Frankenheimer fails to sentimentalize his portrait of Lebiche, as well. This man who devotes himself to the liberation of his country, we should note, never reveals his political beliefs, never provides us with an understanding of his motivations for belonging to the Underground. Presumably, patriotism has prompted him, but we can't be sure. It may be possible that personal reasons — a desire for vengeance, say — drive the character, too. After all, he only commits himself to defeating von Waldheim after the death of Boule. Moreover, it's not clear why, in the film's final moments, he shoots the German officer. Has this killing — a murder, really — been provoked by the sight of the dead men lying along the railroad tracks? Or is it, perhaps, because the colonel, in the moments leading up to the execution, insults the railroad man:

> Here's your prize, Lebiche. Some of the greatest paintings in the world. Does it please you, Lebiche? Do you feel a sense of excitement in just being near them? A painting means as much as to you as a string of pearls to an ape. You won by sheer luck. You stopped me without knowing what you were doing, or why. You are nothing, Lebiche.

A lump of flesh. The paintings are mine. They always will be. Beauty belongs to the man who can appreciate it ... They will always belong to me or to a man like me. Now, this minute, you couldn't tell me why you did what you did.

The Train is one of Frankenheimer's best films, and much of its strength arises from the conflict, the grudge match, which arises between the colonel and Lebiche. The director himself thought this aspect lent the narrative a great deal of momentum

You've got two terrific forces going against each other: one guy whose life is dedicated to stopping the train and the other whose life is dedicated to getting it through. And that's what makes really good movies, I think, why you've got two very strong currents going against each other.[17]

The frequent use of location photography and actual trains also enhance the film, imbuing it with the same gritty realism that distinguishes the war footage we find in *The Manchurian Candidate* and *The Holcroft Covenant*. In addition, a sooty light seems to seep through almost every shot, lending the picture the same semi-documentary look that we find in pictures like Rossellini's *Open City* (1945) and *Paisan* (1946), which Frankenheimer admired. And like these films, as well, *The Train* refrains from glamorizing war, instead reminding us of the great damage it can beget and the cruelty it unleashes.

Black Sunday (1977)

In 1975, the American writer Thomas Harris scored a hit with *Black Sunday*, a sensationalistic thriller about a group of political extremists who launch an attack on the Super Bowl with a blimp. Wanting to capitalize on the "disaster movie" trend which was then flourishing, Paramount Pictures purchased the rights to the novel and rushed the story into development. Robert Evans, the celebrity producer and one time head of Paramount, oversaw the project from its beginning, hiring Ernest Lehman to write the script and casting Robert Shaw, Bruce Dern and Marthe Keller to play the film's leads. Once these aspects of the production were taken care of, he signed Frankenheimer to direct, confident the director was capable of turning the property into a blockbuster. The script was not ready when Frankenheimer came on board, however, and as he waited for Lehman to finish up, he went about making arrangements with the National Football League to shoot actual footage of a Super Bowl game; he also approached the Goodyear Tire & Rubber Company and secured the use of its famous blimp, after promising to present the aircraft in as flattering a manner as possible.

But while he enjoyed these successes, he was disappointed with the script Lehman eventually submitted, worrying that it was too complicated for general audiences; and to correct this, he brought on Kenneth Ross and then Ivan

Moffat to scale the story down.[18] At 143 minutes, *Black Sunday* is still a long film. And with its large cast, its multiple plotlines and the size and scope of the dilemma its characters meet, the movie shares much in common with films like *The Poseidon Adventure* (1972), *Earthquake* (1974) and *The Towering Inferno* (1974). At the same time, it exhibits several of the markers we find in the director's other works. Like *Dead Bang* and *French Connection II*, for example, *Black Sunday* focuses on an obsessive law enforcement official who tracks down and eventually subdues a criminal organization. In this instance, the cop character is an Israeli intelligence agent named Major Kabokov (Shaw); and his outlaw opponents belong to a Palestinian terrorist organization called Black September—the same group which orchestrated the attack on the Munich Olympics in 1972.

As the film opens, Kabokov and his men raid one of Black September's compounds in Beirut, where they find an audio cassette tape which contains the following message:

> The American people have remained deaf to all the cries of the Palestinian nation. But if a foreign people took over the states of Virginia, Georgia and New Jersey and forced the people of those states to leave their homes and lands, would they not feel bitter and betrayed? Therefore understand how we feel, people of America. This situation is unbearable for us. Until you understand that and stop helping the Israelis with arms and money, we of the Black September movement will make it unbearable for you. From now on, you will share our suffering.[19]

Certain that an attack on Israel's most important ally is imminent, Kabokov heads to the United States, where he notifies the FBI. Then he and another Mossad agent named Moshevsky (Steven Keats) set out to find the conspirators, knowing almost nothing about who they are and what they plan to do.

The film's audience, however, is privy to the terrorists' plans, as Frankenheimer frequently directs our attention to their activities. Primarily he focuses on a Palestinian woman named Dahlia (Keller), the person who recorded the ominous message on the cassette tape. Dahlia believes that the only way to effect change in her homeland is through violence, and to realize this, she pairs up with an embittered and insane American blimp pilot named Lander (Dern), whose personality has been damaged by his experiences in Vietnam. Wanting to kill as many people as they can, the couple builds a bomb, which they plan to detonate at the Super Bowl in Miami, where 80,000 people, including the President of the United States, will be in attendance.

Simultaneously, Kabokov conducts his investigation, crisscrossing the country as he searches for Dahlia and the others. Eventually he traces the woman to south Florida, and though he loses her there, he searches her hotel room and finds a program for the upcoming Super Bowl game. Convinced that this must be the terrorists' target, he asks to have the event cancelled, but his idea is ignored. And on game day, exonerating the major's fears, Dahlia and Lander strike, attacking the stadium with a blimp which is loaded with 600 kilograms

Agent Corley (Fritz Weaver) and Major Kabakov (Robert Shaw) search the stands of the Orange Bowl as Lander flies above in *Black Sunday* (Paramount, 1977).

of plastic explosive. Kabokov manages to stop them, however, by hooking a steel cable to the blimp, which allows a helicopter to tow the craft out of the stadium, out to the ocean, where it explodes safely.

Black Sunday offers viewers a frightening examination of the consequences which can follow when hatred festers and people act upon it. And three decades after its release, the film's concerns remain timely, especially in light of the attacks on New York City and Washington, D.C. in 2001, which bear an undeniable resemblance to the events Frankenheimer depicts.[20] The movie still has its problems, though. Its special effects leave much to be desired. Its narrative often tests credulity — especially the climactic sequence with the blimp. And its tone, lacking in irony and humor, is relentlessly, almost deadeningly somber. Several critics have argued, as well, that the film is unnecessarily complicated and that it moves slowly. Vincent Canby, for example, called the picture "boring" and Gary Arnold suggested that it "might be intensified considerably if producer Robert Evans and director John Frankenheimer were in a position to scuttle a reel or two or three or four."[21] And these opinions, to a certain extent, are justified. Just as he does in *Grand Prix* and *The Gypsy Moths*, Frankenheimer cuts often from the film's exciting sequences to quieter, intimate ones, in order to provide viewers with a sound understanding of his characters' personalities, carefully outlining their resentments, their desires, their motives and so forth, a tactic which invariably slows the narrative's pace. All of these factors, no doubt, contributed in part to the picture's stumble at the box office when Paramount released it in March 1977.

Black Sunday is still a fine film. And much of its strength arises from the performances of its principals. Shaw is especially effective as the laconic commando whose taste for killing has soured. And Dern's turn as the crazed vet is also memorable as he creates a villain who is at once frightening and pathetic, while Keller imbues the Dahlia character with a fiery dignity that might remind us of the villainous, but attractive, *femmes fatales* Bette Davis played in films like Wyler's *The Letter* (1940) and *The Little Foxes* (1941). *Black Sunday* is also strengthened by the director's insistence upon making the events which appear on the screen look as authentic and as convincing as possible. And to achieve this, he uses location footage a great deal. Much of the blimp attack sequence, for example, was shot in and around the Orange Bowl in Miami. The scene in which Kabokov and a team of FBI agents chase Mohammed Fasil (Bekim Fehmiu), one of Dahlia's chiefs in Black September, was filmed amidst the old art deco buildings that line Miami Beach. And a conversation Kabokov has with an Egyptian spymaster (Walter Gotell) takes place on the Washington Mall, not far from the Lincoln Memorial.

Frankenheimer includes footage which he filmed at an actual Super Bowl game, too, with shots of real figures from professional football. The quarterbacks Roger Staubach and Terry Bradshaw greet fans at the Miami airport. The coaches Tom Landry and Chuck Knoll — of the Dallas Cowboys and the Pittsburgh Steelers, respectively — lead their teams across the Orange Bowl's playing field. And Joe Robbie, the owner of the Miami Dolphins, makes a brief appearance, as do the television sportscasters Pat Summerall and Tom Brookshier.

Black Sunday's realism is further enhanced by the director's shooting style. He used concealed cameras as he shot city streets and crowd scenes, for instance, allowing him to capture people behaving naturally, unaware that they were being filmed. This technique is used to great effect in the opening sequence as Dahlia travels through congested, downtown Beirut, on foot and by car, trying to get to the compound where the members of Black September are waiting.[22] The director's use of large depth-of-field compositions, mobile cameras and close up shots also adds to the film's immediacy. When Kabokov and his operatives pore through the narrow hallways of Dahlia's compound, the camera follows them closely, tilting, panning, jumping, almost as if it's in the hands of one of the commandos.

It's possible, however, that Frankenheimer's insistence upon verisimilitude, rather than helping the picture's commercial prospects, curbed them. The director may have been too successful at making his characters and their activities believable, and because of this, audiences, wanting a milder and simpler sort of adventure movie, stayed away. A review which appeared in *Variety*, written a week before the film was released, in fact predicted that the picture might have trouble at the box office for this reason.

> [W]hat could work against the film is the curious undertone that, while audiences may flock to cardboard shootouts and disaster films where dozens of artificial characters get slaughtered, it's something else again where the climactic victim is a stadium full of us. Call it a sense of tribal revulsion if you will, but the impact of the film ultimately reaches those primal nerve-endings.[23]

Frankenheimer's unwillingness to demonize the film's heavies may have hurt the picture, as well. Instead of simplifying his portraits of Lander and Dahlia, of depicting them as purely evil creatures, he lets us know why they feel the need to strike out at the world so violently. We learn that Dahlia experienced great trauma as a child growing up in a refugee camp after Israel's victory over the Palestinians in 1948. And Lander, another product of an ugly war, not only lost six years of his life as prisoner in a Viet Cong prison, but when he returned home, he lost his career as a Navy pilot and his marriage, too. Moreover, the director at the same time darkens his portrait of Kabokov, showing us on several occasions that this man, the film's hero, is capable of the same ruthlessness and violence that characterize his enemies: much as we find in *The Train*, in other words, the differences between the film's protagonists and antagonists are not so great. It may be, as well, that Frankenheimer's reluctance to espouse a clear point of view regarding the Israeli-Palestinian conflict, to endorse — or condemn — one side over the other, also alienated viewers. It certainly angered some of them.[24] As Robert Evans recalled in his memoir *The Kid Stays in the Picture*:

> [T]he controversy of [*Black Sunday's*] subject matter caused an uproar.... Why? Telling another terrorist story was not good enough. I had to go a step further, expose the gray area, tell both sides of the complex story.... Blazing across the front page of the leading Jewish newspaper, The *B'nai B'rith Messenger*, was the headline "ROBERT EVANS, HITLERITE." Immediately, notices were put up in Jewish owned stores throughout the country calling for a boycott of the film. That was a gardenia compared to its flip side. The Red Army of Japan threatened to blow up every theater around the world that exhibited *Black Sunday*. To them, it was sacrilegious to the plight of the Arab people.[25]

The Holcroft Covenant (1985)

Frankenheimer begins this film about ideological fanaticism with a prologue which takes place in the final days of World War II. As Allied planes bomb Berlin, a trio of Nazi officers meets in a bunker. In spite of the chaos and destruction which swirl above them, the men seem calm and in good spirits as they place a collection of documents inside a safety deposit box, which they hand over to a Swiss motorcycle courier. When the courier speeds away, headed for one of his country's famous banks, the leader of the little group, a man named Clausen (Alexander Kerst), raises a glass of brandy and makes a toast. "To the covenant," he says, "to our children, to a new and better world." Then, without explanation, Clausen shoots his fellows and himself.

After this striking and enigmatic opening, Frankenheimer moves the story ahead 40 years, turning our attention to Noel Holcroft (Michael Caine), an American architect, who is Clausen's son. Contacted by a Swiss banker named Manfredi (Michael Lonsdale), Holcroft learns that his father (from whom he was separated when he was a baby) and the other men in the bunker siphoned away a fortune from the Third Reich, creating a fund which they hoped their children would use to make amends for the great crimes Hitler and his followers had committed. In order to access the money, though, Holcroft must find the children of his father's partners and get these people to sign the documents which were delivered to Switzerland, the "covenant" Clausen referred to in the prologue. The plan is a ruse, however. Far from being interested in making reparations to their victims, the men in the bunker collected the money in order to bring about the birth of another Nazi Reich. Holcroft does not know this, though, and the well-meaning architect places himself in great danger as he sets out to find the other "heirs" and work with them, never realizing until quite late that these people—a journalist named Johann von Tiebolt (Anthony Andrews), his sister Helden (Victoria Tenant) and Kessler (Mario Adorf), a symphony conductor—have been groomed since childhood to execute their fathers' megalomaniacal schemes.

While *The Holcroft Covenant* is one of Frankenheimer's more flamboyant works, an over-the-top adventure story, packed with murders, chases, explosions, suicides and sordid sex, it is burdened with an ornate script that generally fails to create suspense, a shortcoming which wasn't lost on the few critics who wrote about the movie after its release in the fall of 1985. The review which appeared in *Variety*, for instance, stated that the

> [v]arious scripters credited on *The Holcroft Covenant* have not created a clear narrative line out of Robert Ludlum's complex potboiler novel. Result is a muddled narrative deficient in thrills or plausibility.[26]

Despite its structural problems, *The Holcroft Covenant* is still an interesting movie, thanks in large part to the sophisticated manner in which it was made. Nowhere is this quality more evident, perhaps, than in the prologue which opens the picture. Shot in black and white, the sequence combines actual war footage with material Frankenheimer and his cinematographer Gerry Fisher filmed in the studio, a strategy which imbues the passage with an intense realism. The director's decision to score these scenes from long ago with electronic music is also effective. By juxtaposing old images with contemporary sounds, he draws attention to the interconnectedness of the past and the present, a theme which takes on increasing importance as the film progresses. The starkly

The Film of
ROBERT LUDLUM'S
suspense-packed bestseller
The Holcroft Covenant

Distributed by THORN EMI Screen Entertainment.

Screen
Entertainment

Holcroft (Michael Caine) exposes the conspirators Johann (Anthony Andrews), Helden (Victoria Tenant) and Kessler (Mario Adorf) at a press conference in *The Holcroft Covenant* (Thorn EMI, 1985). Behind Holcroft, to his right, stand Manfredi (Michael Lonsdale, with beard) and his assistant (André Penvern).

lit opening sequence also establishes an ominous mood which carries over into the subsequent film. Throughout the later sections of the picture, on the other hand, Frankenheimer and Fisher frequently use the camera in a charismatic manner, borrowing heavily from directors like Welles, Reed and Lang as they load the screen with deep focus shots, filmed from odd, expressive angles. The movie also gains a great deal from the strong performances of actors like Caine and Lonsdale and the wonderful Lilli Palmer, whose turn as Althene Holcroft, the protagonist's mother, ends abruptly when her character is murdered by Johann, the leader of the neo–Nazi plot.

    The Holcroft Covenant may be hard to follow and lurid — Johann and his sister Helden, for instance, are lovers — but its depictions of anti-democratic conspirators who blend into the everyday world as they plan and execute their schemes links it to both *The Manchurian Candidate* and *Black Sunday*. "It is one of those films," wrote the critic George Perry, "in which nobody is what they say they are and nothing is as it seems."[27] The movie bears some resemblance to *Seven Days in May*, too, as the conspirators, much like General Scott in the earlier film, believe that the dictatorship they intend to impose will be welcomed by the masses. But unlike Scott, these people plan to artificially stimulate the public's appetite for totalitarian rule by using a massive terrorism campaign which they believe will sow fear around the globe. Fortunately, Holcroft learns about this bizarre plot and he exposes it to an international audience at a press conference:

> It's a wonderful idea, gloriously simple. To consolidate every terrorist group into one cohesive, overwhelming force in order to create international crises and political chaos. It's obvious how they'd do it. With four and a half billion dollars behind them and working under inspired leadership, my God, they could blow up ten airliners a week, assassinate any world leader anywhere, turn any religion, race, color or creed against each other, start bloody riots in any city at any time until suddenly the world is reduced to a state of anarchy and panic, ready to accept a strong leader who can restore order and take command.

Ineffectual, mild-mannered and fussy, Noel Holcroft is unusual among the heroes who appear in Frankenheimer's thrillers. Not only does he lack the poise and toughness which distinguish characters like *The Train*'s Lebiche, *Black Sunday*'s Kabokov and *Ronin*'s Sam, but he's also an idealist, a gullible one, whose desire to help others prevents him from thinking clearly and acting prudently. He refuses to take his mother seriously, for example, when she reminds him that Clausen's faith in National Socialism was sincere, and that he was a chronic liar, and that his true intentions for the fortune he and the others built are probably concealed. The same dangerous optimism convinces Holcroft that Helden is sincere when she tells him that she loves him, just a few days after the pair meet. And it is his love for her which clouds his judgment, it seems, in the terrible moments after his discovery of his mother's death. Though he knows that Johann murdered the woman, he fails to consider that Helden may have played a part in it, too. Instead, he worries for her, wondering if Johann will kill her, and so when he heads out to find the woman, he does so not to capture her and bring her to justice, but to save her. He's a parody of the chivalric knight, devoted to his lady, and it his irrational affection which apparently prompts him in the film's final scene to give her his gun, enabling her to kill him; and it is the persistence of this fondness, no doubt, which causes him to cry after the woman decides to shoot herself instead.

Actually, Johann, the film's suave villain, exhibits the personality traits which tend to characterize the director's action heroes. Like Lebiche, for example, he exudes virility and toughness. Like *The Horsemen*'s Uraz, he is a skilled rider — he also wears a thick moustache. And like *Bird Man of Alcatraz*'s Robert Stroud, he is highly intelligent —from Helden, we learn that he is one world's leading authorities on the English pound, of all things. Moreover, Johann's obsessiveness, along with his willingness to set objectives ahead of the welfare of others, are qualities he shares with Sam the CIA agent in *Ronin* and *French*

Connection II's Popeye Doyle. But unlike these characters, Johann has no interest in bringing about some sort of reasonable, understandable improvement in the world. Instead, he longs to seize power, to establish a racist world order, and in this respect, he resembles the vicious extremists Frankenheimer introduces in *Dead Bang*. As he explains to Mrs. Holcroft, just before he shoots her:

> It's been forty years since Nuremberg. Forty years of so-called enlightenment and democracy and what has it accomplished?.... Mr. Truman drops atomic bombs on women and children.... At Yalta, with the sweep of a pen, a senile president condemns a third of the world to communism. Europe, with the zeal of a missionary gone mad, hands over the wealth and resources of Africa to savages who have barely learned to beat a drum. Then you give them tanks and arms to replace their bows and arrows and when your deep freezers arrive they use them to store their fallen enemies 'til Sunday dinner. In America, they vote for law and order whilst shooting down presidents, school children and rock stars in the streets. You see, the world must not be run by the frightened, the ignorant and the weak.

Riviera (1987)

Frankenheimer's first television feature, much like *The Holcroft Covenant*, is serpentine and cluttered, filled with unlikely situations and characters whose personalities seem exaggerated and cartoonish. But it largely avoids the tragedy and the violence which leaves the earlier production occasionally somber and grim, supplying us instead with the same unrestrained, often tongue-in-cheek melodrama which makes similarly themed movies like Fritz Lang's *Spies* (1928) and the 1934 version of Hitchcock's *The Man Who Knew Too Much* such fun.

Primarily, the story follows an ex-spy named Kelly (Ben Masters), who's come to the south of France to open a hotel. But just as he gets started on this venture, Kelly learns that three of his former colleagues have been murdered in Vienna, their covers betrayed by a double agent within "The Bureau," the secretive, anti-Soviet intelligence agency for which he once worked. Angered at this, Kelly asks for his old job back, with the understanding that it will be a temporary commitment. He then sets out, accompanied by a female operative named Ashley (Elyssa Davolos), to find the traitor. As the spies pursue their investigation, Kelly's friend, a European mercenary named Rykker (Patrick Bachnau), offers his services to a woman whose archaeologist father has been kidnapped.

The paths of the characters all cross eventually in Egypt, where Kelly and Ashley make contact with the double agent: using phony pretenses, they persuade him to meet them outside the pyramids in the desert. But before the rendezvous takes place, the two spies join Rykker at an ancient temple and together free the archaeologist from his abductors. Then Kelly and Ashley meet and subdue the traitorous spy, who turns out to be one of their chiefs at the Bureau, an old man named Doc (Shane Rimmer). Kelly then heads back to France,

where he hosts a party to celebrate the opening of his hotel. His recent experiences have rekindled his interest in the spy game, however, and he finds himself wondering, as he meets his guests, if a permanent return to the Bureau
might make him happier.

Frankenheimer did not have control over the final cut of *Riviera*, but the
program still displays much of the visual élan we find in his other work. It
opens, for example, with a marvelous, sweeping shot of a Mediterranean harbor which was filmed from a helicopter, the same technique he used to open
The Gypsy Moths and *The Horsemen*. Throughout the film, as well, several exciting action sequences appear, including a rooftop chase that recalls the opening frames of Hitchcock's *Vertigo* (1958), as well as a car chase that takes place
on the streets of Nice, a scenario Frankenheimer would return to a decade later
in *Ronin*. Moreover, the director's affection for expressive camera angles and
wide angle, deep focus shots reveals itself often, filling the screen with movement, tension and symbolism. In the final scene with Doc, for example, the
director positions the old man between a pair of high walls and beneath a sky
that stretches above like the ceiling of a room, a not too subtle foreshadowing,
it seems, of the cell which awaits him.

Nevertheless, *Riviera* was greatly damaged when its producers re-cut the
film and introduced new material which was shot after Frankenheimer left the
project. This is especially apparent, for example, early in the picture, when a
gang of thugs approaches and threatens a man and a woman on a boat. The
scene, at first, is quite effective as Frankenheimer uses a series of point of view
shots to emphasize the menacing aspect of the heavies and the vulnerability of
their targets. But then the camera abruptly jumps from the tense action on the
boat's deck to the mast of a nearby ship. At the top of the mast sits Kelly, holding a paint bucket and a brush. A witness to what's happening, he grins and
turns over his bucket, dumping its contents on to the bad guys below. This
poorly filmed bit of slapstick, apparently introduced for comic effect, isn't particularly funny and it ruins the suspense which Frankenheimer and his director of photography Henri Decaë have constructed in the previous shots.

According to Frankenheimer it was Michael Sloane, the film's executive
producer, who re-cut *Riviera* and introduced the new footage. Sloane also wrote
the script and the same stale thinking which distinguishes the paint bucket
sequence occasionally creeps into the storyline, too.[28] The gunplay and fights
which take place in the Egyptian temple trade, for example, on the popularity
of Spielberg's *Raiders of the Lost Ark* (1981), while the influence of Zemeckis'
Romancing the Stone (1984) (and *Moonlighting*, ABC's popular television series
which ran from 1985 to 1989) can be detected in the mixture of spatting and
sexual attraction which characterizes Kelly and Ashley's relationship. The climactic revelation of the double agent's identity in the film's closing moments
is not especially original either. Traitorous spymasters have been a staple in espionage novels for decades, as well as the movies which have been adapted from

them. Sydney Furie's celebrated spy film _The Ipcress File_ (1965), for example, also features an intelligence agency chief who sells out his operatives to the Soviets.

Year of the Gun (1991)

In 1984, the American author Michael Mewshaw published _Year of the Gun_, a fictional thriller about an expatriate novelist's entanglement with the Red Brigades, an actual terrorist group that thrived in Italy in the Seventies. Sensing commercial potential in the story, the independent producer Edward Pressman had Mewshaw's novel turned into a screenplay. He invited Frankenheimer to helm the adaptation and the director took the assignment, though he insisted, as he had many times before, on reworking the script before shooting began. Frankenheimer did not enjoy the same latitude when it came to casting, however. "Several actors we wanted turned us down," he told Champlin, a situation which obliged the filmmakers to give the lead role to Andrew McCarthy, a likeable, but unexciting, actor whose previous credits had included a number of light comedies, including _Class_ (1983), _Pretty in Pink_ (1986) and _Weekend at Bernie's_ (1989). The director later came to regret this decision. As he told Champlin: "He's a nice guy and I was happy to have him. But he was just not strong enough for the role."[29]

Several critics reached the same conclusion when the picture opened in the fall of 1991. Janet Maslin wrote: "The smoothly unctuous Mr. McCarthy is never convincing as the rakish, much-in-demand American writer whose activities eventually stir the [terrorists] into a frenzy."[30] Desson Howe suggested that the actor's performance was more appropriate for "an underwear commercial" than an action film.[31] And Hal Hinson, responding to the film's release on video, asked: "If you want to make a serious movie [like this one], why place a lightweight with such limited gifts at its center?"[32] Whether or not the actor's turn as the harried American abroad, caught up in a swirl of bad luck and violence, is as mediocre as the reviewers claimed is debatable. Regardless, his presence failed to muster business for the picture at the box office.

Set in the winter and spring of 1978, _Year of the Gun_ follows David Raybourne (McCarthy), a young journalist who lives and works in Rome. David wants to marry an aristocrat named Lia (Valeria Golino). But he lacks money, and to change this, he decides to write a commercial novel about terrorism in Italy, hoping the effort will land him a spot on the bestseller list. Keeping the project hidden from Lia and his other friends, Raybourne concocts a plot in which the ultraviolent Red Brigades, a radical leftist organization which is committed to "punishing the rich," kidnaps Aldo Moro (Aldo Mengolini), one of the country's most prominent political figures. To lend the book authenticity, David draws heavily from events he reads about in the papers. He also uses char-

Raybourne (Andrew McCarthy) and his lover Lia (Valeria Golino) in *Year of the Gun* (Triumph, 1991).

acters which he models and names after real people, including his acquaintances.

As David works on his novel, an American photojournalist named Alison King (Sharon Stone) arrives in Rome. Soon, she meets the reporter and a short time later learns through contacts that he is writing a book. Suspecting that his book is about the Red Brigades, she asks him if he'd like to have her shoot the photographs for it. David, however, insists that he is not writing about this topic. But the headstrong photographer refuses to accept this and when she gets the chance, she roots around his apartment and finds an early draft of the manuscript. Despite David's subsequent efforts to dissuade her, Alison concludes that the writer has penetrated the Red Brigades, and to find out more, she talks to his friend Italo (John Pankow), a mild mannered college professor. Italo, however, is a Red Brigades sympathizer, and after he hears about the novel from Alison, he breaks into David's apartment, steals the manuscript and turns it over to one of the radical organization's chiefs, a man named Giovanni (Mattia Sbragia).

Much like the terrorists who appear in the novel, Giovanni and his associates have also been planning to kidnap the politician Aldo Moro. And they mistakenly conclude, after finding a description of their scheme in David's book, that someone, a traitor, has been feeding him information. Giovanni then sends some of his people out to capture both David and Alison, and a frantic chase through the streets of Rome follows, ending when the journalists manage to kill their pursuers. After this, David contacts Lia, asking for help. But Lia, like Italo, is a member of the Red Brigades, and she turns her lover, along with Alison, over to Giovanni. The chief does not kill the pair, however. Instead, he takes them to a remote farm house and interrogates them as his operatives attack a convoy of cars in downtown Rome and carry through on the plan to abduct Moro. The Americans are then taken to a mountain, presumably to be executed. Giovanni has Lia shot instead, however, having concluded that it was she who betrayed the group's confidence. As he tells Alison: "Take pictures. Tell the world how we deal with traitors." The film then cuts to the interior of a television studio several months later, where a talk show host asks David about his novel, which, we learn, has become a best-seller. Having contributed her photographs to the book, Alison answers questions, too, but since she is in Lebanon now, covering the country's civil war, she joins the others by satellite.

Year of the Gun, like *Grand Prix*, *The Train*, *Black Sunday*, *Dead Bang* and all of the features Frankenheimer directed for cable television, blurs the lines between history and art by combining imaginary situations and people with real ones. The host of the talk show in the film's final segment, for example, is played by Dick Cavett, the well-known late night television personality. And the Red Brigades on March 28, 1978 indeed kidnapped and later killed Aldo Moro, leaving his body in the trunk of a car on a street in Rome. But the story of David and his friends is the invention of Mewshaw, a fantasy he dreamed up after living in Italy during the period when the Red Brigades was active.

This mixture of reality and fiction also links the *Year of the Gun* to films like *The Battle of Algiers* (1966), *Z* (1969) and *The Day of the Jackal* (1973), but Frankenheimer's thriller fails to reach the heights of its predecessors, and this is not so much the result of McCarthy's underwhelming performance, as it is the director's decision to focus a great deal of attention onto the love lives of his characters.[33] He does this, it seems, to improve our understanding of their personalities, of their motives and their drives. We learn, for instance, that Italo is homosexual and his involvement with the terrorists arose from an affair he had with one of their members. We also learn that David is not above betraying his lover Lia, as he sleeps with Alison at one point.[34] The problem, though, is that so much screen time is given to this dramatic material, a tendency which tends to neutralize the suspenseful aspects of the plot, slowing the story down and sabotaging its emotional impact. As Hinson in his acidic review of the film remarked:

> Timing is essential in the making of a thriller; the director has to know precisely how to parcel out his story, what to withhold from his audience, what to tell it and when. And, in his new spy story, Year of the Gun, Frankenheimer makes serous miscalculations. The other shoe takes forever to drop, and by the time it does we're far beyond caring.

Frankenheimer, however, compensates somewhat for the film's lethargic pace with his craftsmanship, in particular, his efforts to recreate the look and sound and chaos of Italy in the late Seventies. And his success at doing this was not overlooked by the critics, even those who otherwise disparaged the picture. Amy Dawes at *Variety*, for instance, declared, "Frankenheimer and cinematographer Blasco Giuarto do a standout job with the taut, hysterical action scenes, and naturalistic use of Rome backgrounds adds high visual interest."[35] And thanks to the frequent use of hand-held cameras, natural lighting and on-location photography, the picture often looks more like a documentary than a feature, another trait it shares with *The Battle of Algiers*, along with the director's own *French Connection II* and *Ronin*. But much as he does in *The Manchurian Candidate*, *Seconds* and *The Holcroft Covenant*, Frankenheimer also manipulates the camera expressionistically on occasion, using canted-angle shots of darkly lit sets to fill the screen with a sense of menace, underscoring the anxiety and vertigo David experiences as the city he loves turns into a cloistered trap.

We can detect the influence of Carol Reed's cinema in the film's visual aspects, as well. The frequent shots of Rome at night, of the soaring facades of old apartment buildings and the wet, dark streets beneath them, bring to mind the manner in which Reed and his cameraman Robert Krasker filmed the streets of Dublin and Vienna in *Odd Man Out* (1946) and *The Third Man* (1949), two of Frankenheimer's favorite movies. Roger Ebert noticed this resemblance, as well. "There is a long foot chase of a kind we have seen before," he wrote in his review of the film, "but Frankenheimer makes it fresh by using architectural and street details as elements of the chase; it's like one of those chases in *The Third Man* that seem to be defined by the cityscape."[36] The director, in fact, makes an unambiguous allusion to Reed's most famous film during this "long foot chase" sequence. As David and Alison flee their pursuers, they duck into a darkened doorway. where they hide until someone turns on a light, exposing them. This is the same way, we might remember, that Reed introduces Orson Welles' character Harry Lime in *The Third Man*. Just like the two journalists, Lime conceals himself in the shadows of a doorway as he attempts to elude a pursuer. And just as it is for them, he loses his protection when someone switches on a light.

Both films also emphasize the disparity which can exist between appearances and reality, one of Frankenheimer's ubiquitous themes. The gentlemanly Harry Lime is a black market racketeer who fakes his own death in order to escape the police's attention, while the genteel Lia and her soft-spoken cousin Italo are both members of high society, living in fine apartments and driving nice cars, who belong to a radical group which is committed to the destruction of the bourgeois state. As Dawes remarked, "No one is who he seems in this deeply corrupt Italy." Lia and Italo are guilty, as well, of not only deceiving David, but of betraying him, of setting personal interests and ideology ahead of love and friendship, a trait they share with *The Manchurian Candidate*'s Mrs. Iselin and *Ronin*'s Sam. But while their behavior is loathsome, we have to remember that the cousins engage in it because they believe that their actions will help the Red Brigades achieve its goal of creating a better and more just Italy. They may be treacherous and cruel, in other words, yet they also mean well. And in this respect, they recall those men and women in *The Battle of Algiers* who set off bombs in cafés and shoot police officers in the back as they struggle to regain their country's liberty from the French.

CHAPTER FIVE

Oligarchs and Bullies

Again and again in Frankenheimer's cinema we find instances where the short-sighted efforts of individuals bring about tremendous harm for others. In *Seconds*, *Prophecy* and *The Burning Season*, the mercenary objectives of businessmen are addressed. In each of these polemical works, the heavies—the corporate chiefs in *Seconds*, the logging interests in *Prophecy*, the government-backed ranchers in *The Burning Season*—put profit first, callously exploiting customers, polluting the wilderness and dispossessing indigenous populations of their access to natural resources. The same willingness to exploit the vulnerable for self-gain materializes in *The Island of Dr. Moreau*, although ambitiousness and an unrealistic optimism fuel the megalomaniacal scientist's pursuits, not greed.

Seconds (1966)

Frankenheimer's second collaboration with the producer Edward Lewis chronicles the downfall of a New York City banking executive named Arthur Hamilton (John Randolph). Hamilton exemplifies success. He owns a house in Scarsdale, one of New York's nicest suburbs. His wife loves him. His daughter is married to a doctor. He owns a boat and plays golf on the weekends, too. But Hamilton is bored and discontent. And when he learns from his old friend Charlie (Murray Hamilton), whom he thought was dead, that he can have a completely new life, that he can start over fresh, he responds with interest. Following Charlie's directions, Hamilton then visits an office building in the city, the home of a nameless company, where an executive named Mr. Ruby (Jeff Corey) tells him that thirty thousand dollars will buy him a new identity and a new face.

Hamilton declines at first, but under pressure he gives in and the company's staff of plastic surgeons quickly gets to work, transforming his pudgy, plain face into a handsome one. (At this point in the drama, Randolph is replaced by Rock Hudson.) Following his surgery, Hamilton moves to California, to a house that overlooks the Pacific, where he is expected to live his new life as "Tony Wilson," a professional artist. The same listlessness that characterized his former existence returns, though. He begins to lie awake in bed, staring at the ceiling with worried eyes; when his houseman suggests that he meet his neighbors, he growls; and instead of painting, he walks dejectedly along the beach. On one of these walks, however, he meets Nora (Salome Jens), a beautiful divorcee who quickly falls in love with him. But Nora, much like Wilson, is a fake, having been sent by the nameless company to help him adjust to his new life. When Wilson realizes this, he flees California, but the company retrieves him and takes him back to its headquarters. There, he meets his old friend Charlie, who, it turns out, is similarly unhappy with the identity he's received, and in order to be eligible for a new one, he explains, he had to recruit a new client for the company. The new client he found, of course, is Hamilton. Mr. Ruby then explains to the ex-banker that if he wants a new identity as well, he must recruit a new candidate, too. But Hamilton/Wilson refuses and Ruby responds by sending him back to the company's team of surgeons. The doctors do not perform plastic surgery this time, however. Instead, they drill a hole into his head, killing him.

Seconds was met with distaste when it was released in the fall of 1966, turning off critics and audiences alike with its bleak tone and James Wong Howe's disorienting camerawork. And while Frankenheimer attributed its poor performance to poor marketing, the picture's scornful regard for bourgeois mores and practices may have alienated the film's potential audience, as well. *Seconds*, after all, suggests that the pursuit of such standard, middle-class objectives as marriage, career and prosperity not only bleeds people of their time and energy, but their ability to experience happiness. Moreover, the film's everyman hero comes to realize that the pursuit of success can snuff out individuality and free choice, too. In one of the picture's final scenes, he laments to his friend Charlie: "The years I've spent trying to get all the things I was told were important, that I was supposed to want! Things! Not people ... or meaning. Just things." Hamilton's epiphany, of course, plays a part in his destruction, triggering the resistant attitude that prompts the company's murderous response. At the same time, this new understanding he achieves coincides with the awakening of his conscience — the film may end in tragedy, but not before its hero redeems himself. Prior to California and the plastic surgery, we have to remember, the businessman agrees to abandon his family with little hesitation, trading in his duties as father and husband for the new life offered by the company. But after experiencing the loneliness and isolation that come with the transformation, he chooses to act in an unselfish, sacrificial manner, refusing to recruit new candidates for the secretive organization, sparing them from the suffering he's

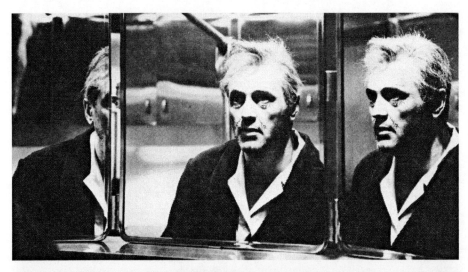

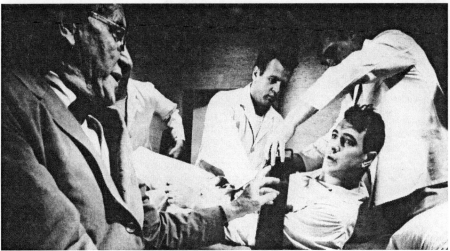

Top: "Tony Wilson" (Rock Hudson) sees his face for the first time in *Seconds* (Paramount, 1966). *Bottom:* In another scene the Old Man (Will Geer) tries to comfort Hamilton/Wilson as he sends him to his death.

known; and he does this with the understanding that it will postpone his own surgery and the relief he thinks it can bring him.

With *Seconds*, Frankenheimer wanted to create a "horrifying portrait of big business" and he clearly succeeded.[1] Led by brutal characters like Mr. Ruby and the mean-spirited Dr. Innes (Richard Anderson), who oversees both of Hamilton's operations, the company in this film dupes its clients with promises of contentment, freedom and romance, then crushes them like grapes.

Ironically, the Old Man (Will Geer), the company's founder, started the enterprise with altruistic ambitions in mind. As he tells the flustered Hamilton, just before he sends him to his death:

> You know, son, when I began this business, I was a young man with an idea. I wasn't aiming to make a lot of money helping others, helping them to find a little happiness. See, I got tremendous comfort in the thought that, in my small way, I was waging a battle against human misery. And I was, too.

But as he goes on to explain, the company's needs for profit moved ahead of its customers' needs for happiness. In fact, the company thrives because the number of "reborns" who do not adjust to their new situations is so high. When they return to the organization's headquarters, they join its sales department, sitting at desks with telephones, tracking leads and luring new customers. And if this doesn't work, they are sent like Hamilton to a place called the Cadaver Procurement Section, to be used later when the company needs to fake a death for a client.

The manipulation of appearances is a ubiquitous motif in Frankenheimer's canon, but it is hard to imagine a more sinister example than the sort we find here. The white collar swindlers who run the company stop at nothing as they try to separate Hamilton from his money. They appeal to his fantasies, tricking him with Nora. They strike at his fears, too. Shortly after he arrives at the mysterious corporation's headquarters, Mr. Ruby and the Old Man shoot a little movie in which Hamilton appears to rape a woman. The picture is a fake, but it has the ability to cause real damage, and this realization weakens the banker, making him receptive to the company's claims about its services. "Isn't it easier to go forward when you know you can't go back?" the Old Man asks in the subsequent scene. Evidently it is, because a few moments later, Hamilton agrees to "sign his life away," much as Faust signed his soul over to Mephistopheles.[2] The Old Man's pleasant manner, as well, is just another aspect of the company's masquerade. "Sakes, boy," he tells Hamilton, knowing the banker's chances of succeeding are poor, "you owe yourself this thing. Begin again, all new, all different. The way you always wanted it."

But why is it that Hamilton, Charlie and the other reborns fail? The picture never provides an explanation. And because of this omission, some critics have argued that the characters' suffering is unwarranted, exaggerated, unbelievable. The director himself felt *Seconds* fell short in this respect. He told Champlin:

> [I]t's a flawed movie. The second act never worked. You never really understood why he couldn't make it in the new life.... As an audience you don't know why it [doesn't work] for Hudson because it's not clear enough that it won't work for anybody.[3]

In the commentary Frankenheimer recorded for this film in 1996, he returned to the topic, suggesting that Hamilton and the others don't "make it" because their transformations are incomplete. The men at the company may give their clients different faces, homes and occupations, but they cannot give them different pasts, and as long as old memories and desires linger, their hopes for a second chance and a second life are deferred. "This movie says you are the result of your experiences, the result of your past. The past makes you what you are today. If you take away your past, you don't exist as a person. And that's what [Hamilton] tried to do and that's why it doesn't work."[4]

The persistence of memory also thwarts the efforts of the conspirators in *The Manchurian Candidate*. And much as he does in the earlier film, Frankenheimer uses expressive compositions in *Seconds* to approximate and convey his central character's anguished frame of mind, moving the camera erratically, framing shots from weird angles and filling them with shadows and harsh lights. The director and his cameraman James Wong Howe make frequent use of extrawide angle "fish eye" lenses, too, to squeeze and stretch their shots across the screen, lending large segments of the film the look of a nightmare. Nowhere is this more successful and unsettling than in the film's final sequence, when the orderlies wheel the screaming Hamilton into the operating room, inject him with a drug and put him to sleep, separating him permanently from his past and all its sorrows.

Prophecy (1979)

After the success of *Jaws* in 1976, Hollywood produced a spate of "monster animal" movies, including *Orca* (1977), *The Swarm* (1978), *Piranha* (1978) and Frankenheimer's *Prophecy*, the story of a massive, deformed bear that runs amok and kills people in the Maine woods. The director was not especially attracted to the idea of making a horror film at first, but after the release of *Black Sunday* in the spring of 1977, he did not have a new assignment lined up. "What happened was that we were working on a group of projects at Paramount and David Seltzer," who'd written the screenplay for Richard Donner's hugely successful *The Omen* (1976) "was able to come up with a script ... that we liked before anything else came so that became the ... picture I did."[5]

Set over the space of a few days, *Prophecy*'s narrative begins in Washington, D.C., when a representative from the Environmental Protection Agency asks Robert Verne (Robert Foxworth), a doctor, to head up to Maine to gather information about a dispute between an Indian tribe and a paper mill. Needing a break from the dreary, run-down city, Verne accepts the offer and flies up to the rugged country with his pregnant wife Maggie (Talia Shire). There, he is met by Isley (Richard Dysart), the manager of operations at the paper mill, who explains to Verne that several lumberjacks and factory employees have recently disappeared in the woods around the plant, the murdered victims, he suspects, of local Indians. The next day, a man from one of the tribes named John Hawks (Armand Assante) approaches Verne, telling him that Isley's allegations are wrong. But the Indians, he says, are nevertheless angry with the paper mill because they believe it has destroyed their land and their health. As Hawks and his sister Ramona explain:

> HAWKS: My people are violently ill. They're beginning to lose their faculties. They stagger and they fall....
>
> RAMONA: I'm a midwife, and I've seen babies born dead, born deformed.
>
> HAWKS: So badly, some have had to be put to death.

After this talk, Vern begins to search for evidence of illegal dumping in the area around the mill and soon learns that Isley's company has been releasing mercury, a toxin which causes mental illness and birth defects, into the water supply for the last 20 years. That night, a giant bear with a horrible, malformed face mauls a group of campers, killing them. This mercury-damaged creature, we realize, is responsible for the disappearances and deaths of the lumberjacks and workers early in the film, not the Indians. When Verne and Maggie find out about the campers, they head to the place where the family died; and there, Maggie finds a hideously ugly, almost dead bear cub which has been trapped in a poacher's net. With help from Hawks and Ramona, Verne saves the poor animal. The creature's mother, the murderous bear, hears her cub's cries, however, and attacks the doctor and his companions.[6] A fantastic chase through the woods at night follows, ending when Verne leaps at the giant bear and stabs it to death with an arrow.

Following the disappointing performance of *Black Sunday* at the box office, Frankenheimer felt the need to make *Prophecy* as commercial as possible. And to do this, he tried to shock his audiences, supplying them with macabre set pieces and hair-raising images at the cost of plot and character development. But the film is not thematically bankrupt. In fact, it delivers a fairly pungent critique of several social problems, and in this respect it resembles movies like *The Day the Earth Stood Still* (1951) and *Soylent Green* (1973), which are similarly interested in enlightening their audiences as they try to scare them. Primarily, Frankenheimer uses his picture to draw attention to the harmful impact industry can have on the environment. As he told *Films and Filming*:

> There is a tower of pollution going on, and I don't think anybody gives a damn about it. And if this picture is a hit, maybe people will come out of it and say, "Hey, we'd better watch what we're doing because we're screwing up the world that we live in."[7]

The film targets other issues, too, including social injustice. The Indian characters in *Prophecy*, for instance, petition the federal government for years before Verne's arrival, asking it to do something about the health problems which have afflicted their community. But despite the seriousness of their claims, they have not received help. The explanation for this inaction, Hawks tells the doctor, is two-fold. First, the people in Washington have made the racist assumption that the Indians are violent, murderous drunks and that their claims lack legitimacy. Second, they seem to be more interested in serving the interests of big business than in protecting the rights of native people, much like the government officials in *The Burning Season*.

The movie addresses urban poverty, as well. Early in the film, Vern visits a squalid, overcrowded slum in the District of Columbia to treat a baby who has been bitten by a rat. The landlord, the infant's mother (Lyvingston Holms) tells Verne, has ignored the woman's pleas for help, responding with indifference to her baby's injury:

> I showed it to him. He say it was chicken pox. I say to him, "There's rats in here." He said, "This is chicken pox." I said to him, "Ain't no chickens in here. There's rats in here and them rats bit my baby." You know what he said to me? He said, "The rats got to have room to live, too."

The poor and the disenfranchised suffer horribly and needlessly, the film again suggests, when those with money and power do nothing.

Prophecy also features strong craftsmanship, including interesting footage of a real paper plant at work and the magnificent Canadian forest, where the feature was shot. As a matter of fact, after its release, a number of critics took notice of the film's technical excellence, but ironically they did so not to praise the picture, but to attack the director. (*Prophecy* yielded Frankenheimer some of the worst reviews of his career.) "Mr. Frankenheimer," wrote Vincent Canby, "treats [his] material with the kind of majesty usually reserved for movies about Cleopatra, Napoleon and General Patton."[8] Canby's remarks fail to recognize, however, that the film's sophisticated, often elegant visual style aids the director as he pursues his thematic goals. Early in the picture, for example, he uses a series of graceful lap dissolves that lead the viewer's attention from the polluted wilderness, where several workers from the paper mill have been killed, to a concert hall in Washington, D.C., where an orchestra is performing. The natural world and civilization, the sequence suggests, are inextricably linked, a sentiment the Hawks character puts into words later when he and Ramona (Victoria Racimo) confront Verne. "What's your concept of the environment?" he asks. "Is it rocks?.... The environment is us. And it's being mangled."

Prophecy is not without its problems, though. Unusual for a Frankenheimer film, it completely lacks humor and the principals, especially Foxworth, give overheated performances, lending much of the picture the same leaden seriousness that mars *The Fixer*, *The Iceman Cometh* and *Andersonville*. But *Prophecy*'s most damaging flaw may be the inadequacy of its special effects. The film's monsters are clearly machines and puppets, they are not very frightening, and their emergence in the middle of the narrative spoils the tension and anxiety the director develops earlier on. We might even argue that *Prophecy* would be more entertaining, and more effective as social criticism, if Frankenheimer had simply left these inane creations out and instead kept the focus on the conflict between the Indians and the polluters.

The monsters aside, Frankenheimer strives for realism and verisimilitude frequently in *Prophecy*. With the exception of Armand Assante, he cast Native Americans to play the film's Indian characters. And much of the picture, again, was shot on location, while the sets which William Craig Smith designed in Los Angeles are naturalistic, effectively approximating the rugged look of the Northern woods. Frankenheimer also used real animals in several scenes to make his depictions of the devastated wilderness more authentic. Unfortunately, the director seems to have set his aesthetic and thematic objectives ahead of the animals' welfare and comfort. This is particularly evident in the sequence in which a raccoon attacks Verne and Maggie in their cabin. At the beginning of the segment, the doctor opens a door and finds a shrieking raccoon writhing on the ground. Moments later, after the mercury-sickened animal attacks him, he strikes at it repeatedly with a shovel. In both instances, it is clear that the raccoon used in these shots is distressed and in pain. And in another scene, a goose is grabbed by its legs and yanked beneath the surface of a lake. Frankenheimer no doubt believed that the need to broaden his audience's understanding of the pollution problem warranted the mistreatment of his animal actors. All the same, his willingness to hurt these creatures runs up against *Prophecy*'s central claim that the environment and its wildlife must be protected and handled with care, a contradiction that injures the film far more, perhaps, than its less than believable monsters.

The Burning Season (1994)

In 1988, three days before Christmas, several gunmen rushed up on a trade union leader named Chico Mendes and shot him dead as he stepped outside of his house in the Acre region of west Brazil. The assassination landed on the front pages of newspapers around the globe, as Mendes had become quite famous in the Eighties, having brought international attention to the Brazilian government's reckless development plans for the Amazon, which entailed burning down the rainforest and displacing its indigenous population in order to make the land suitable for cattle ranching. The activist's death became a much talked about topic in Hollywood, too. As *Los Angeles Times* reporter Claudia Puig wrote in 1994:

> Shortly after [Chico] was assassinated ... the film world fell all over itself in an effort to secure the rights to his story. Steven Spielberg, Robert Redford, Peter Guber, Ted Turner and ex–Columbia head David Puttnam all joined in the scramble for what became one of the most coveted movie projects in Hollywood history.[9]

Following a tremendous campaign, both in and outside of the courtroom, it was the independent producer Peter Guber who landed the property. But then Guber left the project to become chief of Sony Pictures, and the production was taken up by David Puttnam at Warner Bros. The film was then developed over the next several years, with Puttnam hiring William Mastrosimone to write the script. But in 1993, just as shooting was about to begin, the studio cancelled the project, concerned that the story of Chico Mendes and his fight against big business would not bring large audiences into theaters.[10] "There had already been rain-forest movies [*Medicine Man, The Mosquito Coast*] that weren't terribly successful...." Puttnam told *Entertainment Weekly*. "Besides, studios don't generally spend $20 million on a political film, especially one about an unreconstructed Marxist like Mendes."[11]

The script was subsequently passed on to the cable television network HBO, a Warner subsidiary, and Puttnam asked Frankenheimer, who was then completing *Against the Wall*, to helm the picture. Frankenheimer took the assignment without hesitation and soon got to work, inviting the scenarist Ron Hutchinson to revise and shorten Mastrosimone's screenplay, casting Raul Julia to play the lead and recruiting John Leonetti to oversee photography. The film was then shot during the spring of 1994 "in the remote Mexican jungle town of Compoapan in the state of Veracruz.... [which] was chosen for its similarity to Mendes' home."[12]

Filming in Mexico presented Frankenheimer with several problems, the first being the language barrier which existed between him and many of his crew, a problem he also encountered while he was making *The Extraordinary Seaman*. In addition, the climate was terrible. Raul Julia, the film's star, for instance, complained that 107 degree temperatures were not unusual.[13] Moreover, Julia was very ill during the production, and on one occasion had to be airlifted out of the jungle in order to receive emergency medical attention. Later that year, in fact, the actor died.

Despite these challenges, Frankenheimer managed to make a picture which is both coherent and emotionally exacting, an intimate, even sentimental biography that doubles as a critique of unregulated capitalism, drawing a link between greed, environmental destruction and political oppression, a point of view it shares with *Prophecy*, his much less successful horror film from 1979. The film's left wing timbre, in fact, was noted by several critics, including *The New York Times*' John O'Connor, who wrote:

> Directed by John Frankenheimer, whose emotional solidarity with Mendes is never in doubt, *The Burning Season* tells an all-too-familiar Latin American tale of a military-backed oligarchy in which the few get richer and the impoverished many rarely stand a chance.[14]

In Frankenheimer's film, however, the poor enjoy a victory, albeit a small one, over their rich counterparts, thanks to the leadership of Chico.

As the film opens, we meet the future activist as a young boy (Jeffrey Licon). The son of an illiterate laborer, he spends his days extracting sap from rubber trees instead of going to school. Then an advocate for workers' rights named Euclides Tavora (Marco Rodriguez) arrives in the jungle and takes interest in the boy, teaching him to read. The men who run the rubber plantations in the region abduct Tavora, however, and set him on fire, a punishment for trying to unionize the tappers. After this, the film jumps several decades to 1983, to Chico's hometown in Acre, where another activist, Wilson Pinheiro (Edward James Olmos), has arrived, hoping to organize the men who work in the region, as well. Pinheiro is concerned that the tappers' livelihood is under threat, as the government, working closely with land speculators and ranchers, has begun to clear the forest by burning it down. Pinheiro is then murdered, infuriating his friend Chico (Julia), who responds by publicizing the tragedy, using radio to let as many as possible know about the killing.

Chico then takes over Pinheiro's role, leading the union of rubber tappers and organizing non-violent protests in order to slow the rate of the forest's destruction. But he comes to realize that this strategy is inadequate and flies up to Miami, to an economic summit, where he courts environmentalists and uses the media to bring the fires in the rainforest to the attention of the world (much as Robert Stroud in *Bird Man of Alcatraz* uses the newspapers to publicize his plight with the prison officials at Leavenworth). The scheme works, but when he returns to Brazil, Chico finds that he has more enemies than he had before, having enraged government figures, corporate investors and ranchers. Yet despite this, Chico continues to organize protests and galvanize international support, eventually forcing the government to cancel a large road construction plan which will ruin the tappers' way of living and working. But after this success, a rancher named Darli Alvez (Tomas Milian) pays a group of men to silence Chico, and they kill him.

The Burning Season was generally applauded by the critics in the days leading up to its premier in September 1994. *Variety*'s Alan Rich, for example, wrote:

> Admirers of vintage John Frankenheimer ... concerned with his occasional flirtations with self-indulgence and mediocrity ... will rejoice at the presence of the master hand in HBO's *The Burning Season*. Finely textured, beautifully and inexorably paced, the new vidpic joins [his] earlier masterworks in its exploration of the remarkable heroism of unremarkable men.[15]

But praise was not universal. Ken Tucker at *Entertainment Weekly* chastised the director for idealizing his portrait of Chico:

> Julia carefully avoids making Mendes a saint or a fanatic. But he's virtually alone in this effort. The script by Ron Hutchinson and the direction of Frankenheimer cast the subject as nothing less than Brazil's naïve but noble savior. We rarely see him doing anything but making grand pronouncements about justice.[16]

And though he otherwise seems to have enjoyed the picture, referring to it as "another substantial credit in the HBO Pictures library," O'Connor felt that the film was guilty of simplifying the conflict between the poor and the rich:

> The movie makes its points powerfully, although its anger can sometimes be simpleminded. It's not enough that the villainous rancher[s] ... be nasty; they have to be downright vile. The establishment is greedy, wallowing in shifty-eyed schemes; the peasants are saintly, attending Mass when not struggling to make a simple living.

An advertisement for *The Burning Season* (HBO, 1994) which appeared in *Rolling Stone* magazine.

Indeed, far from offering a balanced — and realistic — presentation of the opponents in this land dispute, of giving time to both parties' arguments and points of view, Frankenheimer chooses instead to depict their conflict as a battle between extremes, between very good men and very evil ones. Chico, of course, is one of the good men, and to reinforce this idea, Frankenheimer links him on a number of occasions with saints and martyrs from the Bible. In the first shot of the film, for instance, he circles the camera around a statue of Saint Sebastian, whose body, pierced with arrows, is tied to a post. Then with the same fluid movement, he directs our attention to young Chico and his father, mooring a boat, as they return from a day of tapping rubber. Similarly, when the film moves to 1983, to Chico as an adult, Frankenheimer sets the action in a church, where he cuts between shots of Chico, Wilson Pinheiro (one of the film's other martyrs) and a crucifix which hangs from one of the church's walls. In the final shots of the movie, as well, at the slain hero's funeral, his followers hoist a banner with his face emblazoned on it, as others march with staffs that are topped with crosses, recalling the holy day parades that march down city streets, where the images of saints are lifted high above the ground for others to look at — and worship. And as the mourners carry Chico through the cemetery, we learn from the voiceovers that materialize on the soundtrack that the slain man's actions have won him a degree of immortality, that the Brazilian government set aside a huge plot of land for permanent protection after his death, naming it after Chico and thereby enshrining his memory for years to come, if not forever.

The *Burning Season* ranks alongside *Bird Man of Alcatraz* as one of Frankenheimer's most self-consciously rhetorical films, a "message" movie that makes explicit appeals to the viewer's conscience in order, presumably, to foster some sort of responsive action and lend strength to the cause it champions, in this case, protection of the environment: Raul Julia told the *Los Angeles Times*, "The goal of this film is to bring more awareness of the rain forest to the American people."[17] But while the director created the picture with didactic ends in mind, *The Burning Season* is still an entertaining work, a David-and-Goliath story filled with sex, fights, romance and even cattle drives as Darli Alvez and his sons move their animals through the semi-tropical terrain of central Mexico, where the film was shot. The narrative is also quite suspenseful, as we know from that first opening sequence, when Frankenheimer segues from Saint Sebastian to young Chico, that the film's hero is doomed, encouraging us to wonder as the movie progresses how his death will come about, especially after the killers announce their plans to kill him by leaving a severed goat's head at his front door, the same symbolic gesture which Pinheiro is shown before his murder.[18] And when this happens, when the killers leave the goat's head, we might hope, just as Chico's wife Ilzamar (Kamela Dawson) does, that he will leave the town where they live. But of course we also know at the same time that — loyal as he is to his supporters and his convictions — fleeing is something Chico will not do.

The Island of Dr. Moreau (1996)

Set in the South Pacific, *The Island of Dr. Moreau* tells the story of a United Nations attaché named Edward Douglas (David Thewliss), who winds up on a

The great scientist (Marlon Brando) at work in *The Island of Dr. Moreau* (New Line, 1996).

remote island following a plane crash. Shortly after his arrival on this island, which is owned and overseen by Dr. Moreau (Marlon Brando), a reclusive scientist, Douglas comes to realize that the creatures who live in the jungle that surrounds the doctor's compound are neither human nor animal, but a mixture of both. When he asks about the origin of these beast people, Douglas learns from Moreau that the doctor and his drug addict assistant Montgomery (Val Kilmer) have been using science to breed a new, superior race of beings. But the process has not yet been perfected and Moreau and Montgomery have had to insert electronic devices into their subjects, allowing them to shock the beast people whenever they misbehave. The scientists use drugs to stifle the violent impulses which surface in many of the island's inhabitants, as well. But then a creature called Hyena-Swine (Daniel Ringley) discovers and removes one of these shock devices from his body.

No longer afraid of the doctor and no longer obliged to follow the old man's orders, Hyena-Swine refuses the calming serum Montgomery administers, and soon becomes violent and mean-spirited. An uprising ensues as others follow Hyena-Swine's lead. The rebels first kill Moreau, then Montgomery. They plan to kill Douglas, too, but after a bullet pierces Hyena-Swine, the maddened creature walks into a fire, destroying himself, and the rebellion quickly subsides. Spared a horrible death, the bewildered U.N. envoy then constructs a raft and returns to the open water.

When *The Island of Dr. Moreau* was released in the summer of 1996, it performed fairly well at the box office, but it drew the wrath of critics who objected to the picture's uneven pace, its disappointing special effects and the eccentric performances of its leading men. *People*'s Ralph Novak, for example, charged the movie with being "[m]ore ludicrous than scary," while Todd McCarthy at *Variety* used his review to label it as an "embarrassment for all concerned."[19] But although the feature is certainly flawed, the contempt with which it was met seems overstated and misplaced.

Admittedly, the monsters, much like those in *Prophecy*, are not particularly frightening, but in other areas, the film is quite strong. As always, Frankenheimer builds his narrative with charismatic shots, cramming details and information into each frame as he tries to tell the story with the least dialogue possible. The picture opens, for instance, with a striking, overhead shot of an orange raft floating on the surface of a pale blue sea. A moment later, Frankenheimer and his cinematographer William A. Fraker narrow in on the raft's trio of desperate occupants. Two of these men begin to fight. They each stab one another and fall over the side. Then, a moment later, drawn by the scent of the men's blood, a shark appears and attacks them. Viciousness, the scene suggests, is something which humans share with animals, a theme explored throughout the remainder of the movie.

Hollywood had adapted Wells' novel twice before New Line Cinema and Frankenheimer came to it. The first treatment, titled *The Island of Lost Souls*, was released by Paramount in 1933 and featured Charles Laughton as the scientist. The second version of the story, titled *The Island of Dr. Moreau*, was released by American International Pictures in 1977 with Burt Lancaster in the lead. In each of these, Moreau is depicted as a cruel man, a sadist who refuses to use anesthesia as he "humanizes" his animal subjects with the scalpel. And in each of these somber, serious films, the directors' condemnation of their central character is sweeping and unsubtle. In the New Line version, on the other hand, Frankenheimer's attitude toward Moreau is less clear. The doctor in this film seems to care for his creations, spending time with them, even teaching them to read. Moreover, he is not a vivisectionist, but, rather, a genetic scientist, who painlessly grafts the cells of animals and men together in the test tube. And while the earlier Moreau characters pursue their experiments largely for pleasure and curiosity, the doctor in this film wishes to help the world with his creations. As *Newsweek*'s David Ansen, one of the few critics who appreciated the picture, pointed out: "Brando's Moreau is a cracked idealist."[20]

Frankenheimer's film resembles its predecessors, however, as it warns its audience about the dangers which can arise when men attempt to assume the powers of God and create life. But the manner in which the director treats this theme distinguishes his movie from the others. Unlike the earlier pictures, Frankenheimer's film generally refrains from introducing characters who voice platitudes about the limits of science and the boundaries of knowledge and so

Frankenheimer on the set of *The Island of Dr. Moreau* (New Line, 1996).

forth, a horror film convention that dates back to the silent era. The director chooses instead to poke fun at the people who believe that science can be used to improve upon evolution, casting figures like Moreau and Montgomery in a ridiculous light. Both men, for instance, dress in a bizarre manner. When Frankenheimer introduces Moreau, the great scientist wears a muslin gown and red lipstick, his face coated with a chalky white emulsion that protects his skin from the tropical sun. And the drug addict Montgomery, looking more like a beach bum than a lab assistant, sports surfer shorts and mardi gras beads and wears a wraparound elbow brace that conceals the needle marks on his arm. The two act oddly, as well. In one instance, Montgomery kisses two of the island's female inhabitants, a pair of hideous creatures listed as Sow Lady #1 and Sow Lady #2 in the film's credits. In another instance, shortly after Moreau's death, he begins to dress like his late employer, wearing sheets, his head wrapped in nylon, white powder coating his face. Moreau's behavior is less insane, perhaps, but unusual nevertheless. To keep his head comfortable in the heat, he wears a hat which is made from an ice bucket; and his constant companion, whom he pets and cuddles, is a piano-playing dwarf named Majai (Nelson de la Rosa), who dresses just like his master, wearing gowns, head scarves and wigs.

     Some critics have suggested that Brando's performance is a critique, a grotesque parody of earlier roles he played, particularly his turn as Col. Kurtz in Coppola's *Apocalypse Now* (1979). Both the doctor and the colonel lose their minds when they separate themselves from civilization. And both share a taste for modernist poetry. But while Kurtz is fond of T.S. Eliot, Moreau enjoys W.B. Yeats. In one of the strangest moments in this very strange film, he even has one of his half-human creations read an excerpt from "The Second Coming," Yeats' vision of the end of the world:

> somewhere in the sands of the desert
> A shape with lion body and the head of a man,
> A gaze blank and pitiless as the sun,
> Is moving its slow thighs, while all about it
> Reel shadows of the indignant desert birds.
> The darkness drops again; but now I know
> That twenty centuries of stony sleep
> Were vexed to nightmare by a rocking cradle,
> And what rough beast, its hour come round at last,
> Slouches towards Bethlehem to be born?

And like the maddened colonel, the doctor is an autocrat, who imposes laws of his own devising upon his subjects, using brutality now and then to ensure cooperation. Moreau's personality is softer and more likeable than Kurtz's, though, and his concern for the island's pathetic occupants— his "children," as he calls them — seems real. He chastises Douglas, for example, when the castaway speaks cruelly to the beast people. Yet we can't overlook the fact that it is Moreau who is responsible for what he refers to at one point as "their diminished lives." And in this respect, he resembles the Old Man in *Seconds*, as each of these men are bent on using science and technology to make this world kinder, gentler and more pleasant, and both bring about great suffering as they relentlessly pursue this goal.

CHAPTER SIX

Faulty Command

While the rights of individuals may be of paramount importance in Franken-heimer's cinema, several films address the problems that can arise when people in positions of power set personal interests ahead of the needs of the people they are expected to serve and protect. In pictures like *Seven Days in May* and *The Fourth War*, Frankenheimer considers the threats to national and global security which can develop when military leaders exhibit these tendencies; and in *George Wallace* and *Path to War*, he traces the damage which arises when civilian leaders ignore democratic principles and common sense. Regardless of their positions, however, all of the leaders we find in these pictures are not only incompetent, but dangerous, too, even the somewhat amusing captain in *The Extraordinary Sea-man*, whose mistaken judgment nearly undoes the Allies' efforts to end the conflict with the Japanese in the closing moments of World War II.

Seven Days in May (1964)

Frankenheimer opens this political thriller, his follow up to *The Manchurian Candidate*, with a sequence in which a sepia-colored copy of the U.S. Constitution is slowly split apart by a series of animated numbers that run from 1 to 7. Next, he presents the viewer with a shot of the iron fence that pro-tects the White House's north lawn, and just outside of it, on the sidewalk that lines Pennsylvania Avenue, a demonstration is taking place, with streams of people marching back and forth. Carrying signs and banners, the demonstra-tors are divided ideologically; some support Jordan Lyman (Frederic March), the film's fictional president, while others back James Matoon Scott (Burt Lan-caster), Lyman's nemesis, a Pentagon hawk with political ambitions. After a Scott enthusiast insults one of Lyman's people, the demonstration deteriorates into a riot; and soon the police roll up in paddy wagons and start to strike at

Jiggs (Kirk Douglas) goes to President Lyman (Frederic March) with his discovery of the ECOMCON plot in *Seven Days in May* (Paramount, 1964).

the crowd with their billy clubs. Shot on grainy stock with hand-held cameras, the scene recalls the television news footage of the Mississippi race riots that took place in the early Sixties, when protestors were attacked with similar brutality. This startling scene, which Frankenheimer needed President Kennedy's permission to shoot, is the first, but hardly the last, time the film alludes to contemporary events and crises.[1]

Based on Fletcher Knebel and Charles Bailey II's novel of the same name, *Seven Days in May* was scripted by Rod Serling, with whom Frankenheimer had worked during his *Playhouse 90* days. Serling improved the original story considerably, however, by simplifying its plot and completely rewriting the dialogue, using terse and sarcastic language that recalls the work of tough guy writers like James M. Cain and Raymond Chandler. Set some time in the near future, the picture is a chronicle of the efforts taken by a sitting president to thwart a military *coup d'etat*. Two years into his first term, Jordan Lyman's public approval rating has plunged to 29 percent, following his decision to sign a disarmament treaty with the Soviet Union. Disgusted by what they see as an instance of criminal naiveté, several members of the Joint Chiefs of Staff plan to kidnap Lyman during war games exercises.

Leading the plot is Scott, a decorated four star general. It is Scott's assistant, Col. Jiggs Casey (Kirk Douglas), who discovers the conspiracy, after hearing about a military base called ECOMCON (an abbreviation for "Emergency Communications Control"), which has been constructed in the Texas desert without the president's knowledge. Casey alerts Lyman, who responds by directing the colonel, as well as a senator (Edmond O'Brien) and a presidential aide (Martin Balsam) to collect information that can confirm or deny the scheme's existence. After determining that the plot is real, Lyman confronts Scott, asking him for his resignation — much as Truman asked for Gen. MacArthur's in 1951— though Scott declines. When a confession signed by one of the conspirators suddenly materializes after it was thought lost, Lyman gains the leverage he needs to neutralize the rebellious chiefs. All of them subsequently resign, including Scott, and the crisis dissipates.

Obsessives like Scott appear in many of Frankenheimer's films — *The Young Savages*' Hank Bell, *French Connection II*'s Popeye Doyle and *Dead Bang*'s Jerry Beck all come to mind — but with his access to America's military resources, Scott may be the most dangerous figure in this group. At once charismatic and fanatical, he believes that the "survival of the country" depends upon its ability and its willingness to demonstrate its might. "We've stayed alive because we've built up an arsenal," he tells the president at one point. "And we've kept the peace because we've dealt with an enemy who knew we would use this arsenal." And because he thinks that Lyman's policy have left the nation vulnerable to invasion and nuclear weaponry, he feels free to circumvent the electoral process. Scott evidently doesn't recognize (or care) that his intentions are in many ways just as dangerous to the nation's welfare as an attack from the Soviets. [2]

Lyman understands, though, and he worries that the illegal seizure of power will precipitate World War III. And, rather naively, he hopes to deter the general with rhetoric. "You have such a fervent, passionate, evangelical faith in this country," the president says. "Why in the name of God don't you have any faith in the system of government you're so hell bent to protect?" But because Scott won't negotiate and because the stakes are so high, Lyman feels free to employ any means available to stop the coup, including the use of coerced confessions, secret cameras and, if necessary, blackmail. Lyman and his helpers, it seems, are in many ways just as cold blooded as their enemies; their "dirty trick" tactics, in fact, recall those used by J. Edgar Hoover and his COINTELPRO agents, who, during the Fifties and Sixties, collected personal information on individuals in order to neutralize threats to the nation's internal security efforts; Hoover felt that this threat came from the left, however.

In spite of, or rather because of, these efforts, Lyman and his men manage to save the nation — and perhaps the world — from Scott's short-sighted designs. And with order restored, the U.S. can resume its task of spreading liberty around the globe. In the speech that closes the movie, the president states:

There's been abroad in this land in recent months a whisper that we have somehow lost our greatness, that we do not have the strength to win without war the struggles for liberty throughout the world. This is slander, because our country is strong, strong enough to be a peacemaker. It is proud, proud enough to be patient. The whisperers and the detractors, the violent men are wrong. We will remain strong and proud, peaceful and patient, and we will see a day when on this earth all men will walk out of the long tunnels of tyranny into the bright sunshine of freedom.

These remarks are followed by an image of the Constitution, which once again fills the screen, but this time the document is undamaged and intact.

The Extraordinary Seaman (1969)

The Extraordinary Seaman is based upon a 1967 book by Phillip Rock. It was Rock, in fact, who adapted his comic novel into a screenplay, which he was able to sell to Frankenheimer and his partner Edward Lewis. But although Frankenheimer liked the story the author had developed, he did not like the way Rock's script was written, and Hal Dresner, who'd just finished working on *Cool Hand Luke* (1967), was brought on for revisions.[3] With backing from MGM, Frankenheimer enjoyed a generous budget, allowing him to build a strong cast with stars like David Niven and Mickey Rooney, along with newer talents like Alan Alda and Faye Dunaway. He then headed down to southern Mexico to shoot the picture, and all seemed to go well, despite the production's remote location and the language barrier that existed between the director and some of his crew. But once he returned to Los Angeles and got to work on the film's editing, Frankenheimer realized that things had not gone as smoothly as he'd hoped. Thanks to a misunderstanding with a script clerk, he'd failed to shoot enough film in Mexico; and to compensate for this, he and his editor Fredric Steinkamp added almost 15 minutes of material which they found in various film archives, including newsreels, stock footage and old movies.

While this tactic solved the immediate problem, lengthening the picture's running time to an acceptable 79 minutes, it produced another snag for Frankenheimer. Because the footage was used largely for satiric purposes, it was not protected by fair use laws, and MGM, eager to stay out of court, told Frankenheimer that if he wanted to have his film released he would have to obtain permission from the people who appeared in these clips. But because the director did not like the idea of doing this, he removed the clips which were most likely to arouse a litigious response instead. The tactic worked and after keeping *The Extraordinary Seaman* in limbo for more than a year, MGM, in the fall of 1969, finally released the picture.[3]

The oddly titled film, however, did little business at the box office and the responses it received from critics, at best, were mixed. In his review for *Film Quarterly*, Stephen Farber found much to like in this "genial spoof," but he concluded that the picture was little more than a "minor entertainment ... too obvious in its satire, too narrow in its scope to last."[4] The write-up which ran in *Variety*, on the other hand, was much less receptive:

> "The Extraordinary Seaman" is strictly steerage cargo. A tepid story keel, not entirely — but almost — devoid of amusement strength, has been ballasted with padding newsreel footage and other effect to yield an unstable comedy vessel.[5]

Like *The Train* and *The Holcroft Covenant*, *The Extraordinary Seaman* takes place during the closing days of World War II. As the film opens, a group of American sailors becomes separated from their ship during a training exercise. After a few days on the open sea, the castaways land on a small island in the Philippines. Fearful of being spotted by the Japanese, they head into the jungle which covers the island and soon come upon a river where they spot an old gunboat called the Curmudgeon, which is stranded in mud. At first, the sailors think the craft is abandoned, but then they hear music, a recording of the song "We Sail the Ocean Blue," from Gilbert and Sullivan's *H.M.S. Pinafore*:

> Ahoy! Ahoy! O'er the bright blue sea,
> We stand to our guns, to our guns all day.

The sailors follow the sound to the ship's bridge, where they find a naval officer, a genteel Englishman who introduces himself as Commander Finchhaven (Niven). Wearing a splendid white suit and sipping scotch, Finchhaven persuades the four sailors to help him dislodge the boat, promising to carry them on to Australia in exchange for their assistance.

Subsequently joined by a local businesswoman named Mrs. Winslow (Dunaway), who also longs to leave the island, the captain and his ragtag crew set out to sea. One of the sailors, a lieutenant named Krim (Alda) grows suspicious of the captain, however, after noticing that the stately officer never seems to sleep, eat or get drunk from the whiskey which he ceaselessly drinks. He is also troubled to learn that Finchhaven plans to attack a Japanese ship with the Curmudgeon, although the old gunboat is completely bereft of guns. To answer the American's questions and diminish his fears, the commander tells a story, an extraordinary one. In 1914, at the onset of World War I, he explains, he was given command of the H.M.S. Curmudgeon. And right away, he was given the opportunity to sink a German cruiser, an occasion which would have brought glory to him and his family. But the commander, a drunk, fell off his ship and drowned before this could happen. The shame which this blunder brought to the family name aroused the wrath of his ancestors, who determined that the dead man owed them a great amends for making such an embarrassing error. "They considered the problem for ten years," he says. "And at last ... they decided that I would temporarily be restored to life and returned to Curmudgeon to have another chance to sink a cruiser." And once this is accomplished, he tells Krim, he can return to the grave.

The commander's tale doesn't calm the lieutenant; rather, it convinces

Mrs. Winslow (Faye Dunaway) and friends (Leonard Smith, Richard Guizon) on the deck of the Curmudgeon in *The Extraordinary Seaman* (MGM, 1969).

him that Finchhaven is a lunatic, whose ideas threaten the safety of the others on board, and he responds to this by making plans with them to flee. But when the others set out, Krim and Mrs. Winslow are left behind, thanks to the captain's cunning. They decide to cooperate with Finchhaven, though, and when a Japanese cruiser is spotted, they strap a dynamite charge to the prow of his ship. The captain then rams the enemy craft, destroying it and the Curmudgeon, not realizing that the enemy ship carries two admirals, an American and a Japanese, who've just negotiated Japan's surrender — a blunder which costs the commander dearly. Instead of winning eternal rest, that is, he winds up on a replica of the Curmudgeon, forced to carry about sightseers and children as he waits for another war — and the opportunities at redemption it offers — to materialize.

The Extraordinary Seaman is a bit fluffy and slow, but it offers some rewards to its viewers. The film features exceptional camerawork, for example, from Lionel Lindon, the same cinematographer who'd collaborated with Frankenheimer on *Grand Prix* and *The Manchurian Candidate*. In one especially memorable shot of the Curmudgeon, which Lindon must have filmed from an airplane or a helicopter, we see the ship as it sails across the sun-streaked surface of the Pacific, a tiny silhouette sliding over a sheet of orange and white light. The cast strengthens the picture, as well. Niven is especially good as the cursed sailor. Mincing about the bridge constantly, ogling Mrs. Winslow and ribbing Krim, the seaman is a conceited, silly and often ludicrous character. But although his performance is a send up of the suave military heroes he played in films like Carol Reed's *The Way Ahead* (1944), Carl Foreman's *The Guns of Navarone* and Guy Hamilton's *The Best of Enemies* (1962), the great actor manages, at the same time, to make Finchhaven endearing, often conveying with his eyes the impression that the ghostly captain, for all his bluster, is a sad and desperate fellow. Alda's interpretation of the commander's opposite, the straight laced and hypersensitive Krim, is also effective. An accountant by trade, the lieutenant craves tidiness, organization and structure, and the disarray and chaos that flourish on the decks of the Curmudgeon fray his nerves; and as the film progresses and his anxiety increases, he moves about the ship with increasing clumsiness, banging his head as he runs through a doorway, for instance, stumbling into Mrs. Winslow as she fires her rifle at the enemy, falling over the ship's side. But while these pratfalls and gags are not terribly original, they are amusing because Krim, as Alda plays him, is so serious, self-important and set upon maintaining his dignity, a tendency which makes him preposterous and likeable at once.

Dunaway adds much to the film, too. Steely, calm, sure of herself, the character she plays counterbalances the others' exuberant inclinations. Yet she in many ways is just as absurd as they are: throughout most of the movie, she cradles a rifle in her arms, much as Finchhaven clutches his bottle of scotch. And she is vain, too: in each scene in which she appears, she wears a different outfit and a new, and always glamorous, hairdo. But Dunaway's part is quite small, little more than a series of walk-ons. And as Pratley pointed out, this is because the actress was not a star when *The Extraordinary Seaman* was being made. But between the end of shooting and the picture's 1969 premier, the releases of *Bonnie and Clyde* (1967) and *The Thomas Crown Affair* (1968) had turned her into one of Hollywood's most popular actresses, a phenomenon which prompted MGM to promote the film as a Dunaway vehicle — and a sex comedy.[6] One of the taglines for the posters the studio commissioned, for example, reads:

> STOWAWAY ... SAIL AWAY ... LAUGH AWAY ... LOVE
> AWAY ... WITH DUNAWAY!

Frankenheimer wanted to make his viewers laugh with *The Extraordinary Seaman*, but he was also interested in using it to critique war and the military and, by extension, the United States' involvement in southeast Asia (where, we have to remember, the film is set); and in this respect, *The Extraordinary Seaman* anticipates two better known war satires which also appeared during the Vietnam years, Mike Nichol's *Catch-22* (1970) and Robert Altman's *M*A*S*H*

(1970).[7] And much like these pictures, Frankenheimer's film focuses attention on military leaders, calling into question their competence — and their integrity. Finchhaven, for example, rushes to battle and risks the safety of the people on his boat not for the sake of defending his country and its ideals, but, rather, to relieve himself of the burden his ancestors set upon him. The film's disdain for war is particular to it, we should note; it doesn't show up in Rock's novel. In fact, the Finchhaven we find in the book is a shrewd tactician, not a fool, and his efforts yield success, rather than failure. Instead of ramming a Japanese cruiser, as he does in the film, the commander allows the enemy to seize his gunboat; and once this happens, once the British vessel becomes a Japanese one, he sabotages it, sinking it, and in doing this, unburdens himself of his ancestor's curse.

Frankenheimer's inclusion of newsreel footage and other bits of film also separates his work from its source. And this often bizarre and unflattering material, much like the farcical plot and the actors' campy performances, augments the picture's satirical tone. In one of the clips Frankenheimer uses, for example, Harry Truman's wife Bess struggles over and over to break a bottle of champagne against the fuselage of a bomber. In another, Douglas MacArthur marches pompously through the ocean water as he makes his celebrated return to the Philippines. And in another, a line of goose-stepping Nazi soldiers, thanks to Steinkamp's clever editing, kick their legs like dancehall girls. But these clips, as humorous as they are, appear too often, and as their novelty wears off, their rhetorical effectiveness vanishes, too.

The Fourth War (1990)

With *The Fourth War*, a Cold War thriller appropriately set in winter, Frankenheimer offers yet another compelling profile of an obsessive personality.[8] This time, the director affixes his beam on a misanthropic army colonel named Jack Knowles (Roy Scheider). Since Vietnam, Knowles has been out of sorts, embittered by the United States' inability to defeat its enemy in Southeast Asia and bored over the lack of adventure which has characterized his life since his days in the jungle. The colonel is contemptuous of the bureaucratic decrees and statutes which hold the army together, as well, and his refusal to honor them, along with his resentful attitude, have injured his career. As his friend Gen. Hackworth (Harry Dean Stanton), his commanding officer in Vietnam, explains: "The army's answer was to put him in mothballs, assignments so far out of the way you couldn't find them on a map."

Hackworth is sympathetic to Knowles, however. And because he believes that the officer is still capable of leading soldiers effectively, he assigns him to a base which sits along the Czech-German border, a well-intentioned gesture that eventually leads to the colonel's undoing. Within a few days of his arrival

The cold warriors (Roy Scheider, Jürgen Prochnow) fight in the snow in *The Fourth War* (Kodiak, 1990).

at the base, Knowles takes his men out to the demilitarized zone which separates the two countries. One of the battalion's tanks breaks down, however, and the colonel and his assistant Lt. Col. Clark (Tim Reid) take a walk as they wait for it to be repaired. Surveying the area with binoculars, they spot a defector on the Czech side, running desperately through the snow, pursued by soldiers on horses. A moment later, a Soviet helicopter materializes, and as it attempts to intercept the fugitive, to capture him, it crosses into Germany. Knowles, in response, has one of his soldiers aim a rocket at the flying machine. The strategy works, forcing the craft to retreat. It doesn't help the poor defector, though, who is subsequently shot and killed by one of the soldiers on the ground, a few feet short of the border. Disgusted by this, Knowles raises his pistol and aims it at the man who leads the Soviet soldiers, a Russian colonel named Valachev (Jürgen Prochnow). He collects himself, however, and instead of shooting his enemy, he throws a snowball at him. Valechev responds to this, in turn, by throwing a snowball back at Knowles. But his aim is better, and he actually hits the American. Before Knowles can answer, the Russian climbs into his helicopter and flies away.

His departure does not mark the end of his conflict with Knowles, however. Instead, it precipitates a game of one-upmanship which grows increasingly dangerous. Within a few days of the incident on the border, the American sneaks into Czechoslovakia and captures a trio of Soviet soldiers, tormenting them, humiliating them, and giving them his name to pass on to their commander. A few days later Valechev responds. This time, though, he fires a rocket at the American's jeep, blowing it up. And then, in response to this, Knowles re-crosses the border, heading over to Valechev's base, where he sets fire to a watch tower, much as Popeye Doyle sets fire to the Hotel Tangier in *French Connection II*. But then the Russian changes tactics. Rather than attacking his foe directly, he tries to ensnare him, using a beautiful intelligence agent who calls herself Elena (Lara Harris) to lure Knowles out of Germany. To do this, the agent pretends to be a Czech defector who needs to return to her country to rescue her daughter. Knowles helps her across the border, but he does not trust the woman and once they are inside the country, he follows her to Valechev, and springs on his enemy, but fails to kill him. A chase follows and the colonels wind up on the surface of a frozen lake in the neutral space between Czechoslovakia and Germany, where they engage in a brutal fist fight. Alerted to this, troops from each side of the conflict begin to collect around the lake's shore. And when they train their guns on the combatants, the two men desist, ending their brawl in a draw.

Jack Knowles ranks with Popeye Doyle and Jerry Beck as one of Frankenheimer's angriest and most obstreperous heroes. Like them, he sets his pride and his personal beliefs ahead of the law, public safety and common sense, and in so doing brings injury to others. But while Doyle and Beck may be reckless and self-centered, their objectives and motives have a great deal of merit: Doyle is charged with capturing a murderous drug dealer and Beck has to stop a gang of racist terrorists. Knowles, in contrast, pursues and attacks Valachev for no other reason, it seems, than to settle a score, to get back at the Russian for hitting him with the snowball in the moments after the Soviet soldier shoots the defector. In this regard, Knowles, as well as Valachev, is like a schoolboy on a playground, dead set on proving his toughness. This same destructive machismo, we might remember, characterizes the attitudes and conduct of the hoodlum protagonists in *The Young Savages*. The consequences of Knowles' actions, however, are far more dangerous. By crossing borders and committing sabotage, he runs the risk of escalating the conflict which exists between his country and his enemy's, a frightening thought, given the nuclear stockpiles each nation holds: as General Hackworth remarks, the "private little grudge war" that arises between the two colonels has the potential of turning "the rest of us poor sons of bitches ... into french fries."

Fortunately, this worst case scenario doesn't develop. But there is fallout. We learn from Hackworth's voiceover narration that Knowles is subsequently court-martialed for his actions, and presumably his career as an officer in the U.S. Army is over. Hackworth's narration, which we hear throughout the picture, in fact, is the testimony he gives to military counselors at the trial, following the climactic incident on the lake. And though the general refrains from endorsing Knowles's behavior, he tries to explain it, hoping, it seems, to arouse the judges' compassion. He even suggests at one point that the army bears some responsibility for the contest which arises between Knowles and Valachev:

> It was a challenge he had to accept, gentlemen. Look at it this way. We all know we're talking about a man who's trained to react like this, conditioned, drilled into him. From the day he hit basic training he's been told, "Hey, that's the enemy, bucko, go get 'em." Jack Knowles is a soldier, for Christ's sake, not some candy ass diplomat, who can turn his coat inside out without taking his hands out of his pockets.

But the aggressive temperament which made Knowles a hero in war causes a great deal of trouble for him in peace, setting him against everyone he encounters, it seems, not simply Valachev. When the film opens, the colonel berates a sergeant for not saluting him with enough enthusiasm. When the tank stalls near the border, he upbraids the driver for lacking "combat discipline." And when Clark reports the colonel's first skirmish with Valachev to Hackworth, Knowles rails against him, threatening the subordinate officer and accusing him of "stepping outside" of his duties.

These attacks, of course, are expressions of the colonel's authority, of the power he wields as camp commander. But they also weaken him by arousing the disdain and ridicule of his men, who laugh at him, for instance, after he chews out the soldier over the salute. His hotheaded manner costs him the support of his colleagues, too. Following the harsh rebuke he receives from the angry colonel, for example, the opportunistic Clark sets out to undermine Knowles, providing Hackworth with steady updates on the colonel's various offenses, a strategy which succeeds as the general eventually turns over the command of the base to Clark and promotes him to full colonel. It seems likely, as well, that Knowles' inability to "cope with peace" has contributed to the dissolution of his marriage and the emotional coolness which characterizes the relationship he has with his two sons.

Knowles, in short, is an isolated figure whose difficult personality degrades the quality of his life, a problem which links him again to the Doyle and Beck characters, as well as *Bird Man of Alcatraz*'s Robert Stroud, *The Manchurian Candidate*'s Raymond Shaw and *The Horsemen*'s Uraz. But even these unpleasant people find friends. Stroud has his sparrows and the guard Bull Ransom (Neville Brand). Raymond has Marco. And Uraz has the goat herder Hayatal. But Knowles has no one. Even his champion Hackworth gives up on him eventually, once he recognizes the threat Knowles poses to détente. This realization comes about fairly late in the film, by the way, when the informer Clark tells the general that the renegade colonel has crossed the border to antagonize Valachev. Hackworth says, saddened by the turn of events: "As painful as it is to contemplate, we've got to do something to save the situation." Then, rather ominously, he adds: "We've got to act like we never heard of him."

Knowles' attitude and conduct may estrange him from his peers and family, leaving him at odds with the world and its rules, but there is one person, however, who thinks and acts much as he does, and this, ironically, is Valachev, his mortal enemy. The Russian, as we learn from Hackworth, has been similarly damaged by his military experience. "You see right over there ... is another hero just like you," the general tells the colonel, pointing his finger in the direction of Czechoslovakia. "But he didn't go to Vietnam. He went to Afghanistan. And it was a fucking mess." The two colonels share other similarities. Both are forced, for instance, to work with undisciplined soldiers in obscure outposts. They think alike, too; each, after all, manages to deceive the other with the female intelligence agent. They share a taste for sports cars, as well. And it seems likely perhaps that in other circumstances these men might have been friends, a possibility which perhaps brings to mind Thomas Hardy's famous poem about the wastefulness of war, "The Man he Killed":

> Had he and I but met
> By some old ancient inn,
> We should have sat us down to wet
> Right many a nipperkin!
> But ranged as infantry,
> And staring face to face,
> I shot at him and he at me,
> And killed him in his place.

George Wallace (1997)

Like Orson Welles' *Citizen Kane*, *George Wallace* offers viewers an elaborate character study, a sprawling portrait of a man with an enormous sense of self-importance, who brings tremendous harm upon himself and others as he pursues power. And like *Kane*, *Wallace* employs a non-linear narrative which jumps back and forth in time. The movie opens, for instance, on May 15, 1972, the day the segregationist governor was shot in a shopping center parking lot in Maryland; and it closes two years later, after the governor makes a public apology to a congregation of black parishioners in the Alabama church where his former adversary Martin Luther King, Jr., once preached. In between these sequences, however, the film covers much of the Southern politician's career over the two decades which preceded the assassination attempt, returning on a few occasions to the months immediately following it, a tactic which imbues the movie with a great deal of pathos. By inserting the shooting early in the narrative, and then sporadically drawing attention to its consequences, the director prevents us from ever forgetting that Wallace, though he acted horribly, also suffered horribly.

The film is hardly an apology, however, as—again evoking *Kane*—it focuses much attention on its protagonists' opportunistic personality and his moral recklessness. Early in the picture, for instance, a young, 35-year-old Wallace (Gary Sinise) is taken aside by his mentor Governor James "Big Jim" Folsom (Joe Don Baker), a progressive Alabama democrat who tells his protégé to steer clear of race baiting and allegiances with groups like the Ku Klux Klan. And Wallace at first adheres to Folsom's advice, choosing to court groups like the ACLU and the NAACP, rather than the powerful KKK, when he makes his first gubernatorial run in 1958. But when he fails to win, he repudiates Folsom's fair-minded views and commits himself to an anti-integration platform, declaring to his aides that he will never be "outniggered" again.

Wallace's turnaround, of course, leads to success in the next election, and for much of the remainder of the film, Frankenheimer spotlights the governor's reactionary policies, never hesitating to emphasize their ugliness, never allowing viewers to forget that Wallace adopts them in order to bolster his own political standing. In one of the movie's most memorable sequences, the director recreates the governor's famous 1963 inaugural address, during which he told those in attendance and the world at large that his administration was committed to protecting "segregation today, segregation tomorrow, segregation forever." Interestingly, Frankenheimer had this sequence filmed in black and white, and thanks to this, the material recalls the documentary newsreel footage which was shot during the real Wallace inaugural; at the same time, the director manipulates the camera artfully, expressively, using close-ups, medium shots and long shots to make us aware of the impact his delivery has upon his cheering and applauding listeners; and by doing this, Frankenheimer reveals the great power Wallace and his ideas had over people, much as Leni Riefenstahl does in her depictions of Adolf Hitler and his followers in *Triumph of the Will* (1935).

The film dramatizes a number of other infamous incidents which occurred during Wallace's long career, too, such as the governor's response to the bombing of the church in Birmingham where four African-American girls were killed not long after his first inauguration, a crime some have argued was fomented by his racist rhetoric. We also watch as Wallace takes his stand against the federal government and its insistence upon school integration, holding fast in a doorway at the University of Alabama as President Kennedy's assistant Nicholas Katzenbach (Ron Perkins), backed up by dozens of National Guardsman, pleads with him to move. Scenes from Selma show up, too, with detailed reenactments of the Alabama state police attacking protesters with dogs and fire hoses, which Frankenheimer supplements with footage that was shot by television crews during the 1965 standoff.

The film's portrait of Wallace as a family man is similarly unflattering, depicting him in the early segments of the picture, for instance, as an unfaithful husband, inclined to sleep with beautiful sycophants. And like so many of Frankenheimer's central characters, the governor is an overly ambitious figure, willing to set his own interests ahead of others, in particular the people closest to him. As Lou Grahnke noted in his review of the film, Wallace "values political power over the love of his wife and family"; and Caryn James suggested that the governor is "a man who must be elected to feel alive."[9]

An especially noxious display of this quality reveals itself shortly after

The governor (Gary Sinise) and his second wife Cornelia (Angelina Jolie) after the shooting leaves him paralyzed in *George Wallace* (Turner Pictures, 1998).

Wallace loses his first run for governor, when his first wife Lurleen (Mare Winnigham) comes to comfort him.

> LURLEEN: Honey, I really am so sorry. I just heard. Well, maybe there's some good, huh? Maybe at least now we can head back home, live a normal life.
>
> WALLACE: God damn it to hell, Lurleen! Normal life? That ain't life! I just been hit a blow like this and you want to get on me again about our home life?

Wallace is not above exploiting this woman's love for him, too. For example, when he is forced out of the capitol because of a term limit law, he asks her to run for governor herself, which she does, although she is dying of cancer. And her victory in 1966 is indeed helpful for him, not only allowing him to retain power over the state, but strengthening his standing as a national political player, when he runs for president in 1968. The film intimates, in fact, that Lurleen's death was accelerated by her willingness to help her husband in this way.

But while *George Wallace* is rooted in actual history, it is still a drama, and to make the film as entertaining as possible, Frankenheimer and his writers interpreted the governor's life and career with great license. As the director told Amy Hetzner just as the film was heading into production, "I'm not doing a documentary about George Wallace any more than Shakespeare was doing a documentary about Richard III."[10] Sometimes these inventions enhance the governor's portrait, making him a more attractive figure than he actually was. In the final moments of the picture, for instance, Wallace visits a church in Montgomery where Martin King had preached and apologizes to the congregation. But while this scene is compelling, it is by and large a fiction. As the historian Dan Carter has pointed out, the governor's request for forgiveness

> didn't happen, at least not as depicted in the film. In 1974, as the number of black voters grew, Wallace prepared for his reelection by abandoning the racial rhetoric that marked his hard-fought 1970 campaign and quietly appealed for black political support around the state. In the wake of his successful reelection, Wallace acknowledged the support of black voters by appearing at the Dexter Avenue Baptist Church to welcome the Alabama Progressive Baptist State Convention to Montgomery. The audience warmly, even emotionally, greeted the wheelchair-bound Wallace. But in his remarks he made no apologies for his past actions and he defensively insisted that he had been a defender of states rights in the 1960s, not a racist. The acknowledgement that he was wrong, the pleas for forgiveness, would come much later in his life.[11]

The filmmakers' departures can often be uncomplimentary, too, though, and this aspect of the script played a large part in arousing the wrath of George Wallace's relatives in the weeks before shooting began, prompting them to threaten legal action. In particular, the Wallace family was incensed over the invention of a character named Archie, a black trustee who lives in the governor's house, who at one point contemplates killing the governor with an ice pick; they were upset, as well, by a scene in the teleplay which had Wallace attempting suicide; nor did they appreciate the way Lurleen was portrayed. As George Wallace, Jr., explained to Hetzner: "There's no need to create the fiction of an attempted suicide on the part of my dad or an alleged murder of my dad by an orderly at the governor's mansion, or portraying my mother in such a way that she was not." To a certain extent, the producers answered the Wallace family's requests by eliminating the suicide scene, and adding a disclaimer at the end of the picture:

> During successive administrations, trustees from Alabama state prisons have served Alabama governors, including George Wallace. The character, Archie, was created for dramatic purposes to reflect a viewpoint concerning this turbulent period of American History.

But what exactly is this viewpoint? The telefilm's executive producer Mark Carliner, speaking to the *Los Angeles Times*, suggested that Archie (Clarence Williams III) serves a metaphorical function, that he's an illustration "of rage," evoking the quiet, but powerful anger which Wallace's actions and beliefs generated in Alabama's African-American population.[12] At the same time, Archie and Wallace become friends of a sort late in the film, after the governor is shot. It is Archie, who drives the governor to the church and pushes him down the aisle and stands beside him as the politician makes his appeal. And it is Archie who, in the film's touching final scene, tucks the injured man into his bed and bids him goodnight. *The Baltimore Sun*'s David Zurawik, as a matter of fact, described the relationship which develops between the men as a "real love story."[13] The friendship-between-enemies theme, of course, materializes often in Frankenheimer's oeuvre. The prison guard Bull Ransom grows close to Robert Stroud in *Bird Man of Alcatraz*, the guard named Michael Smith and the prisoner Jamaal grow close in *Against the Wall* and the CIA agent Sam and the freelance terrorist Vincent grow close in *Ronin*. Wallace's transformation, the profound personality change which follows the shooting, is a familiar trope, too, of course, bringing again to mind *Against the Wall*, as well as earlier films like *The Horsemen*, *French Connection II* and *The Challenge*, in which all the main characters are similarly redeemed by their encounters with pain.

Path to War (2002)

Frankenheimer's final film, much like *George Wallace*, tracks the descent of a politician, showing us the ways in which ambition and power can blur judgment. The picture opens on January 20, 1965, the night of Lyndon Johnson's first — and only — inaugural ball. Having defeated his opponent Barry Goldwater handily, the president (Michael Gambon) now possesses a great deal of political collateral, and with a carefully selected group of advisors, he sets out to put his mark on domestic policy, hoping to create what he refers to as the Great Society, a new America which will work harder to eliminate social ills like poverty and racism.

But before Johnson can really make headway in this direction, problems flare up in Vietnam, as the Soviet-backed forces from the northern part of the region enter into conflict with their adversaries in the south. Concerned that a communist victory will jeopardize global stability, as well as his political standing, Johnson follows the advice of his Secretary of Defense Robert McNamara (Alec Baldwin) and orders the U.S. military to begin a strategic series of bombings, hoping this will bring Ho Chi Minh to the negotiating table. The plan fails, however, and Johnson, ignoring the counsel of dovish advisors like George Ball (Bruce McGill) and Clark Clifford (Donald Sutherland), proceeds to escalate America's involvement in the conflict, eventually sending over ground troops.

Unfortunately, the campaign distracts Johnson from his social programs, and as the situation overseas worsens, his popularity falters. Student demonstrations begin to spring up as allies like Martin Luther King, Jr. (Curtis McClarin) turn away and throw their support to the anti-war effort. The president's advisors abandon him, too, including McNamara, leaving Johnson frustrated and bitter. His friend Clifford, however, stays on, becoming Secretary of Defense, hoping this will strengthen Johnson's chances as he pursues another presidential term. But in March 1968, the president holds a press conference

Michael Gambon as Lyndon Johnson in *Path to War* (Avenue Pictures / Edgar J. Scherick Associates, 2002).

in which he articulates a major shift in foreign policy, telling his audience that the United States will soon withdraw the bulk of its troops from Vietnam. And then, just before the film ends, he makes the following statement:

> With America's sons in the fields far away, with America's future under challenge right here at home, with our hopes and the world's hopes for peace in the balance every day, I do not believe that I should devote an hour or a day of my time to any personal partisan causes or to any duties other than the awesome duties of this office — the presidency

of your country. Accordingly, I shall not seek, and I will not accept, the nomination of my party for another term as your president.

The war, we realize, has not only defeated the United States military, but its commander-in-chief, as well.

Although the director came to this film fairly late in its development, *Path to War* nevertheless exhibits many if not all of the markers that distinguish his other pictures. Once again, we find that Frankenheimer's *mise en scene* is characterized by a high degree of realism, thanks to his use of sets and costumes which look authentic and his decision to cast several actors who physically evoke the men they are playing, especially Gambon as LBJ, Sutherland as Clifford, Chris Eigeman as Bill Moyers (the president's press secretary), and Frederick Forest as Gen. Earle Wheeler, Chair of the Joints Chief of Staff. And just as he does in *George Wallace* (as well as in the opening prologue of *The Holcroft Covenant*), the director frequently blurs the lines between history and artifice by combining archival footage of actual events with new material he and his crew shot. The director's partiality for deep focus photography and long takes reveals itself frequently, too, as he tends to frame his actors in the foreground and background sections of each shot, creating dynamic compositions that compensate somewhat for the occasionally sluggish pace of Giat's "exposition heavy" script, which devotes so much attention to what Johnson and his confreres said to one another during their planning sessions.[14] Tom Shales, who wasn't bothered by this aspect of the movie, pointed out: "[T]he path to war is paved with meetings— meetings in the Oval Office, at the Pentagon, in Lyndon and Lady Bird Johnson's bedroom, and virtually wherever a meeting can be held."[15]

This emphasis on conversation and dialogue, rather than physical action, lends the film a theatrical quality, bringing to mind, perhaps, the director's 1973 interpretation of *The Iceman Cometh*. *Path to War*, of course, will remind us, as well, of *Seven Days in May*, which also tells the story of a Cold War–era president who finds himself stuck in a political swamp, at odds with the American public, his fellow politicians and the nation's military leaders. But while the earlier picture is a suspense piece, a thriller built upon a "what if" scenario, *Path to War* is a true-to-life character study, recalling *George Wallace* and *The Burning Season* as it examines the effects pressure and strife can have upon the psyche. But rather than showing us how pain can ennoble an individual, as the earlier pictures do, *Path to War* seems to suggest quite the opposite, emphasizing the psychological and spiritual harm which befalls Johnson as his political ambitions, his dreams of social progress for America and his hopes for stability in Vietnam come undone. And for several critics, this focus on Johnson's fall from grace and the anguish it caused him brought to mind Shakespearean characters like Macbeth and Hamlet, whose misguided thoughts and policies bring about chaos for their kingdoms, their armies, their subjects and themselves. Shales wrote: "[This] portrait of Johnson is an American dream turned

Shakespearean tragedy." Frankenheimer himself made this comparison on a number of occasions, too:

> I tried to show the destruction of the man from the height of his popularity to being alone and disgraced. All in the course of four years. And what happened to this country while it was all happening. They're two parallel stories.... [B]asically, this is a modern-day King Lear. This is the destruction of a bigger than life giant.[16]

And much like the destruction which besets Macbeth, Hamlet and Lear, LBJ's is self-imposed. He can blame no one for his downfall but himself, though he tries throughout the later portions of the film to make the argument, somewhat pathetically, that his decisions have actually been forced upon him, that a host of factors—ranging from Ho Chi Minh's refusal to meet at the negotiation table to Robert Kennedy's decision to run for president—have obliged him to escalate the war. He also blames his counselors, refusing to acknowledge that not only is it he who picked them, but it is he, and only he, who has the power to decide upon which suggestions to adopt and implement. But toward the end of the film, his friend Clark Clifford reminds him of the responsibility he holds, his culpability, saying: "You decided. Against all your natural instincts, against the whole of your life experience—you decided." We might argue, perhaps, that these harsh words connect with the president, that they contribute to his decision to curtail the war effort, which he announces in the film's final, climactic sequence. And if this is so, then we might begin to regard *Path to War* in a more optimistic light, perhaps. While the picture tracks Johnson's spiritual ruin, it presents us at the same time with another instance in the director's canon of a man who becomes, after experiencing intense suffering, a less harmful person, if not a better one—the same scenario we find in both *The Manchurian Candidate* and *Reindeer Games*.

CHAPTER SEVEN

The Misuse of Force

Frankenheimer's distaste for public servants who misuse and abuse the power of their positions also materializes in *I Walk the Line, French Connection II, Dead Bang* and *Ronin*. But the main characters in all of these films are not military or political leaders, but police officials of some sort, charged with preventing crimes and subduing criminals, and in each, the hero cannot abide by the laws he is expected to enforce. But while other "rogue cop" films like Fritz Lang's *The Big Heat* (1953), Don Siegel's *Dirty Harry* (1971) and even Sydney Lumet's *Serpico* (1973) suggest that sometimes this behavior is necessary and perhaps admirable, Frankenheimer's police pictures regularly draw attention to the problems it can generate. The strength of democratic society rests upon the rule of law in his cinema and whenever its protectors set personal objectives before duty, the potential for anarchy and human suffering escalates.

I Walk the Line (1970)

Taking its title from Johnny Cash's famous song, Frankenheimer's first film for Columbia begins with Sheriff Henry Tawes (Gregory Peck) cruising along a country road in his patrol car. After a dilapidated truck driven by a little boy (Freddie McCloud) rushes past him, a chase commences, ending when the truck crashes. The young driver runs off into the nearby woods, but instead of following him, Tawes walks over to the stranded vehicle and finds a beautiful teenaged girl (Tuesday Weld), sitting on the passenger's seat. "I'm Alma McCain," she tells him and then explains that she was the driver. Though Tawes does not believe the girl, he forgives the accident and lets her go. This act of mercy may seem benign, but it actually precipitates the sheriff's subsequent fall from grace.

Alma is the daughter of a moonshiner named Flint McCain (Ralph

All for Love: As Alma (Tuesday Weld) watches at right, Tawes (Gregory Peck) wrestles with her young brother, Clay (Jeff Dalton, left), in *I Walk the Line* (Columbia, 1970).

Meeker), who decides to make an ally out of Tawes by having the girl seduce him. Flint's scheme works and when a Treasury agent named Bascomb (Lonny Chapman) shows up in Tawes' county, looking for illegal stills, the sheriff shields the McCains. He does this solely for Alma, first to win her heart and later to persuade her to leave her family and come with him to California. But as Tawes follows his Lorelei, Bascomb and a deputy named Hunnicutt (Charles Durning) continue their search for moonshiners. Playing a hunch, Hunnicutt heads over to the McCains' property, and there he is murdered, after he shoots the family dog and tries to rape Alma. Upon learning about the deputy's disappearance, Tawes drives out to the McCains' place and finds Flint burying the dead man's corpse. Once again, the sheriff forgives the moonshiner's crimes and offers his help. This gesture, though, is hardly selfless. He will do this, he says, if Flint promises to give him Alma, and Flint accepts the sheriff's terms.

Betrayal is a staple in Frankenheimer's cinema, and it materializes in *I Walk the Line*, too, as Flint reneges on the deal and leaves the mountain valley where the film is set, taking his daughter with him. And once he discovers this, Tawes sets out to find Alma, racing along worn out roads of the valley until he catches up with the same dilapidated truck that caught his attention at the start of the film. Convinced that she is being held against her will by her family, Tawes tells the girl to come with him. She refuses and a fight breaks out. The sheriff shoots Flint, wounding him, then Alma sinks a meat hook into Tawes' chest. Broken hearted and aware, for the first time, perhaps, of the impossible nature of his dreams, the sheriff watches as the McCains roll away in their truck. To reinforce our understanding of his isolation, Frankenheimer closes the film several seconds later with a freeze frame shot of Tawes, kneeling in the rain alone, eyes wide with sorrow.

Like *Seconds* and *The Iceman Cometh*, *I Walk the Line* is a tragedy, a record of a man who destroys himself as he pursues happiness; and like the protagonists in these films, Sheriff Tawes thinks he can improve or escape the circumstances which frustrate him. His motives are understandable, perhaps: possession of Alma will enable him to get free of his loveless marriage and his dull job. But in the sheriff's county, there seems to be a caste system of sorts in place which prohibits people from crossing class lines. And thus when he sets his sights on the moonshiner's daughter and begins to dream of a new life, a quasi-bohemian existence removed from his middle-class obligations, he invites disaster. As Frankenheimer explained to Pratley, "[H]e thinks he can be reborn, that he can change his whole life. This is a theme of mine, the fact that your life cannot change — you are what you are, and you have to live with that."[1]

A film very much of its time, *I Walk the Line*, like *In the Heat of the Night* (1967) and *Easy Rider*, suggests that cops in America are a loutish bunch who have difficulty doing the right thing. To sharpen his critique, Frankenheimer presents each of the police characters in this picture in an unflattering, almost satirical manner. Overly emotional and prone to bad judgment, Tawes may be the most buffoonish of the lot, but Bascomb and Hunnicutt hardly escape the director's attack. The federal man is an especially grating character, who wears a loud suit, preens in front of mirrors and cracks dirty jokes. At one point, he even tells the sheriff that a new brothel might make the unnamed town where the film is set more livable. Hunnicutt is just as slimy. When Frankenheimer introduces him, he positions the camera behind the deputy's back, directing our attention to one of the lurid men's magazines he likes to read at his desk in the courthouse. And though the deputy is fairly diligent about doing his job, his objectives are less than sincere. Driven by envy and mean-spiritedness, his interest in the McCains only develops when he discovers the link between them and Tawes. Shutting them down can hurt the sheriff, he realizes. The same motive, no doubt, compels him to attack Alma.

I Walk the Line is a memorable film, greatly strengthened by Peck's sympathetic interpretation of the sheriff and David Walsh's cinematography. Recalling the Depression-era photographs of Walker Evans, Walsh uses his camera to document the ugliness of rural poverty, focusing frequently on the rusting machinery and ruined houses that pock the Tennessee landscape, where much of the film was shot. These images of real objects and locations lend the movie a great deal of authenticity. Occasionally, they serve a figurative function, as well, allowing Frankenheimer to move the plot and convey his pessimistic point of view with a minimum of dialogue and exposition. As the opening credits roll, for example, a sequence of disparate shots—of ravaged faces, junked cars and Tawes driving—flash across the screen as a particularly mournful version of Johnny Cash's "I Walk the Line" plays in the background. Several inferences arise from this sequence. First, it establishes the film's setting as a wasteland. Second, it tells us that the citizens in this community are as stranded and as dead as the cars that litter their weedy lawns. Third, it suggests that Tawes, despite his healthy appearance and the mobility of his vehicle, is somehow linked to these symbols of decline and failure.

Frankenheimer's use of Cash's music throughout the film is also quite effective. The Man in Black's folksy, funereal ballads—with titles like "Face of Despair" and "Flesh and Blood"—magnify the film's dark mood considerably. They also function much like lyrical odes in classical drama, commenting upon the actions, motives and predicament of the story's principal characters.

French Connection II (1975)

In 1971, 20th Century–Fox scored a huge hit with *The French Connection*, a hard-boiled thriller about the largest heroin bust in New York City's history. Directed by William Friedkin and starring Gene Hackman as Det. Eddie "Popeye" Doyle, the picture presented a gritty, but sympathetic portrait of the police at work. In 1972, wanting to capitalize on the picture's success—it won five Academy Awards—Fox decided to produce a sequel, a continuation of Doyle's pursuit of Alain Charnier, the French drug lord who eludes capture at the end of Friedkin's film. As the studio wanted the story to take place in Marseilles, a port city in the south of France where heroin production thrived in the late Sixties and early Seventies, it asked Frankenheimer, who spoke French fluently, to helm the project.[2]

French Connection II was shot on location in Marseilles in the summer of 1974, and as the movie opens, Doyle (Hackman) arrives in the port city, the bright sun burning relentlessly above him. The only person who can identify Charnier (Fernando Rey), Doyle has been sent by his supervisors to assist the Marseilles police as they search for the elusive kingpin. The assignment is a ruse, however. A large portion of the heroin confiscated by the NYPD in the first film has disappeared and removing Doyle to France prevents him from investigating his fellow detectives. Vulgar, loud and not too smart, Doyle alienates himself quickly from his French counterparts, a group of "narcs" led by the level-headed Henri Barthelmy (Bernard Fresson). Annoyed by Barthelmy's cautious approach to law enforcement, Doyle soon sets out on his own. In his porkpie hat and Hawaiian shirts, he cuts a clownish figure on the foreign city's streets and he is quickly spotted and subsequently abducted by Charnier's men. Imprisoning him in a slum hotel, Charnier injects Doyle with heroin, with the hope that this will loosen his lips. The tactic breaks the detective, transforming him into a helpless addict. But it doesn't yield any useful information and Charnier returns the captive to the police. As he explains to Doyle, just before he frees him: "We take you back, Doyle, to your friends. They are looking for you everywhere and making it difficult for me to operate."

Renewal invariably follows demoralization in Frankenheimer's pictures and the same happens here. Forced by Barthelmy to quit his addiction "cold turkey," Doyle suffers terribly, bursting into tears at one point. But he makes it through and sets out on his own to locate the hotel where he was kept prisoner. Once he finds it, he sets the building on fire and snags one of Charnier's men. The goon provides information which eventually leads Doyle and his French counterparts to the lab where Charnier's people process heroin. Charnier rushes off, though, as the police close in, just as he did in the first movie. But Doyle, weak and limping, runs after him and a chase commences through the congested city, ending when the detective spots his adversary sailing out of the harbor on a yacht. Drawing his gun from the holster he wears on his ankle, Doyle fires two shots into Charnier's chest, presumably killing him. But Frankenheimer closes the movie at this point, denying his viewers a denouement of any sort, leaving open the possibility that the pursuit may continue in the future.

French Connection II is an often harrowing examination of the dangers that result when people flout the law for personal gain. Charnier, of course, may be the most offensive example of this criminal self-centeredness. A bon vivant, he uses the money he earns from his drugs business to make his life exceedingly comfortable, spending it on fine clothes, hunting trips and beautiful women. His success, however, rests upon a willingness to exploit human weakness, a great sin in itself. Yet, as Frankenheimer shows us, it also has a terrible, imitative effect, breeding a culture of addicts and thieves who, like Charnier, seize upon the weak. Such is the case with the old woman (Cathleen Nesbitt) in the hotel, the one who steals Doyle's watch. The problem not only transcends gender, age and nationality, but occupation, too. A sleazy U.S. Army general (Ed Lauter) is one of Charnier's collaborators, for instance, and there are the crooked members of the narcotics squad in New York, as well, who have stolen, and probably sold, the heroin that was seized in the first film.

Though Doyle has no apparent interest in financial gain, he is similarly guilty of flouting the law for private reasons, sidestepping civil liberties and human rights when they interfere with his pursuit. To some degree, this brutal approach is effective, leading him and Barthelmy to Charnier's heroin. But it is also ugly and somewhat fascistic, recalling the brutish methods of the interrogators in movies like Rosselini's *Open City* and Melville's *Army of*

Shadows (1969). Early in the film, for instance, Doyle amuses himself as he explains to a suspect:

> I'm going to take you right down there into that alley there. See, right down there. Start on your throat, right here. I'm going to bust everything in it.... Then your belly. Start working on your belly, I'm going to hit you so fucking hard in the belly, it's going to break your backbone.... Then I'm going to work on your arms. I'll set 'em over a curb. And I'm going to use them for a trampoline. I'm going to jump up and down on them. Right? Then your kneecaps. One. Two. Kneecaps. Oatmeal. I'm going to make oatmeal out of your fucking kneecaps. And when I get done with you, you are going to put me right in Charnier's lap.

In another instance, he brutalizes a man in an alley with his fists and knees. Yet Doyle, despite these repellant qualities, is difficult to reject completely. Far from his New York City stomping grounds, the detective, like the fish on the tables that appear at the beginning of the film, is out of his element, completely separated from people who think, act and speak like him. Certainly, he behaves in a ludicrous manner frequently, translating the word "mayonnaise" into French and ordering "el scotcho" at a bar, for instance, but the character's basic problem, the alienation felt by the émigré, is hardly unique or strange; and because of this, in spite of his many defects, he is recognizable, understandable and sympathetic.[3]

Like the first *French Connection*, Frankenheimer's picture is a "police procedural," a film that traces the efforts of law enforcement officials as they conduct an investigation. In the middle of this movie, however, the director breaks from the genre's most important convention by halting the detective hero's search, confining him first to the cell-like room of the hotel and then the basement jail of the Marseille police station. Some critics have denigrated this turn in the narrative. Roger Ebert, in his 1975 review, complained that it brings "the movie to a standstill. The plot, the pursuit, the quarry, are all forgotten during Hackman's one-man show, and it's a flaw the movie doesn't overcome."[4] These sequences do slow the story's pace a bit, but they nevertheless serve an important thematic function. In many of Frankenheimer's films, extreme suffering gives rise to important changes in his protagonists' personalities: the amputation of Uraz's gangrenous leg in *The Horsemen* leads to humility and self-reliance; Rick's burial in *The Challenge* strengthens the boxer's loyalty to Sensei Yoshida; Sam's shooting in *Ronin* solidifies his friendship with Vincent. For Doyle, the dialectal torture of addiction and withdrawal restores the drive and commitment that characterized his pursuit of Charnier in the first film. During the first third of *French Connection II*, he is distracted and ineffectual, spending much of his time drinking, carousing and picking fights with the people who can help him. But following the experience with heroin, he returns to the dirty Marseilles streets single-minded, not only avoiding drink and women, but working closely with Barthelmy. He may or may not capture (or kill) Charnier — we aren't allowed to know — but he certainly scores his revenge with the two bullets he fires into his chest.

Popeye Doyle (Gene Hackman) takes to the streets, searching for his foe Charnier in *French Connection II* (20th Century–Fox, 1975).

Though *French Connection II* is one of the bleakest pictures Frankenheimer made, it is also one of the most thrilling, thanks to set pieces like the burning of the Hotel Tangier, the flooding of the dry docks and the final chase, when Doyle runs after Charnier along the Marseilles harbor. The director realized that the exaggerated quality of these scenes could arouse disbelief and thus he tried to make them seem as authentic as possible. He explains on the commentary he recorded for the film's DVD release:

Doyle (Gene Hackman) and Barthelmy (Bernard Fresson) on a raid in the slums of Marseilles in *French Connection II* (20th Century–Fox, 1975).

> The key to doing a movie like this is to make every incident, every moment of the movie as real and believable as you can. Once you, the audience, feel betrayed by me, once you feel out of the movie, once you feel, "Oh, these are only actors and this is fake and this doesn't look right," then the movie's over for you, then everything that happens after that doesn't work. But if I can keep you involved and keep you believing this looks right, this looks real, then I'm doing my job. And that goes for the costumes, that goes for the sets, that goes for the extra that's way in the back of the room. One little thing that's not right can turn you off the whole movie.

To achieve the verisimilitude he needed to make these scenes work, the director used several tactics. He and his cameraman Claude Renoir employed shooting techniques borrowed from *cinéma-vérité*, filming Marseilles' buildings, its streets and its citizens, for example, with handheld cameras and hidden cameras. He and production designer Jacques Saulnier built sets which they modeled after real places, like the city's police station, a jail and a bottom rung hotel. And Charnier's lab, incredibly, was built under the guidance of a group of Corsican heroin dealers who had taken an interest in the film. The director also hired non-actors whenever he could.[5]

When *French Connection II* opened in the spring of 1975, the reviews it received were generally favorable and its performance at the box office was decent. Even so, the sequel's receipts failed to meet the expectations of the studio and the project marked the end of Frankenheimer's relationship with Fox. Interestingly, the director's next picture, *Black Sunday*, which he shot for Paramount, also features a law enforcement official who leaves his country to hunt criminals. But while Doyle circumvents the law whenever it proves to be an obstacle, Kabokov, *Black Sunday*'s Mossad agent hero, sets public interests ahead of private ones as a rule, and his methods are generally more effective — and much deadlier — than those of the New York detective.

Dead Bang (1989)

During his years in live television, Frankenheimer shot several programs which were based on real events, a practice that carried over into *Bird Man of Alcatraz*, *Grand Prix* and *The Fixer*. More than 20 years would pass after *The Fixer*, however, before the director brought another "true story" to the screen, *Dead Bang*. The project first came about when he was approached by Jerry "Bulldog" Beck, a detective in the Los Angles County Sheriff's Department. While investigating a homicide, Beck had discovered — and neutralized — a national network of neo–Nazi terrorists, whose activities were endorsed and protected by local officials. The detective's experience interested Frankenheimer, and the two men, with screenwriter Robert Foster, put together a script. When Don Johnson, the popular star of the *Miami Vice* television series, was cast to play Beck, the movie's box office potential looked promising. But after its release in the spring of 1989 the picture flopped, a development which arose in part from the conflicts he had with Johnson, though poor reviews may have contributed to its disappointing run, too. It's also possible, perhaps, that audiences were simply not interested in watching a thriller that explored a subject as unpleasant as militant racism. Arguably, Costa-Gavra's *Betrayed* (1988), the story of an FBI agent who penetrates a group of "white power" extremists, had failed for the same reason.

As he does with many of his action films, Frankenheimer builds *Dead Bang*'s plot around a chase. Early in the morning on Christmas Eve, an L.A. cop is shot and killed. Assigned to the case, Det. Jerry Beck (Johnson) spends the day reviewing police records, searching for potential suspects. A listing for a paroled robber named Robert Burns (Frank Military) arouses the detective's interest and the next day, he and Burns' parole officer, a man named Webley (Bob Balaban), visit the home of the suspect's mother. Instead of Burns, though, they find his brother John (Tate Donovan), a college student, who tells them that he does not know where Robert is.

Later that day, Burns and several of his friends attack a Mexican cantina in Arizona, emptying the bar's cash register and killing all the customers. An alert local police chief notifies Beck and the detective leaves Los Angeles immediately. In Arizona, Beck and the chief visit a ranch where Burns is believed to

Chief Dixon (Tim Reid) and Beck (Don Johnson) search for white supremacists in *Dead Bang* (Lorimar, 1989).

be hiding. Burns is there, in fact, and he eludes the cops; but, as he rushes off, he leaves behind a cache of documents, a collection of "hate" propaganda, maps and an address book. Beck then drives out to Oklahoma, to interview Reverend Gebhardt (Michael Higgins), one of the people listed in the book. Once there, he is joined by a fastidious FBI agent named Kressler (William Forsythe). The men then visit Gebhardt, the leader of a white supremacist organization called the Aryan Nation Church of Christ. Surprisingly genial, the pastor describes the church's mission to the detective. "The [church], Mr. Beck, embodies the nucleus of what America once was and will be again.... White and pure, cleansed of its present racial impurities." He also claims that he is not familiar with Robert Burns. The fugitive, however, has come to the church for sanctuary and — much as Charnier spots Doyle in *French Connection II*— he spots Beck as the cop scours the property, searching for him.

That night, Burns springs on Beck while he is driving his car, threatening to kill him, but Beck saves himself by crashing his vehicle into an oncoming police car. He also sets fire to a stream of gasoline which has leaked onto the street, causing an explosion. The drastic nature of these responses troubles his supervisors in Los Angeles and Beck is called back for a psychiatric evaluation, which he only passes after he threatens the doctor. He then returns to the case and flies out to Colorado, where he meets Dixon (Tim Reid), a black police chief. Joined by Kressler, the men pay a visit to a paramilitary training camp which is operated by the Aryan Nation Church. Their search yields nothing until Beck discovers a concealed door, which leads to Burns' hiding place, an underground bunker. A firefight commences, ending when Beck shoots the fugitive. As the man dies, he tells Beck that he did not shoot the cop in Los Angeles. A moment later, Burns' brother John appears. With his gun drawn, he explains that he committed the murder in order to demonstrate to his brother his contempt for the police and his commitment to white supremacism. Taunted by Beck, John fires several shots rapidly, missing his target and emptying his gun. Beck then emerges and shoots the young man, killing him. Later, at a press conference, Kressler takes credit for the investigation's success and Beck and Dixon, now friends, say goodbye to one another.

Dead Bang, despite its sensationalistic plot, is an effective and unsettling film. Ostensibly, it is another police procedural, a movie about the efforts taken by a cop to capture a cop killer, and in this respect, it resembles such conventional fare as Daniel Petrie's *Fort Apache, The Bronx* (1981) and Roberto Faenza's *Corrupt* (1983). But the picture also examines the power which anger and hate acquire when they are organized by sophisticated ideologues who crave revolution and the elimination of democracy, the same theme Frankenheimer explores in *The Manchurian Candidate* and *Seven Days in May*. And much like the Mrs. Iselin and General Scott characters in the earlier pictures, the fanatics in *Dead Bang* are familiar with American mores and conventions and they use this understanding to screen their activities and schemes. When John Burns appears in the film for the first time, for instance, he wears a sweatshirt with a college logo embroidered across the chest. The garment functions as a sort of disguise for him. Literally, it hides the incriminating neo–Nazi insignia tattooed to his arm. It also signifies to Beck that John is different from the scruffy bikers and hoods—the criminals—who occupy his mother's house. Thanks to the sweatshirt and the associations it generates, John manages to arouse Beck's trust, rather than his suspicion, an error in judgment which proves to be pivotal in terms of the plot's development.

Dead Bang takes its title from a slang term used by the police in the United States to describe a criminal investigation that produces successful results with minimal effort. "Dead bang," in other words, is synonymous with words like "easy" and "trouble-free" and "undemanding." Beck's investigation is anything but easy, however, owing in large part to the cunning and duplicity of characters like the Burns brothers and Reverend Gebhardt. Beck is also hindered by the obnoxious nature of his own personality. An alcoholic with a bad temper, he frequently attacks people with foul language and threats. Such behavior has contributed to the collapse of his marriage. It also weakens the relationships he has with colleagues, a serious problem given the collaborative nature of

Frankenheimer on the set of *Dead Bang* (Lorimar, 1989).

police work. When Beck asks Webley to help him on Christmas Eve, for instance, the parole officer, having been treated rudely, refuses, and the delay which results gives Burns and his friends time and opportunity to leave Los Angeles without interference. Similarly, when Beck sneers at Kressler's wholesome views, the agent retaliates with a report that leads to Beck's temporary suspension, interrupting the investigation and enabling Burns to escape from Oklahoma to Colorado.

Prior to the film's release, Frankenheimer told the *Los Angeles Times* that he hoped *Dead Bang* would appeal to the same audience that had made Richard Donner's police comedy *Lethal Weapon* (1987) a huge hit.[7] To a certain extent, the films do resemble one another. The pairing of a white cop with a black cop is the most obvious likeness, of course. And each film makes use of crude humor frequently. Early in the picture, when Beck and Webley visit the home of Burns' mother, a cagey biker rushes out of the building. Beck runs after the man on foot, eventually catching him, but the chase upsets his stomach, and he throws up on the fugitive. Beck then presses a billy club into the biker's throat and asks him questions which the man refuses to answer. After Beck threatens to throw up again, however, the biker supplies the detective with information. The appropriateness of material like this, in a film that examines a problem as serious as white supremacism, may be debatable. At the same time, it enables the director to draw a comparison between authoritarian conduct and vomit.

Ronin (1998)

Interest in Frankenheimer revived after the success of his cable television features and in 1997 he was invited to direct *Ronin* for MGM. Featuring a pulpy script by J.D. Zeik and Richard Weisz (a pseudonym for David Mamet), the film enjoyed good reviews upon its release, winning praise for the intensity of its action scenes and Robert De Niro's performance as Sam, the picture's tough guy protagonist. Anthony Lane, in his review for *The New Yorker*, wrote:

> In the manner of director Jean-Pierre Melville, whom he knew and admired, Franken-
> heimer likes to launch his action sequences from patches of somber suspense; [his
> characters] sit around in hotel rooms, then go out for a chase. After a while, you stop
> counting the chases—they just get longer and louder, and it's like watching the revival
> of a forgotten art form; the fact it's done with a minimum of special effects make it all
> the more stirring.[8]

Ronin's scenario, on the surface, is a familiar one. Honoring the conventions of the "caper" picture—a genre exemplified by movies as diverse as *The Asphalt Jungle* (1950), *Rififi* (1954), *The Italian Job* (1969) and *The Getaway* (1972)—the film follows the adventures of several criminals as they plan and execute a heist. In this instance, the crooks are mercenaries, hired by a pair of Irish nationals named Deirdre (Natascha McElhone) and Seamus (Jonathan Pryce) to steal an aluminum suitcase from a group of arms dealers. Meeting in Paris, the five contractors who make up this team—an ex–CIA operative (Robert De Niro), a French assassin (Jean Reno), an East German computer expert (Stellan Skarsgård), a British weapons specialist (Sean Bean), and an American driver (Skipp Sudduth)—are not told what the box contains and why their employers want it. But it is not important to them, the ambiguous objective of their assignment. What matters really is the fee they expect to collect for their services. And though this pursuit of money brings the men together, it also divides them. Midway through the film, the East German, whose name is Gregor, disappears with the box, just as the group secures it from the arms dealers; he then heads off to sell its enigmatic contents to a Russian mobster. This treachery causes the original group to split into rival factions and a chase commences, as Sam (the CIA man) and Vincent (the assassin) compete with Deirdre and Seamus to find the traitor first.

The double cross, of course, is one of the caper genre's most frequent motifs. It also surfaces frequently in Japanese samurai movies, in pictures like Kurosawa's *Yojimbo* and *Sanjuro*, where the bodyguard character played by Toshiro Mifune uses subterfuge to serve his own, money-driven interests. That Frankenheimer wants his audience to make a connection between his contemporary mercenaries and the samurai of legend is fairly obvious. As the film opens, a series of titles appears, explaining that

> In feudal Japan, the warrior class of Samurai were sworn to protect their liege lords
> with their lives. Those Samurai whose liege was killed suffered a great shame, and they

Deirdre (Natascha McElhone) and Sam (Robert De Niro) keep an eye out for the enigmatic suitcase in *Ronin* (MGM, 1998).

were forced to wander the land, looking for work as hired swords or bandits. These masterless warriors were no longer referred to as Samurai, they were known by another name: such men were called Ronin.

"Ronin," which translates into English as "men on the wave," aptly describes the desperate characters who people this film.[9] With the Cold War over, these spies and assassins have lost their jobs, and they have not been able to adjust to the new employment situation fostered by the new world order. Because of this inability, or unwillingness, to change, they are men out of time — alienated drifters who have lost the projects and obligations that once gave their lives purpose, identity and security. Moreover, they kill for a fee.

Later, however, Frankenheimer complicates our understanding of the ronin concept by introducing an anecdote about masterless samurai who act collectively and selflessly. After Sam is shot, Vincent brings him to another out-of-work spy named Jean-Pierre (Michael Lonsdale), who removes the bullet and saves the American's life. Once he recovers from the surgery, Sam meets Jean-Pierre in a room where the older man has constructed a diorama with toy samurai warriors and a miniature fortress. This battle scene, Jean-Pierre explains, is taken from a Japanese folktale.

JEAN-PIERRE: "The 47 Ronin," do you know it? Forty-seven samurai whose master was betrayed and killed by another lord. They became ronin, masterless samurai ... disgraced by another man's treachery. For three years, they plotted, pretending to be thieves, mercenaries, even madmen. Then they snuck into the castle of their lord's betrayer and killed him....

SAM: Nice. I like that. My kind of job.

JEAN-PIERRE: There's something more. All 47 of them committed *seppuku*, ritual suicide in the courtyard of the castle.

SAM: Well, I don't like that so much.

JEAN-PIERRE: But you understand it?

Sam: What do you mean?

JEAN-PIERRE: The warrior code — the delight in battle. You understand that, yes? But also something more. You understand there is something outside of yourself that has to be served. And when that need is gone, when belief has died, what are you? A man without a master.

SAM: Right now, I'm a man without a paycheck.

Jean-Pierre: The ronin could have hired themselves to new masters. They could have fought for themselves. But they chose honor.

The shame and humiliation wrought by the loss of a retainer, by the destruction of one's career, we see, does not force men into lives of crime automatically, nor does it completely destroy the clan, or group, that originally brought them together. Arguably Frankenheimer uses this story to highlight and contrast the moral and social weaknesses that characterize the band of ronin in his film. Simultaneously, however, the interdependence and allegiance of the 47 parallels that which develops between Sam and Vincent after Gregor's betrayal. Like the samurai, the two men are bound together by a loyalty that persists in spite of and because of the danger that surrounds them. For Frankenheimer, shared crises and loyalty, rather than affection, almost always build and preserve friendships. Such is the case with *French Connection II* and the mutual dependence that arises between Popeye and Barthelmy. And the same can be said of the ties that bind Raymond and Marco in *The Manchurian Candidate*, Senator Clark and President Lyman in *Seven Days in May* and Smith and Jamaal in *Against the Wall*. The director, incidentally, felt that friendship is the film's central theme.[10]

He may not have recognized that this relationship has a serious flaw in it. Sam, after all, is not an ex–CIA agent, though he leads Vincent and the others to believe differently. As he explains to Deirdre late in the movie, "Don't you understand? I never left." Sam, the film infers, has been assigned to track down the suitcase in order to keep it from Seamus, who, it turns out, is a political extremist, a terrorist set on destroying the peace process in Northern Ireland. Without Vincent's friendship and aid, Sam cannot achieve this goal; and were it not for CIA man's deception, his betrayals of the professional criminal's trust, it seems unlikely that Vincent would help as he does. It is Vincent, we should note, who kills Seamus; and thanks to his death, negotiators are able to arrange a truce that calms the divided country, as we learn from a series of voiceover radio reports. This armistice, however, is just as problematical and ironic as Sam and Vincent's friendship. The actions which have preceded it, the car chases and gunfights, have injured and killed dozens of innocent people.

Ronin performed only moderately well at the box office in the U.S. But in the years since its premier, this picture, much like *Reindeer Games*, has enjoyed strong sales in retail stores.[11] It seems unlikely that its enduring popularity is the result of the director's analyses of complicated human relationships, however. Rather, it is more likely the result of the film's stylized treatment of violence and the slangy, hard-boiled manner in which the characters talk to one another, traits it shares with *Reservoir Dogs* (1992), *The Usual Suspects* (1995) and *The Boondock Saints* (1999), which have also become "cult" favorites. Frankenheimer takes pains to make his film exciting, too, packing it with suspense as often as he can. Honoring several of Hitchcock's injunctions, he places his characters in constant peril, frequently introducing danger into mundane and familiar settings. A man shoots at a girl in a playground, for instance. A sniper murders a skater in an ice rink. Turbo-powered sports cars race against rush hour traffic. And fireballs rip through the scenic tunnels of Paris. Frankenheimer manages to make these improbable scenes believable by shooting on location with hand-held cameras, a Steadicam and cameras which he had mounted to cars, a technique that imbues the picture's spectacular chase scenes with the same documentary realism that characterizes the auto race footage in *Grand Prix*.

Is *Ronin* an important film? Maybe. It certainly is an entertaining one; and, aesthetically, it is very satisfying. The chiaroscuro lighting that shows up so frequently gives the picture a rich, noirish look, reminiscent (like *Year of the Gun*) of Reed's *The Third Man*. And Elia Cmiral's minimalist score, curling through the soundtrack like a snake, compounds the menace and tension that Robert Fraisse, the film's director of photography, creates with his camera. Moreover, the film is rich with references to other pictures, particularly to those of Jean-Pierre Melville. The links between *Ronin* and *Le samourai* (1967), for instance, are fairly clear, as each film self-consciously compares its central character to the masterless warriors who once struggled to work, and survive, in old Japan; and Frankenheimer, like Melville, has set his story in France. (The old spy who operates on Sam shares Melville's first name, as well.) The American director also borrows from some of the French director's more obscure titles. For example, *Ronin*, like *Bob le flambeur* (1955), opens with a shot of Montmarte at night. And *Le doulos* (1962) chronicles the friendship that exists between a police informer and a gangster; this relationship, like Sam and Vincent's, is dependent upon one friend's willingness to deceive the other.

It is hard not to notice, however, that *Ronin* is much more accessible to contemporary audiences than the films it pays homage to. Perhaps this is because of Zeik's and Weisz's simple, but unabashedly melodramatic, script. Or perhaps it is because *Ronin* is not yet an "old" film. The world it renders, filled with traffic jams, shiny cars and glass skyscrapers, more closely resembles the one we live in. Just as important, *Ronin* is a film about terrorism and the occasionally disastrous consequences which follow from efforts to check it. In our post-9/11 world, these issues remain pertinent. It seems likely, in fact, that as long as the current situation holds, as long as extremists continue to blow up train stations in Madrid and London and shoot filmmakers on the streets of Amsterdam, *Ronin* will escape the datedness that weakens even the best genre movies, even Melville's.

CHAPTER EIGHT

Outsiders

Many of Frankenheimer's films feature characters who refuse to abide by the conventions of society. Sometimes these figures rebel against what they regard as injustice; such is the case with Yakov Bok in *The Fixer* and Chico Mendes in *The Burning Season*. Sometimes it is the security and ennui of bourgeois culture which they cannot accept, as we find in *Seconds*, *The Gypsy Moths* and *Impossible Object*. The protagonists who appear in these films to a certain extent are tragic figures, in the sense that their willingness to stand up to social pressure and to expose themselves to pain and sorrow arouse our admiration and pity. We cannot say the same, perhaps, for the marginalized figures who appear in *The Young Savages*, *99 and 44/100% Dead!*, *52 Pick-Up* and *Reindeer Games*, who differ from Frankenheimer's other non-conformists in one very important way: they express their distaste for society and its rules in a violent manner, breaking laws for self-gain and, occasionally, killing those who interfere with their plans.

The Young Savages (1961)

Based on Evan Hunter's 1959 novel *A Matter of Conviction*, *The Young Savages* follows the efforts of a New York City prosecutor as he investigates the murder of a blind Puerto Rican teenager. When the film opens, the blind boy Roberto Escalante (José Perez) sits with his sister Louisa (Pilar Seurat) on a stoop outside their Spanish Harlem tenement. Simultaneously, a trio of young hoodlums from an Italian-American street gang called the Thunderbirds march through the kids' neighborhood. The three boys approach Roberto and spring upon him with switchblade knives. A chase follows and the killers race through the barrio's rubble-strewn streets, trying to elude the police. But they are quickly captured, and once in custody, they claim innocence, explaining that they killed Roberto out of self-defense.

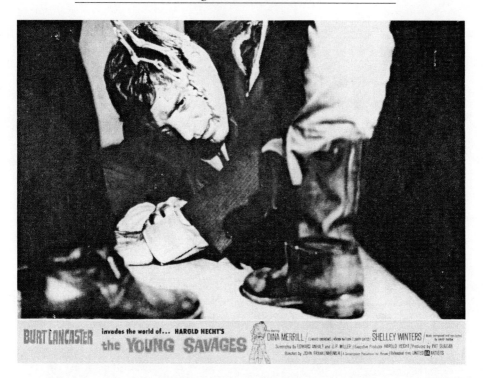

A group of juvenile delinquents attacks Hank Bell (Burt Lancaster) in *The Young Savages* (UA, 1961).

Sensing that a conviction will help him politically, the city's District Attorney (Edward Andrews) asks one of his assistants, Hank Bell (Burt Lancaster), to prosecute the case against the three suspects—whose names are Danny (Stanley Kristien), Arthur (John Davis Chandler) and Anthony (Neil Nephew). Bell, née Bellini, grew up in the same tough neighborhood as the killers and even dated one of the boy's mothers (Shelley Winters) years earlier. In fact, when this woman learns that Bell wants to send the defendants to the electric chair, she pleads with him, swearing that her son Danny could never murder anyone.

Undeterred, Bell continues to build his case, interviewing witnesses and the victim's family as well as members of the Thunderbirds and their rival gang the Horsemen. Along the way, he learns that Roberto, though blind, was a "warlord" in the Horsemen and a pimp for his prostitute sister Louisa. He also learns that the knife Roberto used against the three Thunderbirds, the basis of their self-defense argument, was actually a harmonica. Bell then heads home convinced that his efforts against the Thunderbirds are justified. But on the subway, he is "stomped" by a group of teenagers, and he responds to this attack by choking one of the assailants, nearly killing him. Frightened by his conduct, Bell begins to question the soundness of his beliefs, and when he shows up for the trial, he sabotages the case, successfully arguing that the three deserve light sentences, if not acquittal. His effort is helped when it is revealed through questioning that Danny, though present at the murder, did not actually stab the blind boy.

Frankenheimer had little time to prepare *The Young Savages*, his second movie, but he nevertheless managed to invest the picture with stylistic features that characterize his television work, using wide angle, deep focus shots, in particular, to imbue the film with a documentary look that somewhat compensates for its stagy plot. He and his director of photography Lionel Lindon also enhanced the film's realism by shooting much of the picture on location in upper Manhattan, using actors, who, like the characters they played, had run into trouble with the law. As the director told the *Los Angeles Times* in 1960: "We have cast [the film] very accurately. We found a theater in downtown Manhattan with just the boys we wanted — kids who had really been through the mill as so-called juvenile delinquents. We flipped for them."[1]

But although these qualities strengthen *The Young Savages*, the picture at the same time suffers from a certain sanctimoniousness. As Pauline Kael noted, "You're awfully conscious that the picture means to be hard-hitting; it sometimes succeeds, but a lot of it is just worthy."[2] And in this respect, the film anticipates a number of other "message" movies the director subsequently made, including *The Fixer*, *Prophecy*, *The Burning Season* and *Andersonville*. Nevertheless it seems likely that *The Young Savages'* earnest tone and its efforts at arousing compassion for the killers owe as much to Lancaster as Frankenheimer, as the actor believed that movies "should appeal to people at the higher levels" and serve as "the voice of society."[3] (Ambitions of this sort would guide — and weaken — *Bird Man of Alcatraz*, too.) But despite these high-minded intentions, the film at the same time has a sensationalistic quality. Throughout it, Frankenheimer makes use of conventions and iconography which can be traced to the rash of low-budget juvenile delinquent films which flourished in the late Fifties, such as the picture's garish title and the slangy, fatalistic talk of its teenaged thugs. The movie's plot also borrows liberally from a 1959 "juvie" feature directed by Paul Stanley called *Cry Tough*, in which warring gangs, much like the Thunderbirds and the Horsemen, attack one another on the streets of Spanish Harlem. And Jody Fair, the actress who plays Danny's girlfriend Angela in the film, was cast because of her background in pictures like *High School Confidential!* (1958), *Hot Rod Gang* (1958) and *Girls Town* (1959).

This combination of high-mindedness and exploitation, arguably, is one of the defining traits of Frankenheimer's cinema, surfacing as well in *Seconds*, *I Walk the Line*, *Black Sunday* and *Against the Wall*. The picture's thematic concerns anticipate later efforts, too, especially its preoccupation with the ambiguity of appearances. When the picture opens, for example, the director trains the camera on the blind Roberto, who plays a harmonica as his sister Luisa purchases a snow cone from a sidewalk vendor. This image of children having fun is both hopeful and wholesome; yet, as subsequent events reveal, it is false. Roberto is his sister's pimp and the two, as they sit together above the passing crowd, are presumably waiting for clients to call. Frankenheimer emphasizes the disparity between appearances and reality in the scene which immediately follows this one, too. But this time, the film's characters, rather than its viewers, are deceived. As if summoned by the sound of Roberto's harmonica, the Thunderbirds rise up from the Harlem streets and approach the Escalante kids. Startled, the blind Roberto lifts his hands above his head, and his harmonica, glinting in the sunlight, blinds the boys, confusing them, encouraging them to mistake the musical instrument for a knife.

The Young Savages, to a certain extent, is a mystery story as well as a social exposé, and Bell is the film's detective figure. His job isn't easy, though, thanks again to the breach that exists between the way things seem and the way they actually are: his only sources of information — the witnesses, friends, family members and suspects he interviews— tend to give him nothing but *bad* information. When Bell questions Angela in the fish market, for instance, she denies her role in the crime; then, when she breaks down and tells him that she hid the killers' knives in a car, she provides a misleading description of the car's make and color. Similarly, all of the Thunderbirds claim innocence when the police first bring them into the station and they refuse to answer Bell's questions. The killers do this, we should note, out of self-interest: to admit guilt is to strengthen the state's case and to help Bell send them to the electric chair. The strategy is futile, as their efforts only strengthen the lawyer's belief that the boys, who actually *did* act out of self-defense, are guilty of first-degree murder.[4]

But while many of the characters in *The Young Savages* distort (or ignore) the truth in order to serve their needs and ambitions, Danny's lie — about his involvement in the killing — is self-destructive. For Bell, the lie is symptomatic of a personality which has been "twisted" by poverty, prejudice and violence, the "strange social order" that characterizes the boy's Harlem neighborhood. The same pressures, ironically, have also influenced — and damaged — Bell. Wanting to leave behind his poor roots and his Italian heritage, he has struggled in his adult life to create a new identity for himself, far removed from his past; and through assimilation and social climbing, his efforts have succeeded, leading him to a good career, prosperity, a pretty wife, and a comfortable, spacious apartment, which is located high above the dirty streets of his youth. But it dawns on Bell, after he nearly kills his attacker on the subway, that his efforts at denying and hiding the past have been acts of self-betrayal and they've hurt him. This insight comes about while he and his wife Karin (Dina Merrill) stand on a balcony. Embarrassed and bitter, he reminds the woman of an argument they had several nights earlier, when she addressed him using the name he was born with, not the one he adopted:

> There's something else you said. "Old Hank Bellini." Danny DiPace said it, too. "What's the matter, Mr. Bellini? You ashamed of being a wop?" My old man was ignorant. He thought the way to be a good American was to change your name. It was always easy for me to explain: "My father did it." Now I realize I was glad. I was secretly glad my name was Bell instead of Bellini. It was part of getting out of Harlem.

Prior to this epiphany, Bell is guilty of what Sartre called *mauvaise foi*, or bad faith, having embraced the ideas of others in order to avoid forming his own. The discovery liberates his thinking, however, as his subsequent conduct demonstrates. No longer interested in upholding the status quo, because he no longer accepts it, he uses his time in the courtroom to defend, rather than condemn, the Thunderbirds, the representatives of the past he tried to abandon.

99 and 44/100% Dead! (1974)

Set in the future in an unnamed American city, *99 and 44/100% Dead!* chronicles the exploits of Harry Crown (Richard Harris), an Irish assassin who—much like *The Train*'s Lebiche and *Reindeer Games*' Rudy—sets loyalty and friendship ahead of self-interest. As the picture opens, a mobster named Uncle Frank (Edmond O'Brien) hires Harry to undermine the efforts of Big Eddie (Bradford Dillman), a rival crime boss who wants to muscle in on Frank's operations. To begin to do this, Harry sets out to find and kill Marvin "Claw" Zuckerman (Chuck Connors), one of Eddie's enforcers. Joined by Tony (David Hall), a young hoodlum, Harry locates Claw in a brothel, torturing a prostitute with his prosthetic hand. Claw escapes, though, by threatening to kill Baby (Katherine Baumann), the prostitute. A few nights later, Frank sends Harry and Tony out to destroy a shipment of whisky Eddie has ordered. When the pair approaches a convoy of delivery trucks, however, they encounter Claw and his men, who, having been tipped off, are waiting for them with machine guns. Nevertheless, Harry and Tony manage to destroy the whiskey and escape.

Eddie responds to this attack by having Baby kidnapped, after learning that she and Tony are in love. A tip from a friend, though, leads Harry and Tony to the elementary school where Buffy (Ann Turkel), Harry's romantic interest, is a teacher. There, they find Baby in a classroom, tied up, a bomb taped to her thighs. The three get out safely, but, almost immediately, Eddie has Buffy abducted. Harry and Tony then search for her in a large commercial laundry, where they meet resistance from the racketeer's men, including Claw. Harry manages to eliminate Claw, though, by pushing him into a vat of boiling chemicals. After this, Harry looks for Eddie, finding him with his gun pressed into Buffy's belly. But before he can act, Uncle Frank shows up, firing his gun at Eddie, knocking his enemy to the ground and freeing the captive. As the injured man lies dying, he explains to Frank that Clara (Janice Heiden), Frank's mistress, has been a spy, feeding him information about Frank's operation. The

Harry Crown (Richard Harris) makes an explosive exit in *99 and 44/100% Dead!* (20th Century–Fox, 1974).

action then jumps to one of the city's harbor ports, where Harry and Buffy board a luxury ship as Frank dumps the bodies of Eddie and Clara into the ocean water.

To a certain extent, *99 and 44/100% Dead!* is, as *Variety* described it, a "genre lampoon."[5] In particular, it makes use of the iconography and conventions that distinguish action-adventure films and crime thrillers in order to honor and poke fun at them simultaneously. Wearing earth tone leisure suits and a Prince Valiant haircut, Harry Crown is a parody of the modish underworld characters Michael Caine brought to the screen in films like *Deadfall* (1968) and *Get Carter* (1971). The men who work for Eddie look buffoonish, as well; though they wear the same, stylish black-suit-and-tie outfits Hollywood gangsters have been wearing since the Thirties, they are all middle-aged and flabby underneath, more interested in eating than in making rough with their boss' enemies. Similarly, the ridiculously named Claw Zuckerman, with his prosthetic arm and its kinky attachments, recalls the strange henchmen characters who appear in some of the early James Bond movies, as well as Kien Shih's one-handed villain in the Bruce Lee adventure *Enter the Dragon* (1973). But Claw is more sinister than silly. A sadist, he likes to brutalize women by tying them up, beating them and, in Buffy's case, shooting them with drugs.

In fact, his arm was cut off by Harry years earlier when the Irishman caught him "messing a woman in Frank's bathroom."

As ambitious as it is, *99 and 44/100% Dead!* often drags, brought down by the overheated performances of its principals and Robert Dillon's trite script. But there are still several moments in this strange picture which sparkle. When the film begins, for instance, a thudding melody materializes and a series of images, reminiscent of the drawings which appear in comic books, flashes across the screen. Frankenheimer follows this vibrant montage moments later with a chase scene in which a pair of black sedans race along a crowded wharf, wheeling in and out of tight spaces as their drivers fire guns at one another. The sequence is interesting because the shots, bursting with action, are linked together without transitional cuts, much like the panels of a comic strip. Throughout the film, in fact, Frankenheimer evokes the look of comics, using simple, but dynamic, visual compositions, which he fills with bright colors, melodramatic scenarios and exaggerated characters.

Some critics have read this aspect of the film's *mise en scene* as a conscious nod to Pop Art, the artistic movement that flourished in the Fifties and Sixties in which artists like Andy Warhol and Roy Lichtenstein called into question the divisions between fine art and popular culture by painting soup cans and cartoon characters. Pop Art has also been interpreted as an *attack* on the customs and attitudes which comprise and foster popular culture in the West. Lichtenstein, for instance, felt that his paintings drew attention to "the most brazen and threatening characteristics of our culture, things we hate, but which are also powerful in their impingement on us."[6] Arguably the same sentiment guides *99 and 44/100% Dead!*, too. More than a lampoon of crime movies and more than an homage to comic books, it appropriates the icons and conventions that characterize these art forms in order to critique the cultural beliefs and values they represent.

Frankenheimer uses this strategy, in particular, to denounce the role big business plays in the United States by linking it to organized crime. When Claw tortures Baby, he wears a business suit and removes the prosthetic attachments for his arm from a briefcase. The brothel where the scene takes place, looks like an office suite, filled as it is with desks and prostitutes who dress themselves like secretaries. Uncle Frank and Big Eddie may be mobsters, but they are businessmen, too, competitors who wage a war with one another when one attempts to horn in on the other's share of the bootleg liquor market. Dressed like tycoons and driving luxury cars, these black market capitalists thwart the law whenever they can, but at the same time enjoy the support and patronage of society's mainstream leaders, including politicians and religious figures. A raking shot of Frank's living room, for example, stops on a photograph of Richard Nixon, which is addressed to the crime boss "with admiration"; and in the park where Eddie tries to recruit Harry midway through the film, a cardinal in a red miter can be seen grinning and fawning as he chats with a pack of the racketeer's men.

On a number of occasions, as well, Frankenheimer includes pieces of Pop Art in his shots—like the "love doll" sculpture in Buffy's bedroom and its enormous counterpart which appears on a city street in a later scene. He also alludes to some of the movement's artists and their works. The wall paper in Buffy's apartment is reminiscent of the "found art" collages Robert Rauschenberg created. The highly stylized images that appear in the opening credits sequence resemble Lichtenstein's famous comic strip paintings. The film's first shot of an American flag recalls the series of flags Jasper Johns painted. The film's last shot, a drawing of an explosion with the word "Wham!" written across, alludes to one of Lichtenstein's better known paintings, a piece named *Whaam!* And the film's title, a re-working of an Ivory Soap slogan, like Andy Warhol's famous Brillo box sculpture, draws attention to and calls into question the overly optimistic manner in which large corporations pitch their products to the public.

52 Pick-Up (1986)

Frankenheimer spent much of his time in the first half of the Eighties working abroad on projects like *The Challenge*, *The Holcroft Covenant* and *Riviera*. For *52 Pick-Up*, an adaptation of a crime novel by Elmore Leonard, he returned to the United States. He was not the first director to bring the book to the screen, however. Rather, it was J. Lee Thompson. Thompson's adaptation, released in 1984 under the title *The Ambassador*, however, departed significantly from its source, introducing political intrigue into the plot and moving the story from Detroit to the Middle East. Frankenheimer, in contrast, wanted his interpretation to adhere closely to its source. To ensure this, he hired Leonard to work on the script; and for the most part, the film and the novel are quite similar, though Frankenheimer was obliged to shoot in Los Angeles, rather than Detroit, to save on production costs.[7] The changed locale matters little, though, as the L.A. depicted in this picture, despite its sun and palm trees, is as much a moral dead zone as the version of Detroit which shows up in Leonard's novel: both cities are places where violence proliferates, appearances are at odds with reality and selfishness thrives, at least temporarily.

As the film opens, Harry "Mitch" Mitchell (Roy Scheider), a rich engineer, pays a visit to the apartment of his mistress, a model named Cini (Kelly Preston), intent on ending their affair. But when he arrives, he is met by a trio of masked blackmailers who have secretly filmed his trysts with the woman. The leader of this group, an adult movie theater manager named Raimy (John Glover), makes the businessman an offer: if he hopes to keep his unfaithfulness hidden from his wife Barb (Ann-Margret), an aspiring politician, he must pay them $105,000. Mitch does nothing at first and says nothing to the police as the publicity which might arise might hurt Barb's political ambitions. A few nights later, though, Mitch tells Barb about his affair. The news hurts her and he has to move out of his home, but the revelation of the truth, he thinks, nullifies the threat posed by the blackmailers, and he tells them that he will not pay. Raimy and his crony Bobby Shy (Clarence Williams III), a pimp/hit man, respond by abducting Cini and murdering her with a gun they've stole from Mitch. They also film the killing and after showing it to the businessman, they tell him that he must now pay the gang $105,000 annually.

Once again, Mitch refuses to go to the police. Instead, he tracks down the blackmailers through Cini's prostitute friend Doreen (Vanity). He then confronts Raimy, who, it turns out, is an accountant as well as a pornographer, and invites the villain to review his books. Afterward, Raimy, a bit disappointed, remarks: "Like a lot of people who make a lot of money, you don't seem to have any." Mitch then offers him a one time payment of $52,000 (hence the film's title) and Raimy accepts. The proposal buys Mitch time, which he uses to set the three blackmailers against one another, telling Raimy that one of the crooks named Leo (Robert Trebor) is a snitch (a lie) and telling Bobby Shy that Raimy plans to keep the money for himself (another lie). The counterattack works to a certain extent: Leo and Bobby Shy both get killed. But late in the film Raimy kidnaps Barb, injects her with heroin and rapes her. This move, he thinks, will ensure Mitch's cooperation. It does and Mitch meets the kidnapper on a bridge in Long Beach with the money. He also offers Raimy his sports car, which he accepts. But once the killer climbs inside, the doors lock automatically (Mitch's handiwork) and a recorded message explains that the car will explode in ten seconds. Raimy tries to get out, but can't, and the car blows up.

52 Pick-Up is a sex thriller, cut from the same rough cloth as Lawrence Kasdan's *Body Heat* (1981) and Bob Rafelson's remake of *The Postman Always Rings Twice* (1981). And like these movies, it is an example of what the critic Alain Silver has referred to as "neo-*noir*," a self-conscious style of filmmaking that makes use of the stylistic and thematic traits of *film noir*, the famous cycle of dark American crime films which flourished after World War II.[8] Throughout the film, Frankenheimer and his director of photography Jost Vacano fill the screen with heavy shadows, for instance, mimicking the expressive, low-key lighting schemes used by cameramen like James Wong Howe (*Sweet Smell of Success*, 1959), John Alton (*The Big Combo*, 1955) and Woody Bredell (*The Killers*, 1946). Subtle references to specific *films noirs* also surface. When Mitch is forced to watch the murder of Cini on the television set, Raimy stands near him, aiming a flashlight at the prisoner's head. The chiaroscuro lighting and the placement of the figures we find here recall the scene in Billy Wilder's *Sunset Boulevard* (1950), when Gloria Swanson and William Holden sit in her home theater watching silent movies as a projector, positioned behind them, pierces the darkness with hard white light. The fight between Mitch and Raimy in the projection room of Raimy's theater also recalls the fight scene that takes place between Robert Ryan and Paul Douglas in Lang's *Clash by Night* (1952).[9] At one point in Frankenheimer's film, as well, Raimy is depicted shooting porno-

Mitch (Roy Scheider) confronts Raimy in the projection room of an adult movie theater in *52 Pick-Up* (Cannon, 1986).

graphic material with a movie camera pressed to one eye; a black patch, much like the one Raoul Walsh wore, covers the other. Walsh, of course, directed the early *noir High Sierra* (1941) and the later *noir White Heat* (1949), which, like *52 Pick-Up*, ends with an explosion.

Filmed on location, frequently with handheld cameras, much of 52 *Pick-Up* has a rough, semi-documentary look to it that at times recalls *nouvelle vague* crime thrillers like Malle's *Frantic* (1958) and Godard's *Breathless* (1959). Some critics have objected to this trait, however; Janet Maslin, in her review, for instance, referred to the picture as a "slapdash, unsightly production."[10] But while *52 Pick-Up* does have an irregular, almost improvisational aspect to it, it is in actuality a carefully structured work. Throughout it, for example, the director uses imagery to announce and develop the film's themes. Consider the opening sequence. First, we have a full shot of Mitch, swimming in a narrow "lap" pool, which is followed by a close-up of Barb, watching him at a distance from a window in their palatial house. As he dries himself with a towel, Mitch looks up at his wife and she peers down at him. They say nothing, but their facial expressions are anything but happy. The distance between them, Frankenheimer infers, is more than physical. A few moments later, with the incident in Cini's apartment, the explanation for their emotional estrangement becomes evident: Mitch, bored in the marriage, has turned his attention to a young lover. Infidelity, we should note, is another *film noir* staple, the catalytic event that triggers the violence and tragedy in films like Wilder's *Double Indemnity* (1944), Lang's *The Woman in the Window* (1945) and de Toth's *Pitfall* (1948).

But unlike these films, *52 Pick-Up* focuses little attention on the affair itself, and more on its consequences, tracking Mitch's efforts to repair, rather than escape from, his marriage. Instead of walking out on Barb permanently, he comes home. Instead of going to the police and seeking their help and arousing publicity, he confronts the blackmailers by himself. Instead of simply letting Raimy, the man who drugs Barb and rapes her, drive away with the money, he kills him on the bridge. And these efforts, it seems, work. Barb may be devastated after her experience, but, in the last shot of the film, as the couple walk away from the burning car, they embrace. The distance between them has disappeared.

Kirk Honeycutt has argued that *52 Pick-Up* "is all about [Mitch] seeking redemption through ... action."[11] We might add that the picture is also about Mitch restoring his freedom, his ability to control his life, through action. For much of the film, though, Mitch is a trapped man, and Frankenheimer uses visual clues to underscore and emphasize his situation. The picture's opening shot shows him swimming, framed by the edges of his pool. The scene when Raimy and the others first confront him takes place in a close, windowless bedroom. When Mitch watches the videotape, the superimposed reflection of his face appears on the small, framed screen.

Mitch's fortunes change, though, when he begins to respond to his tormentors in a new manner. Rather than negotiating with or trying to ignore them, he makes up his mind to attack the men. And much as he employs symbolism to emphasize Mitch's lack of freedom in the early scenes, he uses it again to convey this change in the character's outlook. Frankenheimer explained to Champlin:

> He's got to decide to go out and kill those guys. It was a crucial decision for him to make, and the audience has got to understand what's going on inside of him, how it's driving him crazy and now he's got to do it.[12]

To make the audience understand, the director associates Mitch's epiphany with the position of the sun in the sky as he drives his car from his house to the desert and back. Confused and upset when he sets out, the weather, appropriately, is dark and rainy; in the next shot, though, when he stops the car in the desert, the light of the rising sun is just visible; then, when he returns to his home in the city, the sky is bright with light. It is at this point that he begins his deadly campaign.

Acting quickly and decisively, Mitch makes use of the same underhanded methods his adversaries have used against him — taking compromising pictures of Leo and Bobby Shy, framing Leo, tricking Raimy and trapping him with the car. Raimy and Mitch, as a matter of fact, share a great deal in common. Both come from working class backgrounds. They dress alike, wearing sports jackets and shirts without ties. They enjoy the same types of cars — and women. And they both engage in criminal activity when it suits their needs. But Mitch is the better cheat, though, and this is why, at the end of the film, he has his wife and freedom back, while Raimy and the others are dead.

Reindeer Games (2000)

Set in Michigan's Upper Peninsula, *Reindeer Games*, like *Ronin*, focuses on the efforts taken by a group of criminals as they plot and execute an elaborate robbery. The film opens, however, in a prison yard. Under grey, snowing skies, a convicted car thief named Rudy (Ben Affleck) and his cellmate Nick (James Frain) chat about what they plan to do when the state releases them on parole in a few days. For Rudy, freedom means having the chance to eat good food and visit his family. For Nick, it means spending time with Ashley (Charlize Theron), the beautiful woman with whom he's been corresponding through a "pen pal" program for several months. Before the release date arrives, however, a convict (Dana Stubblefield) attacks Rudy with a knife, but inadvertently stabs Nick instead, killing him. The tragedy upsets Rudy considerably, yet when he leaves the prison, and spots Ashley waiting for Nick in the parking lot, he passes himself off as his dead friend (which is easy because Ashley has never seen Nick). The ruse works and Ashley takes Rudy to a motel and makes love to him. Afterward, however, her brother Gabriel (Gary Sinise) and his three friends Merlin (Clarence Williams III), Pug (Donal Logue) and Jumpy (Danny Trejo), break into the motel room and beat Rudy up. Gabriel, mistaking Rudy for Nick, has learned from reading his sister's letters that Nick once worked as a security guard in an Indian casino called the Tomahawk near the Canadian border. Tired of the trucking life, Gabriel wants to rob the casino and retire; and Nick/Rudy, he reasons, can help him.

Rudy responds to this by telling the crazy trucker and his cronies the truth about the situation and they decide to kill him. But Rudy then manages to convince the dim-witted criminals that he's been lying, and they take him, along with Ashley, up to the casino. When he escapes from the back of the casino and runs across the frozen surface of a lake, Ashley follows, trying to help him. She falls through the ice, however, and Rudy jumps in the water to help. The effort saves the woman, but it loses Rudy his freedom and that night, Gabriel and the others take him to another motel where they handcuff him to a bed. Once again, though, Rudy escapes. But once again, he turns around to help Ashley, wanting to get her away from Gabriel. He finds her, though, in an indoor swimming pool with her brother and watches with sadness and horror as they begin to have sex.[13]

Simultaneously, Gabriel's men return to the motel and Rudy is forced to return to his room. The next day, Gabriel, his associates and a reluctant Rudy,

Rudy (Ben Affleck, center) reluctantly agrees to help his captors (Clarence Williams III, left; Danny Trejo) pull off the heist in *Reindeer Games* (Dimension, 2000).

each dressed up in Santa Claus costumes, enter the Tomahawk with heavy firearms and proceed to rob it, though Pug, Merlin and Jumpy are killed. Ashley and Gabriel then drive Rudy to a cliff where they plan to murder him. Ashley, however, shoots Gabriel first and a moment later, the real Nick shows up. He faked his death, he explains, as part of a plan to trick Rudy into meeting Ashley and helping her with the robbery. The pair also tricked Gabriel — who it turns out is not really Ashley's brother — for the same reason. Nick and Ashley, whose real name is Millie, then tie up Rudy and set him behind the steering wheel of a car, which they plan to push over the cliff's side. The experienced car thief, however, manages to start the car. He crushes Nick with it, then sends it off the cliff with Ashley/Millie clinging to the hood. After sending Nick over the cliff, as well, Rudy takes the money that was robbed from the casino and heads off for his parent's nearby home, along the way shoving bundles of cash into people's mailboxes.

Frankenheimer's last theatrical picture is as much a comedy as it is a violent melodrama, and in this respect, it resembles *99 and 44/100% Dead!* But unlike the earlier picture, *Reindeer Games* is often funny, thanks to Ehren Kruger's charismatic script and actors like Williams and Sinise, who play their nut case characters with unrestrained zest. Stuffed as it is with sex, foul language and grotesque violence, the film also recalls Quentin Tarantino's trashy, but entertaining trio of crime films, *Reservoir Dogs*, *Pulp Fiction* and *Jackie Brown*

(1997). But despite the over-the-top performances and cartoonish scenarios, the film shares much in common with Frankenheimer's more serious works, especially with its inclusion of characters who use deceptive behavior to serve their own ends. In fact, when the picture missed its original December release date, its title was temporarily changed to *Deception*. As Frankenheimer explained to Gary Arnold, the film's producers

> thought it would be a struggle to build an ad campaign around the title with Christmas behind us instead of ahead of us. So Miramax did a lot of title research, and we settled on *Deception*, although no one was ecstatic about it. It didn't seem to promise the payoff we were seeking in the old Hitchcock tradition of *Spellbound* and *Notorious* and *Vertigo* and all that. So after brooding about it, we ... went back to the original title.[14]

The original title, of course, is a reference to "Rudolph the Red-Nosed Reindeer," the popular Christmas song about a mistreated reindeer who turns a physical shortcoming into an asset.[15] Frankenheimer told Arnold that Kruger wrote the script with the song in mind and allusions to its storyline appear throughout the film often. When, for instance, Rudy sends Ashley over the cliff into the Christmas Eve night, the front of the car is on fire, burning brightly like the reindeer's famous nose when he pulls Santa's sleigh. And when the truckers torture Rudy, which they often do, they tend to laugh at him — Merlin giggles, for example, when he presses a gun against the back of Rudy's head — and call their prisoner names, like "convict," "Romeo" and worse. And like his reindeer counterpart, Rudy is ridiculed by his fellows because he is different from them. Primarily, it is his intelligence, his ability to think quickly, which separates him from the others. At one point, for example, Gabriel chides Rudy, snarling, "You think you're so smart."

Rudy is also capable of compassionate, helpful behavior — Ashley's rescue, for instance — which the truckers are not. But although the film honors the song's storyline frequently, it departs from it, as well. Unlike the famous reindeer, Rudy has no interest in joining in with his companions, and unlike Rudolph's friends, who come to recognize the reindeer's usefulness and begin to love him, Rudy's cohorts decide to kill Rudy once they think his usefulness has been exhausted. The film also makes an attempt to let the audience know what a "reindeer game" is — something the song alludes to, but never makes clear. After Rudy explains to Gabriel that he is not Nick and then reverses himself, the self-satisfied trucker, believing that he has persuaded Rudy to tell the truth, says, "I read your letters, convict. Don't play no reindeer games with me." In the context of this film, in other words, a "reindeer game" is a lie.

During the film's promotional campaign, Frankenheimer told a number of interviewers that he had didactic objectives in mind when he made *Reindeer Games*. Reasoning much like the American writer Flannery O'Connor, he believed that the film's exaggerated depictions of crime and cruelty could lead audiences to a greater appreciation of ethical behavior. He explained to the *Detroit Free Press* that effective thrillers "have resonance, something you mull over after you leave the theater. And the best ones have a moral."[16] Unfortunately, the director was never very specific about which moral lessons he hoped the movie would transmit, though it seems certain he wanted to caution viewers about the dangers of violence, dishonesty and greed. All of the heavies in the film engage in this sort of behavior, after all, and all of them die painful deaths. But Rudy survives, perhaps because he has more goodness in him than the others. And perhaps it is because, unlike them, he is more interested in aiding people than in hurting them. The ending of the film, for instance, might be interpreted as Rudy's repudiation of the harmful tendencies which characterized his past: rather than taking things from his neighbors, as he did when he was a car thief, he now gives them gifts. Frankenheimer, in fact, intended the scene to be read this way:

> I believe that the protagonist makes a very moral choice at the end of this movie. He's somebody who, through all his life, has done the wrong thing, has used his intelligence and charm, has always taken the easy money, all that has landed him in jail in the first place, being a car thief. And then, at the end he has a choice, and he makes the right choice. I like that choice.[17]

The director apparently did not recognize, however, that Rudy's actions are not wholly honorable. The money he passes on, it must be noted, doesn't belong to him. Rather, it belongs to the Indian tribe which owns and manages the Tomahawk casino. Rudy's final good deed, his "very moral choice," in short, is a criminal act. And just prior to this sequence, we have to remember, Rudy murders Nick in cold blood, pushing the injured man over a cliff.

Much like *French Connection II* and *52 Pick-Up*, *Reindeer Games* bears the influence of *film noir*. Though the director shot the movie in color, for example, he wanted it to have the same monochromatic look that characterizes the older movies.

> [I]n this picture, there's hardly any color. We [did] it in the laboratory, but also by being very meticulous in the choice of location, in the choice of set dressing — no bright colors in anything — choice of costume — all of the costumes are earth tone or black or gray.[18]

Frankenheimer and his director of photography Alan Caso also borrowed from the earlier films' low-key lighting schemes, saturating their shots with sinister shadows. The inclusion of a *femme fatale* in the cast of characters is something else *Reindeer Games* shares with *films noirs*.[19] Much like the female leads in movies like *The Lady from Shanghai* (1948) and *Double Indemnity*, Ashley uses sex, beauty and sweetness to conceal her motives and manipulate her admirers, while her actions and ambitions lead to her undoing. Yet Ashley is, perhaps, more sympathetic than her predecessors. She may be driven by her desire for money, but unlike many women in *noir*, she comes from a lower income background, not an affluent one. The grinding economic conditions of Rust Belt America, Frankenheimer seems to suggest, are as much to blame for her rotten tendencies as greed. As she tells Rudy:

There's no future for people like you and me. The places we come from — bland towns, mill towns, small lives. No future, just more of the same. If you want a future, you've got to stand up and steal it.

Ashley has no future, of course, while Rudy does. And as he heads back to his parents' home in Sidnaw, Michigan, a bland mill town, he seems to be happy.

CHAPTER NINE

Prisoners

Frankenheimer's heroes often find themselves trapped in situations which cause mental and physical anguish, ranging from unhappy marriages (*Seconds, I Walk the Line, Impossible Object*) to problems with drugs and alcohol ("The Days of Wine and Roses," *French Connection II*) and physical impairments (*Grand Prix, The Horsemen, George Wallace*). And with varying degrees of success, these characters extricate themselves from their traps. The banker in *Seconds* undergoes radical plastic surgery in order to change his identity. The junkie Popeye Doyle refuses to use heroin. Ignoring his pain, the driver Scott Stoddard returns to the race car circuit. But in the four films Frankenheimer made about prisons—*Bird Man of Alcatraz, The Fixer, Against the Wall* and *Andersonville*—the protagonists completely lack the ability to change their conditions, restricted as they are by walls and bars and the tyranny of their captors. But under the pressure of confinement, many of the characters we find in these movies experience a sort of spiritual liberation, growing stronger, more resilient, more accepting of fate. In short, their bodies may be confined, but as a consequence of this, their minds and hearts become free.

Bird Man of Alcatraz (1962)

Although he dropped out of school in the third grade, was convicted of killing two people and spent more than 40 years of his life in solitary confinement, Robert Stroud became one of the world's preeminent experts on bird diseases, publishing two well-received books on the subject. Moved by this unlikely achievement, a social worker named Thomas Gaddis wrote a book-length profile of the convict's life, which he titled *Birdman of Alcatraz*. Published in 1955, Gaddis' biography was in turn adapted by a writer named Guy Trosper into a screenplay, which was eventually picked up for development by

Harold Hecht, upon the insistence of his partner Burt Lancaster. As Lancaster's biographer Kate Buford wrote, the story of the prisoner's rehabilitation "appealed deeply" to the actor's soul.[1]

Set over a 50 year period, *Bird Man* opens in 1912 as a train delivers Stroud (Lancaster) to Leavenworth Federal Prison in Kansas, where he's being sent to serve out a 12 year sentence for having killed a man in Alaska over a prostitute. An incorrigible bully, the prisoner can get along with no one — except his mother (Thelma Ritter), for whom he feels an almost incestuous affection. (Frankenheimer's next two films, *All Fall Down* and *The Manchurian Candidate*, also feature intense, unhealthy mother-son relationships.) And this emotion gets the best of him when, after a couple of years, Mrs. Stroud travels from Alaska to visit her son at "The Big House." But because she arrives on a day when inmates are prohibited from meeting guests, the old woman is sent away. And when Stroud learns about this, he lashes out, first assaulting and then killing a guard, outraging the prison's warden, Harvey Shoemaker (Karl Malden). The courts sentence him to death for this, but he is spared after his mother goes to President Wilson and secures a clemency. The U.S Attorney General sees to it, however, that the prisoner pays dearly for his crime, ordering him to spend the rest of his life in solitary confinement.

That same year, 1920, Stroud finds a fledgling sparrow in an exercise yard, which he nurtures and trains, teaching it to fly and perform tricks. The progress he makes with the creature impresses the prison's new warden and he permits Stroud to keep the bird — and acquire hundreds more over the next several years. But in 1927, an outbreak of septic fever begins to kill the animals, a disease for which, at that point in time, there was no cure. Desperate to save his companions, the prisoner reads what he can about bird ailments in books borrowed from the Leavenworth library. He experiments with several homemade serums, too, eventually developing a formula which works. The crisis arouses Stroud's interest in science and he eventually becomes an expert on bird health. He also begins to publish articles on the subject in journals, a development which wins him a following, a cult of devotees.

One of these people, an entrepreneurial widow named Stella Johnson (Betty Field), visits him, certain that she and the prisoner can build a thriving business by selling his remedies to bird owners. The plan works, but its success irks the men who run the Federal prison system, a group which now includes Harvey Shoemaker; and they decide to take Stroud's birds from him. Ever defiant, Stroud responds to this by marrying Stella, an act which becomes a front page item, publicizing the prisoner's conflict, arousing the public's sympathy and stymieing the administrators' efforts. The victory is not without consequences. Jealous of Stella, Mrs. Stroud tells her son to end his relationship with her; and when he doesn't, she turns on him, thwarting his subsequent efforts to obtain parole. The prison officials punish him, too, transferring him in 1942 to Alcatraz, the country's toughest penitentiary, forcing him to leave

Robert Stroud (Burt Lancaster) at work in his cell in *Bird Man of Alcatraz* (UA, 1962).

behind his birds and his research. This development saddens Stroud, but it does not break him, and he soon begins a new project, a book about the history of Federal prisons. But the prison's warden, who happens to be Harvey Shoemaker, confiscates the manuscript, troubled by its allegations that the American corrections system uses repressive measures to control its population. But while this loss hurts him, too, Stroud again rebounds, not succumbing to self-pity or hate, the traits which characterized his personality when he began his stay in prison.

The film then moves to 1953, to a riot that breaks out, which the elderly inmate, now a man of peace, helps to end. Following this, Frankenheimer cuts to an exterior shot of Alcatraz and the San Francisco harbor, one of the few bits of footage in the picture which was shot outside of the studio. As a boat lands at one of the docks, we learn from Tom Gaddis (Edmond O'Brien), who is standing on the wharf, watching the craft, that the Bureau of Prisons has finally recognized Stroud's rehabilitation; and now, after 43 years in solitary confinement, the prisoner is being sent to a low security prison in Missouri, where he will again be able to mix with other men.

Bird Man of Alcatraz enjoyed high ticket sales when United Artists released it in July 1962. It also aroused critical approval, winning reviewers over with the richness of its characterization, of the light it sheds on the complex, often contradictory personalities of people like Stroud and the men and women who interact with him. John Scott at the *Los Angeles Times*, for example, wrote:

> *Bird Man of Alcatraz* must be regarded as a grim, off-beat prison picture, unusual in that it concentrates attention on the psychological aspects of confinement, rather than on the superficial bang-bang action of most prison dramas.[2]

And the review which appeared in *Variety* argued: "In telling, with reasonable objectivity but understandably deep compassion the true story of Robert Stroud, it achieves a human dimension way beyond its predecessors."[3] Lancaster received much acclaim, too, and in fact his performance was later nominated for an Academy Award. A.H Weiler at *The New York Times*, for instance, applauded the actor for interpreting the role with "realism, nuance and restraint," a tactic which enhances the film's believability and makes the convict more sympathetic. (It might be argued, however, that Lancaster's efforts at making Stroud endearing are perhaps too successful, that his portrayal of the murderer as a sort of saint, a jailhouse Albert Schweitzer, strains credulity.)

Weiler also argued that Lancaster's Stroud is an existential character, a man whose life takes "on meaning and substance" once he begins to pursue the projects which engage his attention. He wrote:

> One cheers for the idea that, at long last, his profound love of these dumb creatures, a love accentuated by his confinement, results in his development as a man of science and the author of a definitive tome on the illnesses of birds and their cures.[4]

And in this respect, the film anticipates *Grand Prix, The Gypsy Moths* and *The Horsemen*, as they also feature protagonists who place little value on what others think of them, instead defining themselves by their actions, by their ability to do what they want to do, not what they are told to do.

Lancaster believed that the prison system in the United States was "outdated and outmoded," that its insistence upon retribution, rather than rehabilitation, stripped inmates like Stroud of their sense of worth, as well as their rights; and he hoped the film would bring this problem to the public's attention, and, perhaps, trigger reform.[5] The actor's point of view surfaces rather explicitly late in the film, when Shoemaker, the rigid warden at Alcatraz, finds Stroud's critique of the federal prison system, a discovery which infuriates him.

> SHOEMAKER: Do you think that I want to go on punishing you? Now, we've grown old together in penitentiaries and in all that time I've only asked one thing from you — cooperation. The only thing I've gotten back was defiance. Not once have you ever shown a sign of rehabilitation.
>
> STROUD: Rehabilitation?
>
> SHOEMAKER: Yes, rehabilitation.
>
> STROUD: I wonder if you know what the word means. Do you?

SHOEMAKER: Now don't be insulting.

STROUD: The unabridged Webster's International Dictionary says it comes from the Latin root *habilis*. The definition is: "to invest again with dignity." You consider that part of your job, Harvey, to give a man back the dignity he once had? Your only interest is in how he behaves. You told me that once, a long time ago, and I'll never forget it. "You'll conform to our ideas of how you should behave." And you haven't retreated from that stand one inch in 35 years. You want your prisoners to dance out the gates like puppets on a string with rubber stamped values, impressed by you, with your sense of conformity, your sense of behavior, even your sense of morality. That's why you're a failure, Harvey, you and the whole science of penology. Because you rob prisoners of the most important thing in their lives, their individuality. On the outside, they're lost, automatons, just going through the motions of living. But underneath there is a deep, deep hatred for what you did to them. First chance they get to attack society, they do it. The result? More than half come back to prison.

Lancaster, moreover, was convinced that Stroud was a victim of juridical overkill, and he wanted the picture to help the prisoner, who died just one year after the film's theatrical run, in his pursuit of a parole or pardon. Stimulating viewers' interest and arousing their sympathy was thus imperative, and to achieve this end, the actor and Frankenheimer, along with the film's scenarist Guy Trosper, were not unwilling to enhance their portrait of Stroud, eliminating aspects of his history and his personality which were unattractive, while inventing details where were more dramatically effective than actual facts: the Federal Bureau of Prisons never confiscated Stroud's critique of the American penal system; the real Stroud killed a guard when his brother, not his mother, was prevented from visiting him at Leavenworth; the real Stroud was a jailhouse bootlegger, too, who used his lab equipment to ferment birdseed and distill liquor, which he and complicit guards sold to other prisoners. The real Stroud also had a psychopathic personality, and he remained mean-spirited until his last days, never developing the mild temperament which makes Lancaster's interpretation of him so endearing.

Frankenheimer, for the most part, was pleased with *Bird Man of Alcatraz*, but he felt that the film would have been stronger if he'd enjoyed greater control on the set. But because he entered the production late and because of his leading man's insistence upon managing every aspect of the project, his influence over the picture's creation was limited. The director wasn't even present in the cutting room when the movie's editor Edward Mann, closely supervised by Trosper and Lancaster, put the film's final cut together.[5] Nevertheless, many of the themes and motifs we find in later, more personal films materialize, most notably the individual's refusal to bend to authoritarian measures and the depiction of suffering as a positive phenomenon, a corrective force which can make a person stronger, kinder and more humane. We ought to note, as well, that the picture presents us with an early display of the realist shooting techniques Frankenheimer would utilize regularly in his subsequent work, especially the long take and the shot-in-depth, as well as the occasional expressionistic flourish, such as the thick shadows, for instance, which conceal Shoemaker's face when he warns Stroud in Leavenworth that someday his birds will be taken from him.

The Fixer (1968)

Before its publication in the fall of 1966, Bernard Malamud sent a copy of his novel *The Fixer* to Frankenheimer and his partner Edward Lewis, hoping the filmmakers might be interested in turning this story of a Ukrainian Jew who is unjustly accused of murder and placed in prison into a movie. The director responded to the work with great interest and he and Lewis purchased the property, after which they hired Dalton Trumbo to write the adaptation.[6] Before production on the film could begin, however, Frankenheimer went down to Mexico to shoot *The Extraordinary Seaman*. By the summer of 1967, though, the Malamud project was well underway, with the leading roles all cast; and in the fall of that year the director, his actors and his crew flew out to Budapest to shoot the adaptation. According to *The Washington Post*, which ran a feature about the production, Frankenheimer and Lewis chose to film *The Fixer* in Hungary, rather than the United States, in order to save money — approximately $3 million.[7] But thanks to the tremendous bureaucratic inefficiency of the Hungarian government, the director was met with numerous frustrations and obstacles daily, a problem which created tensions on the set between him and Trumbo, as well as one of the film's stars Dirk Bogarde; it also added several weeks to the shooting schedule.[8]

Like *Bird Man of Alcatraz*, *The Fixer* is a story about redemption, about the moral awakening a man experiences under the combined pressures of confinement and isolation. Its narrative is rooted in real history, as Malamud loosely based the hero of his novel, Yakov Bok (Alan Bates), upon a Jewish bricklayer named Mendel Beilis, who, just like Bok, was taken into custody by the Tsar's secret police in 1905 and charged with the murder of a Christian boy. Although Frankenheimer simplifies Malamud's interpretation of the story, his film is still lengthy (130 minutes) and complex.

The picture opens in the rustic village where Bok, an impoverished, and embittered, handyman, has lived his whole life. Hoping to earn a better living, he heads out for Kiev, but upon his arrival in the Ukrainian capital, he learns that Jews are restricted from working outside of the Jewish ghetto, and to improve his chances for finding work, he decides to pass himself off as a Christian. One night, the fixer finds a drunk lying in the snow. This old man, whose name is Lebedev (Hugh Griffith), wears a badge that marks him as a member of the Black Hundred, an anti-Jewish organization, and Bok decides to leave him alone. But then the man's daughter Zinaida (Elizabeth Hartman) appears, and she persuades Bok to carry the old man home. The next day, not realizing

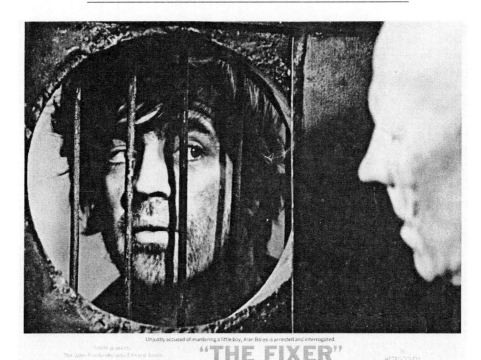

Unjustly accused of murdering a little boy, Alan Bates is arrested and interrogated.

MGM presents
The John Frankenheimer-Edward Lewis
Production

"THE FIXER"

METROCOLOR

The weary prisoner Bok (Alan Bates) arouses a guard's sympathy in *The Fixer* (MGM, 1968).

that he is Jewish, Lebedev rewards the fixer, offering him a large sum of money if he'll work on his house. The situation makes Bok nervous, but he does his job well; and soon after, Lebedev asks him to take over the operation of a brick plant he owns. Bok then moves to the brick factory, where he watches over the other workers, in order to stop them from stealing. But then he is arrested and jailed, charged with rape, thanks to a false claim Zinaida files against him.

The accusation is eventually dropped, but not before it is revealed that Bok is Jewish. A vindictive prosecutor named Grubeshov (Ian Holm) then charges him with a second crime. A dead boy has been found near Lebedev's brickyard, and this killing, Grubeshov has concluded, must be the work of Jews, of Bok in particular. But while the lack of evidence prevents the prosecutor from filing formal charges against the suspect, it doesn't stop him from putting Bok in prison. And for several years, the fixer is forced to endure solitary confinement and torture as ruthless officials and malicious guards attempt to wear him down mentally and physically in order to draw out an admission of guilt. Bok wins one ally, though, an investigating magistrate named Bibikov (Bogarde), who believes that the boy's killers is his mother (Georgia Brown);

Bibikov learns, as well, that the Tsar is exploiting the fixer's predicament, using it to rile up hatred in the general population in order to make himself more popular. But the magistrate, unfortunately, is murdered before he can help Bok. The fixer never concedes guilt, however. In fact, he demands a trial, which the officials refuse. But as the years pass and the story of his unjust imprisonment becomes widely known and threatens the Tsar's grip on power, the government grants Bok his wish. The movie ends shortly after this, with Bok arriving at a courthouse in Kiev, a crowd of onlookers cheering as he climbs the building's front steps.

In spite of the problems Frankenheimer experienced as he made *The Fixer*, he was confident that he had created an important film, an incisive examination of anti–Semitism and political repression. But when MGM released the picture in December 1968, his expectations were disappointed for the most part, as many of the reviews which appeared were unfriendly. Objecting to its violent content and solemn tone, Renatta Adler at *The New York Times*, for example, described the movie as "an unremittingly, unenlightening depressing experience."[9] The write-up in *Variety* dismissed the picture as "a ponderous diatribe against injustice."[10] And Charles Champlin complained in his review for the *Los Angeles Times*: "Frankenheimer's telling of the story is so strident, so heavy-handed, so charged, that it becomes less a human drama than a theatrical pageant and so works against its own intentions."[11] Roger Ebert also disdained the picture. But he directed his attack primarily onto the film's dialogue, arguing that it is overly expository and philosophical, that it strives to enlighten audiences, rather than entertain them. The filmmakers, he wrote, "have missed no opportunity to give us speeches telling us what is happening and what it all means."

Ebert was especially irritated by the film's last spoken line, which appears on the soundtrack as a voiceover. As the fixer nears the top of the courthouse steps, his weary voice intones: "The name is Yakov Bok. A Jew. An innocent man. Also your brother." Ebert objected to these remarks on the grounds that they state what should be obvious to most people by the end of the picture. He wrote:

> Frankenheimer has already spent more than two hours introducing us to Yakov Bok, and convincing us of his Jewishness, his innocence and our brotherhood with him. That is what the film is about. Why, then, do we have to be told? Why do we have to have the moral spelled out for us, as if the film itself meant nothing?[12]

Ebert may not have realized, perhaps, that Bok's final words are addressed to a judge: just before he says them, we hear the sound of a gavel striking a hard surface. And thus the inclusion of the line serves an important narrative function, letting us know that Bok makes it into the courtroom, that he isn't killed or doesn't fall down dead, before he can plead his case. But Ebert's comments, as well as those of the others who rejected the film, still carry weight. Indeed, *The Fixer* is one of Frankenheimer's "talkiest" pictures, and the dialogue, thick with platitudes and profundities, is often preposterous. (We should note, though, that the characters we find in Malamud's novel also tend to speak in an elevated manner.) In addition, *The Fixer* suffers from structural problems, as the director was forced by Lewis to shorten the picture drastically before its release, creating gaps in the narrative and abrupt leaps across time and space which disorient the viewer. "[I]t was a severely, severely compromised picture," he explained to Champlin.[13] Condemnation of *The Fixer* was not universal, however. The film received four Golden Globe nominations, including Best Picture, and Bates' performance was nominated for an Academy Award. Moreover, the movie drew praise from some powerful critics, such as *Life*'s Richard Shickel, whose review refutes the charge that the film is too violent. He wrote:

> That Yakov's time in jail [is] unpleasant and that the movie is unrelenting in spelling out the details of that unpleasantness cannot be denied. But there is no attempt to exploit them for merely sensational effect. They are dramatically necessary for a story that is an uplifting hymn to the human spirit.

For Schickel, Bok is an everyman figure, with whom most people, regardless of their nationality or faith, can identify. "He is ... [a]nything but a born hero, he is devious, even rather cowardly — a very ordinary man."[14]

And yet this unremarkable person, our "brother," has the will to defy tyrants and the ability to thwart their objectives. In addition, as his situation worsens, he acts with increasing selflessness, becoming a better person, the more he suffers. Through flashbacks and voiceovers, we learn, for example, that Bok was a hard person before he left his village for Kiev; and that he rejected his wife Raisl (Carol White) because she could not bear a child. But several years into his incarceration, Raisl visits him. And he learns from her she has had another man's baby. This news pains him at first, but when she asks for him to sign a paper that asserts that he is the child's father, he agrees — because doing this will help her. Similarly, his refusal to confess, to admit guilt for killing the Christian boy, is done not so much out of pride, or even self-interest, but of concern for other Jews, as a confession, he suspects, will be used by anti-semites to justify pogroms and purges and other horrors. He rejects an offer of amnesty from the Tsar for the same reason.

Moral transformations like this occur frequently in Frankenheimer's canon. The zealous prosecutor Hank Bell in *The Young Savages* abandons his opinions about the boys' guilt when he realizes they have been shaped by prejudice. Likewise in *Bird Man of Alcatraz*, the one-time killer Robert Stroud, after shedding his self-absorption and self-pity, devotes himself to science and medicine in order to save the lives of the birds he comes to care about and love. And much like Stroud, who writes an unflattering book about the American prison system, and Chico Mendes, the hero of *The Burning Season* who publicizes the role Brazilian politicians have played in the destruction of the rain forest, Bok becomes a dissident of sorts, a harsh critic of the political status quo, radicalized by the suffering he's endured at the hands of government men.

But trapped in his solitary cell, stripped of all but some rags and, for a while, a copy of the New Testament, he has no way of communicating his subversive ideas, of finding an audience for them. But then, when he is visited by one of the Tsar's officials, Count Odoevsky (David Warner), and is offered the pardon, which he refuses, he gets his chance.

> BOK: Wise I never was. Something in myself has changed, your honor. I feel less and I hate more.
> Odoevsky: Whom do you hate?
> BOK: Tsar. Government. You. All those who lack the insight, you might call it, that creates in a man charity, respect for the most miserable.
> Odoevsky: I've been misinformed about you, Bok. Your dossier is that of a completely apolitical man.
> BOK: There's no such thing as an apolitical man. "Where there's no fight for it, there's no freedom." Spinoza said it best.
> ODOEVSKY: He was a Jew.
> BOK: He said, "You can't stand still and let yourself be destroyed." He said, "If the state acts in ways that are abhorrent to human nature, then it's the lesser evil to destroy the state."

Surprisingly, Bok's criticism of the count and the despots he serves, as dangerous as it is, yields victory for him. Immediately after Odoevsky leaves the fixer's cell, he tells the prosecutor Grobeshevsky to file an indictment, triggering the process which will lead Bok to the courtroom and his trial. When individuals resist tyranny, the film demonstrates, they weaken it.

Against the Wall (1994)

Against the Wall is Frankenheimer's quasi-fictional interpretation of the prisoner uprising which broke out at the Attica Correctional Facility in upstate New York in 1971. The film opens, however, with a montage of clips taken from actual news footage which was filmed in the late Sixties and early Seventies. A shot of Robert Kennedy lying on the floor of the Ambassador Hotel with a hole in his head, for instance, flashes on the screen then the bodies of the students killed at Kent State and the burning streets of riot-torn Watts. The director then cuts to the quiet streets of Attica, to a barber shop, where a young man with long hair is sitting, chatting with a barber. This is Michael Smith (Kyle MacLachlan), a 22-year old expectant father, who has decided to become a corrections officer at the local prison, drawn by the pay the position promises.

Once Smith has his hair cut, he heads over to "The Factory," the locals' name for the prison, to start his new job. That same morning, a black militant named Jamaal X (Samuel Jackson) arrives at the facility. The film proceeds to follow the two men, cross cutting between them, as they experience their first day at Attica. And from this, as well as several subsequent scenes, we learn that the conditions in this prison are terrible, that the institution's senior officers, contemptuous of their charges, handle the inmates roughly, screaming at them, threatening them, pushing them, conducting needless (and humiliating) strip searches, as well as ignoring their requests for basic needs, like functioning toilets and clean underwear. We also learn that the spirit of protest which has materialized throughout the country in response to Vietnam has begun to manifest itself inside The Factory, too. But the inmates are not interested in the war. Instead, they want the prison's superintendent and his guards to do a better job of recognizing their human rights. The abuses continue, however, adding to the inmates' frustration and rage, and one morning, when a gate in one of the facility's tiers malfunctions, several prisoners, headed by a psychopath named Chaka (Clarence Williams III), rise up and overwhelm their guards, wresting their keys from them and liberating the others from their cells.

In the course of the riot which follows, several guards are captured, including Smith. And these men are brought outside to the prison's yards, surrounded by thousands of rowdy inmates who remember the mistreatment they've received. But Jamaal, who emerges as one of the unplanned uprising's leaders, recognizes that if the hostages are killed, the "Attica brothers" will lose their ability to negotiate with government officials; and thus he protects them from the likes of Chaka and the other sadists. The officers still receive harsh treatment, however, as their captors force them to demoralize themselves in exchange for clothing, food and bathroom privileges. But Smith refuses to join in with the others, even though it arouses their scorn, as well as the attention of Chaka, who thinks it might be best to kill him before he can cause trouble.

Jamaal, in contrast, comes to respect Smith for his unwillingness to bow, recognizing the non-conformist guard as a kindred spirit. And he recruits him to speak to a news crew, to tell the outside world that the hostages have not been tortured or killed, hoping that his testimony will aid the prisoners in their efforts as they negotiate with state government officials for better living conditions. But the effort fails: on the fifth day of the standoff, New York's governor Nelson Rockefeller puts an end to the negotiations and orders law enforcement officials and soldiers to raid the prison. And once again, Frankenheimer fills the screen with horrendous violence as the liberators rush into the yard, firing indiscriminately at the inmates as well their hostages, their vision impaired by tear gas. Several men are killed, in fact, including Chaka, Jamaal and Lt. Wiesbad (Frederick Forrest), the fascistic chief of the guards, while Smith is injured critically, shot several times in the stomach by one of his friends, a constable in the Attica police department.

Against the Wall provides viewers with what seems to be a fairly accurate account of the Attica tragedy, an impression which is enhanced by the manner in which the film was shot. To make the action on the screen look as spontaneous and real as he could, the director eschewed studio sets and artificial light, and made frequent use of portable cameras, especially the Steadicam.

As he told Charles Champlin for a piece which appeared in the *Los Angeles Times*:

> I had a discussion with the young cameraman, John Leonetti, and I said, "This has to look like a documentary." I don't want anyone coming away and saying, "This is brilliantly composed." I want people to look at this movie and say, "My God, this is a newsreel."[15]

And to enhance this quality further, Frankenheimer had his editor Lee Percy refrain from using fades, dissolves and other transitional cutting techniques.

The film is not without its expressive aspects, though. After the uprising, the director uses long takes and point of view shots to follow the movements of characters like Chaka and Jamaal as they roam the yard. This fluid camerawork not only lends the sequences momentum, but also underscores the fact that these men, who for years have been locked up and shackled, now have the ability to move freely. Many of the director's favorite themes materialize, too. Much as he does in *The Island of Dr. Moreau*, he uses the film to focus on the violent consequences that can follow when one group uses force to subdue and dominate another. He also emphasizes the similarities that can exist between opponents and enemies, a theme he explores in *The Train*, as well as *Black Sunday*. At first, when the prisoners assume control over the guards, they display the same vindictiveness and meanness of spirit which was shown to them when they were captives. The suffering they've experienced, it seems, has done nothing to dissuade them from acting cruelly themselves. To the contrary, their experiences have created an appetite for revenge, which they, in their newly acquired positions of power, have the freedom to satisfy.

Frankenheimer's film was not the first television drama based on the Attica disaster. In 1980, ABC broadcast a similar re-creation of the five-day standoff, titled simply *Attica*. Interestingly, this picture won an Emmy for its director Marvin Chomsky in the Outstanding Direction in a Limited Series or Special category—the same award Frankenheimer won for *Against the Wall* in 1994. And while the two features share much in common, as they both strive for documentary realism, use ensemble casts, and emphasize the legitimacy of the inmates' demands, if not their methods, the latter picture offers richer depictions of its protagonists, providing viewers with information about their interests, their objectives and their motives, as well as tracking the ways in which the events which precede and follow the uprising shape and alter these people's personalities.[16]

This is especially apparent in Frankenheimer's treatment of the Michael Smith character, whose personality continually evolves as the narrative progresses. We learn early on, for example, that this young man doesn't enjoy the idea of becoming a guard, but because he is poor and his wife is pregnant, he must. And after making this decision, changes in his manner and his conduct quickly follow. Not only does he transform his appearance (shedding his long hair and, perhaps, the anti-establishment sympathies it symbolizes), he quickly embraces the outlook of the other officers at The Factory, allowing himself to regard the prisoners as something less than human, treating them with unnecessary force as he obeys the orders of his supervisors, even if they disagree with his morals. "You're changing!" his wife Sharon (Anne Heche) tells him at one point, with a mixture of sorrow and contempt. But Smith's willingness to follow orders vanishes after the inmates take the prison, after they beat him up in the metal shop he supervises. When they tell him to defecate in front of the other guards, he refuses. When the guards tell him to humiliate himself in order to receive a pair of shoes from the inmates, he refuses, too. And while he never offers an explicit explanation for these actions, he hints to Jamaal, after the news conference, that he cares more about his dignity than the approval or disapproval he receives from others, an attitude he didn't have (or wasn't willing to reveal) prior to the crisis and the anguish he's experienced.

Andersonville (1996)

In the spring of 1994, just before he left for Mexico to shoot *The Burning Season*, Frankenheimer was asked by his friend Ethel Winant, an executive at the TNT cable television network, if he'd like to helm a film about Camp Sumter, a Civil War prison in Andersonville, Georgia, where several thousand Union soldiers died. The director was averse to the idea at first, having just finished *Against the Wall*. "'Do I want to shoot another prison picture?' he asked himself. 'That's all I need: I'd be remembered for the three A's and three ages of prison movies: Alcatraz, Attica, Andersonville.'" Winant nevertheless remained enthusiastic about Frankenheimer's involvement. "She wouldn't take no for an answer. She called, came to see me, nagged and eventually prevailed." But Winant's persistence alone did not sway him. Rather, it was her willingness to meet several of his requests, giving him, for instance, a 60-day shooting schedule, an unusually long stretch of time for a television production, but which he thought was "the bare minimum for adequate coverage" of a subject as grim as the one they hoped to bring to the screen.[17]

Frankenheimer got to work on the Andersonville project in the summer of 1994, spending several months shaping and enhancing the movie's narrative with the writer David Rintels (who'd already spent almost three years researching and working on its script). He cast his actors, as well, recruiting several people he'd collaborated with previously, such as Frederick Forrest and Carmen Argenziano, while giving one of the film's central parts, the role of the young soldier Josiah Day, to Jarrod Emick, a Broadway actor who'd never before appeared in a major movie. And just as he had on *Against the Wall*, Frankenheimer insisted upon making the film's sets look as authentic as possible. To do this, he had the picture's production designer Michael Hanan and a crew of construction workers build "a full scale model" of the prison over a 15 acre plot of land outside Atlanta, "using numerous old photographs [of the original site] as a guide."[18] The film opens in June 1864, as a platoon of Union soldiers (Company 1 of the 19th Massachusetts Volunteers) are captured by Confederate forces in the Virginia woods and transported by train to a massive, open-air stockade in southwest Georgia. Bewildered, as much by the filth of the prison yard as the tremendous number of detainees it holds, the soldiers are quickly set upon by a gang of thugs called the Raiders, who hope to separate them from one another in order to attack and rob them of their valuables. Fortunately, a watchful prisoner intervenes, steering the new arrivals away from the bandits. The rescuer, it turns out, is a man named Dick (Gregory Sporleder), a member of Company 1; but because he is emaciated, bearded and covered in dirt, he is not recognized at first by his comrades. He then tells them his story, that he was injured in battle, captured and brought to Andersonville several months earlier. And now, with the knowledge he's acquired, he wants to help his friends survive their time in the camp, providing them with information about which people to avoid and how to stay healthy. Dick also introduces the men to a group of Pennsylvania soldiers who are digging an escape tunnel, and wanting to help, the Company 1 soldiers, led by a corporal named Josiah Day (Emick), ask to join in the dangerous work. As the men toil, they make progress; but they are interrupted when the Raiders stage a violent attack, resulting in many injuries and the death of Dick.

Outraged by this, a pair of soldiers from Company 1 named Limber Jim (Peter Murnik) and Tobias (Andrew Kevorit) begin to talk about plans for retaliation, but they are discouraged by Willens (Charles Lawlor), one of the Pennsylvania men, who tells them that such an effort might compromise their ability to finish the tunnel. Sadly, however, when the diggers attempt their escape a short time later, some are killed and the rest are captured, including Josiah and the Company's crippled sergeant, McSpadden (Frederic Forrest), who was severely injured on the battlefield early in the film. The survivors of the failed run are then placed in the stocks that have been built outside the prison by the camp's commandant, Captain Wirz (Jan Triska), who keeps them there exposed to the elements for several days before he lets them go. Several weeks then pass and, one day, as new prisoners arrive, the Raiders come to take their things. But this time, Limber Jim intervenes. Instead of steering the new men away, though, he rallies his friends and they rise up against the villains, subduing them.

A kangaroo trial follows in which the prisoners try the Raiders, convict several of them of murder and then hang them. More time passes and as the conditions grow worse, several Union soldiers, drawn by the promise of rations and freedom, agree to join the Confederate army. The men in Company 1 hold out, however, and as the film approaches its conclusion, it seems as though their patience and fortitude will be rewarded, as Wirz tells them that a prisoner exchange has been organized, and they will be returned to the North. Franken-

A scene from the trial of the Raiders in *Andersonville* (Turner Pictures, 1995).

heimer then uses a series of panning and tracking shots that follow the men as they leave, which he follows with a pull away shot, revealing a field that is dotted with hundreds, perhaps thousands of marble headstones, a solemn reminder of the tremendous number of men who lost their lives at the camp.

TNT first broadcast *Andersonville* over two nights in March 1996, almost a year after Frankenheimer and the film's editor Paul Rubell completed the film. Thanks to heavy promotion, the movie drew high ratings, as well as a great deal of advance coverage in the press. The reviews which appeared, however, were for the most part mixed, as many critics found much to praise in the film's visual authenticity, its emphasis upon recreating the look — and the horrors— of Andersonville, but found fault in its plot, complaining that the narrative moved too slowly and its protagonists, as well as the predicaments they find themselves in, were overly familiar. Tony Scott at *Variety*, for example, wrote: "Some of *Andersonville* plays like old-hat World War II movies or *The Great Escape*."[19] Caryn James complained: "Despite the Civil War surroundings, we've seen too much of this before, in everything from 1930's gangster films to *Stalag 17*.... [T]he script lets [the director] down with one-dimensional characters."[20] Woody West at *The Washington Times*, in contrast, described the picture as "an excellent piece of television." At the same time, he felt that Frankenheimer failed to provide viewers with an adequate understanding of why the events which appear on the screen happened. "[T]he drama occurs in something of a vacuum," he argued. And he went on to suggest that the film would have been greatly served if it opened with a series of explanatory titles.[21]

Andersonville is the weakest of the cable movies, an exceedingly long (and heavy-handed) critique of barbarism and administrative ineptitude, shot through with a cloying sentimentality, as Frankenheimer devotes much too much screen time emphasizing the friendship and love which grow between the men of Company 1 as they endure their time in the prison. It's possible that these critiques might be more penetrating and his efforts to celebrate the good soldiers more palatable, if he had provided a better historical context for the film, as West suggested, perhaps telling us more about the origins of Camp Sumter, for instance, as well as the Confederacy's reasoning for allowing the camp's inmates to suffer as they did and its refusal to conduct prisoner exchanges.

Frankenheimer, however, was not particularly interested in creating an educational resource for students of the Civil War. Rather, he sought to make a film that would arouse his audience's interest and move their hearts, the objectives of all good storytelling. When David Rintel's screenplay was published by Louisiana State University Press in 1996, for instance, the director explained in the Foreword that: "David said to me during the production that he didn't want to sacrifice history to drama and I, as a director, had to respect that; nevertheless, drama is my business and I tried to build it wherever I could find it."[22]

We should note that Frankenheimer does provide some historical information about the camp and its inmates. But this material appears in the film's closing moments, with series of titles that appear on screen. We learn, for example, that "In 1864-65, more than 45,000 Union soldiers were imprisoned in Andersonville. 12,912 died there." Another tells us: "The prisoner exchange never happened. The men who walked to the trains were taken to other prisons, where they remained until the war ended." And then a final title flashes on the screen, letting us know that the man who perpetrated this deception, the camp's commander, was punished severely for treating so many people so badly: "After the war," we read, "Wirz was hanged, the only soldier to be tried and executed for war crimes committed during the Civil War."

Andersonville is unusual in Frankenheimer canon as it is the director's only costume drama, a period piece set long ago. But it is still very much one of his films. The director's taste for naturalistic, documentary-like photography reveals itself often, as he fills the screen with long, unbroken tracking shots that rake the prison yard, showing us the miserable captives as they eat, dance, fight and die. And again we find, as we do in *The Train*, a situation where men living under authoritarian conditions come together, as their suffering imbues them with a sense of both solidarity and purpose, giving their lives worth and meaning. And as we find in *Against the Wall*, *The Iceman Cometh* and *Path to War*, the film features an ensemble cast. But unfortunately the dramatis personae generally lack the complexity and the contradictory traits which usually distinguish the director's protagonists and antagonists elsewhere. For example, the men who make up the Massachusetts Volunteers all seem to possess

Frankenheimer on the set of *Andersonville* with actor Robert David Hall (Turner Pictures, 1995).

sterling characters, committed as they are to helping one another, while their enemies, the Raiders, are presented as bestial types, completely selfish and completely repellant.

But there is one character in the film who stands out, and this is Wirz. With his German-Swiss accent, his vitriolic manner and his injured arm which hangs across his chest in a sling, the captain is at once threatening and preposterous, vaguely reminiscent, perhaps, of Col. Saito (Sessue Hayakawa), the Japanese commandant who oversees the prison camp in Lean's *The Bridge on the River Kwai* (1957). And though Wirz may be, as West described him, "a sociopath — or in terms now archaic, evil — who is unmoved by the cruel captivity, degradation and deaths of those in his charge," he is perhaps pitiable, too, as much a captive of Andersonville as his prisoners and, just like these men, an anguished soul. As Mel Gussow suggested: "[T]here are moments ... when it seems as if Wirz hates himself, or at least is trapped in a hopeless situation."[23] But the captain is just one character amidst thousands, and his appearances, while memorable, are too brief and too infrequent, and in the end, Frankenheimer's Civil War story drags, a dull, message movie which never manages to transcend its well-meaning intentions.

Appendix:
Two Short Films

"Maniac at Large" (1992)

In 1992, a cable television producer named Gilbert Adler asked Frankenheimer if he'd like to direct an episode of *Tales from the Crypt*, HBO's popular
anthology series. The idea of returning to television did not appeal to Frankenheimer at first. The pay Adler was offering was not great and the production's
budget would be low. But he nevertheless accepted because he needed work,
thanks to the commercial failure of the last three films he'd made, *Dead Bang*,
The Fourth War and *Year of the Gun*. The opportunity of shooting a television
program on film, something he'd never had a chance to do during his days as
a live director at CBS and NBC, interested him, as well.[1]

Titled "Maniac at Large," the program is set in a public library. Its narrative centers around a character named Margaret (Blythe Danner), a clerk whose
inability to cope with stress leads to trouble for her co-workers. As the show
opens, all seems to be normal and safe at Margaret's library. A tranquil light
streams through the windows, people sit at desks quietly reading and a watchful security guard (Clarence Williams III) stands near some bookshelves. But
then the camera drifts over to the front page of a newspaper. "Maniac at Large!"
a headline shouts. The announcement upsets Margaret when she picks up the
paper and the subsequent discovery of a switchblade knife on one of the tables
in the reading room leaves her feeling worse. Can it be that the killer is in the
library? The mousy clerk's anxiety only increases as the day progresses. Anyone, it seems, might be the killer. One of the patrons (Adam Ant) frightens her
when he enthusiastically suggests that the next victim will be a woman. Another
patron attacks a book — a collection of nude photographs— with a knife. Another
screams at her, rattling the doors to get into the library, after the building is

OUTRAGEOUS 1950s EC COMICS!

CRIME

NO. 27
MAY

2⁵⁰
4⁰⁰ CANADA

SuspenStories

CRIME

JOLTING TALES OF
TENSION
IN THE
EC TRADITION!

closed for the night. Worked into a frenzy by the end of the shift, Margaret arouses the pity of her boss Mrs. Pritchard (Salome Jens), who invites the harried woman up to her office in order to calm her down. Mrs. Pritchard's efforts only agitate her, though, and the clerk, grabbing the switchblade she found earlier in the day, proceeds to stab her boss to death. Margaret, it turns out, is the maniac at large.

Frankenheimer and his crew had just four days to shoot the show, but the finished product nevertheless displays a great deal of technical virtuosity and stylistic flare, thanks to the director's meticulous, pre-production planning of his shots and the skill of cameraman John Leonetti, who would collaborate again with Frankenheimer on *Against the Wall* and *The Burning Season.* Throughout this little film, Leonetti's camera moves frequently, gliding restlessly over the library's walls and its floors and patrons, stopping only now and then to focus on some sinister image, like the damaged pages of the erotic book Margaret finds in the library's basement or Mrs. Pritchard's bloody corpse. The camera's frantic movement, of course, correlates with the clerk's agitated state of mind, showing us the world as she sees it. To make the picture more unsettling, the filmmakers also use pitched camera angles and expressive, chiaroscuro lighting, a strategy that lends sections of "Maniac at Large" the same distorted look that characterizes early German horror films like Murnau's *Nosferatu* (1922) and Leni's *Waxworks* (1924), as well as Lang's *M* (1931), which also focuses on a murderer's anguished personality.

And while the film's expressionistic shooting style arguably separates it from much of the director's later work, at the same time, the picture is guided by one of his favorite themes, the discrepancy between appearances and reality and the harm this phenomenon can have upon people. In many of the movies which address this topic — pictures like *I Walk the Line, Black Sunday* and *Reindeer Games*— the protagonists are duped by liars and schemers who exploit their ignorance, their goodwill or their trust. Alma plays on the sheriff's heart strings in order to protect her father's still. Landers tricks his colleagues into letting him fly the blimp during the Super Bowl game. Ashley convinces Rudy that she loves him. But no one beguiles or deceives Margaret. Her bewilderment arises from within, a symptom of mental illness. Not only is she afflicted with a variety of amnesia that forces her to forget the role she's played in the murders of her victims, but also, like the protagonist in Hitchcock's *Suspicion* (1941), she suffers from an overactive imagination, finding dangers where none exist. These misperceptions, in turn, ratchet up her anxiety, eventually trigger-

Opposite: The story upon which "Maniac at Large" (HBO, 1992) is based first appeared in the February-March 1955 issue of *Crime SuspenStories*, an illustrated magazine published by Entertaining Comics. The story was featured on the magazine's cover. In 1999, Gemstone Publishing reprinted the issue, the source for this image.

ing her final, violent outburst. "I don't like being afraid all the time," she says to Mrs. Pritchard after she kills her.

Frankenheimer told Pratley that he regarded "Maniac at Large" as an example of an "Edgar Allan Poe story."[2] The tale which appeared originally appeared *Crime SuspenStories*, however, was written for the magazine (by an uncredited writer), not Poe. Yet the influence of the great author is nonetheless pronounced — on both the comic story and its adaptation — particularly when we consider stories like "The Black Cat" and "The Tell-Tale Heart," which similarly feature protagonists who become killers when their anxiety gets the best of them. Frankenheimer's film may bring another of Poe's works to mind, as well, the mystery story titled "The Purloined Letter," in which a thief conceals a letter by setting it "beneath the nose of the whole world" instead of stashing it in some hiding place. Like the thief, Frankenheimer sets the real maniac beneath our noses; and from the film's opening moments all the way up to the climax, he encourages us to look for the killer elsewhere, tricking us with red herrings like the crazy patron who bangs on the doors, the other who enjoys talking about serial killers and the pervert in the basement with the knife. The film prevents us from seeing things as they are, in other words, and suggests perhaps that we share more in common with the poor, insane woman than we might think.

"Ambush" (2001)

In 2000, BMW asked Anonymous Content, a production company that specializes in online advertising, to create a series of short action-adventure films about a professional driver who carries his clients around in a BMW sports car. The producers originally planned five films for *The Hire*, as the project came to be titled, and drafted five directors to shoot them — Ang Lee, Won Kar-Wai, Guy Pierce, Alejandro Gonzales Inarittu and Frankenheimer.[3]

Frankenheimer was asked to work on the series because the chase scenes he'd shot for *Ronin* had impressed the project's producers. Wanting the director to do for BMW what he'd done for Mercedes-Benz in the earlier picture, they asked him to emphasize the prowess of their automobiles and their ability to perform well under great physical strain. They spared no expense, providing him a generous budget, a comfortable 10-day shooting schedule and several BMWs which he was allowed to damage and destroy as he saw fit.[4]

On April 26, 2001, *The Hire* had its internet debut, and met with instant success, drawing more than 100,000 viewers in the first two days of its run.[5] Media and film critics responded to the campaign with interest, too. Elvis Mitchell at *The New York Times*, for example, declared: "The BMW films tingle with zest in a way that car ads don't anymore."[6]

Frankenheimer's contribution to the series, a six-minute piece titled

"Ambush" may be the best of the lot. Written by Andrew Kevin Walker, the story opens *in medias res*, with the unnamed central character (Clive Owen) and his passenger (Tomas Milian) shooting along a dark road in a black sedan. A van rolls up beside the car and a masked man (Franklin Jones), leaning from the passenger window, aims a pistol at the driver and explains that the character played by Milian is "carrying two million dollars in stolen, uncut diamonds."

If the driver wants to avoid trouble, the man in the mask says, he'd better pull over. The terrified passenger pleads with the driver, however, explaining that he has swallowed the diamonds. "They will cut me wide open!" he cries. The appeal works and the driver decides to escape rather than cooperate. He speeds up, slows down and swerves in and out of oncoming traffic as the gunmen in the van fire at him. Then he turns off the main road onto another road which is unlighted and finds an area where construction equipment is stored. There, he tucks his car behind a bulldozer.

A moment later, the van, racing at full speed, enters the area, crashes into one of the heavy machines and explodes. The film then cuts to the Diamond District in downtown Los Angeles. As the driver drops off his charge, he asks him, "Tell me, what you said about swallowing the diamonds, was it true?" Instead of answering, the client chuckles mischievously. As he wanders off toward a jewelry store, the driver rolls away in his heavily damaged car.

"Ambush" may be little more than a long commercial, but Frankenheimer was given a great deal of creative legroom as he shot it, and the picture exhibits many of the stylistic traits we find in his feature films, including the use of a desaturated color scheme, wide depth of field, location photography and several close up shots of the principals' tense faces. The director's almost obsessive interest in achieving authenticity surfaces in "Ambush," too, and rather than building the film's chase sequence with process shots and computer generated images, he used real cars and stunt drivers and real crashes and explosions. To further enhance the sense of immediacy — and the viewer's emotional response — he mounted cameras to the vehicles, as well, just as he'd done in both *Ronin* and *Grand Prix*.[7]

Some of Frankenheimer's favorite motifs show up in "Ambush," too. Each of the film's three main characters, for instance, employ disguises and deception of some sort. The passenger tricks the driver by telling him that he's swallowed the jewels. The driver uses the lack of light in the construction area to camouflage his darkly colored car. The gunman and his associates, much like the blackmailers in *52 Pick-Up* and the members of the Red Brigades in *Year of the Gun*, all wear ski masks to hide their faces. Seeing things as they are can be difficult, the director again reminds us, if not impossible.

Frankenheimer also calls into question the moral distance between the film's heroes and heavies, much as he does in *The Train*, *French Connection II* and *Ronin*. Clive Owen's character is primarily a mercenary, a person who offers his services to any customer who is willing to pay him what he asks. He may have a streak of good in him. He eventually decides to help the passenger. At the same time, the passenger is a jewel thief. Moreover, saving him threatens the safety of other, innocent drivers on the road. Reading the gunmen proves to be difficult, as well. They may fire upon the driver and pursue him, but they are trying to recover jewels which have been stolen from them. They are violent men, certainly. Their leader speaks in a sinister manner, too. And thus it seems likely that they are professional criminals of some sort. But can we be sure? After all, they might be like Kabokov and his men in *Black Sunday*, a coterie of foreign agents who do not feel the need to abide by the laws of other countries as they pursue a suspect. It seems unlikely, perhaps, but we can't eliminate the possibility completely. The truth of who these men are is as concealed from us as their faces.

Filmography

The Young Stranger—1957 (83 minutes)

PRODUCER: Stuart Millar, R.K.O.
SCRIPT: Robert Dozier, from his teleplay "Deal a Blow"
PHOTOGRAPHY (B & W): Robert Planck
EDITOR: Robert Swink, Edward Biery, Jr.
MUSIC: Leonard Rosenman
CAST: James MacArthur (Hal Ditmar), Kim Hunter (Helen Ditmar), James Daly (Tom Ditmar), James Gregory (Shipley), Whit Bissell (Grubbs), Jeff Silver (Jerry), Eddie Ryder (Man in Theater)
SUMMARY: A teenaged boy runs afoul of the police and his family after defending himself against a bullying movie theater manager.
RELEASE: March, Universal
AVAILABILITY: LD

The Young Savages—1961 (100 minutes)

PRODUCER: Pat Duggan, a Harold Hecht Production, Contemporary Productions
SCRIPT: Edward Anhalt, J. P. Miller, from Evan Hunter's *A Matter of Conviction*
PHOTOGRAPHY (B & W): Lionel Lindon
EDITOR: Eda Warren
MUSIC: David Amram
CAST: Burt Lancaster (Hank Bell), Dina Merrill (Karin Bell), Shelley Winters (Mary Di Pace), Telly Savalas (Gunnison), Stanley Kristien (Danny Di Pace), John Davis Chandler (Arthur Reardon), Neil Nephew (Anthony), Jose Perez (Roberto), Vivian Nathan (Mrs. Escalante), Pilar Seurat (Louisa), Edward Andrews (District Attorney Cole)
SUMMARY: A murder investigation prompts a New York City prosecutor to reconsider his views about class identity and prejudice.
RELEASE: May, UA
AVAILABILITY: VHS, LD

All Fall Down—1962 (111 minutes)

PRODUCER: John Houseman, John Houseman Productions
SCRIPT: William Inge, from James Leo Herlihy's novel.

PHOTOGRAPHY (B & W): Lionel Lindon
EDITOR: Fredric Steinkamp
MUSIC: Alex North
CAST: Warren Beatty (Berry-Berry), Brandon De Wilde (Clinton), Eva Marie Saint (Echo), Angela Lansbury (Annabell), Karl Malden (Ralph)
SUMMARY: After returning to his home in Cleveland, a gigolo impregnates and abandons his girlfriend. She then dies, breaking the young man's heart.
RELEASE: March, MGM
AVAILABILITY: VHS

Bird Man of Alcatraz — 1962 (147 mins)

PRODUCER: Stuart Millar, Guy Trosper, Norma Productions
SCRIPT: Guy Trosper, from Thomas Gaddis' *Birdman of Alcatraz*
PHOTOGRAPHY (B & W): Burnett Guffey
EDITOR: Edward Mann
MUSIC: Elmer Bernstein
CAST: Burt Lancaster (Robert E. Stroud), Telly Savalas (Feto Gomez), Thelma Ritter (Elizabeth Stroud), Karl Malden (Harvey Shoemaker), Whit Bissell (Dr. Ellis), Betty Field (Stella Johnson), Neville Brand (Bull Ransom), Edmond O'Brien (Tom Gaddis)
SUMMARY: While serving out his sentence in solitary confinement, a murderer becomes an expert on bird diseases.
RELEASE: July, UA
AVAILABILITY: VHS, LD, DVD

The Manchurian Candidate — 1962 (126 mins)

PRODUCER: George Axelrod, John Frankenheimer, Frank Sinatra, M.C. Productions
SCRIPT: George Axelrod, from Richard Condon's novel
PHOTOGRAPHY (B & W): Lionel Lindon
EDITOR: Ferris Webster
MUSIC: David Amram
CAST: Laurence Harvey (Raymond Shaw), Frank Sinatra (Marco), Angela Lansbury (Mrs. Iselin), James Gregory (Senator Iselin), Yen Lo (Khigh Dhiegh), Henry Silva (Chunjin), Janet Leigh (Rosie), John McGiver (Senator Jordan), Leslie Parrish (Jocie Jordan)
SUMMARY: Psychiatrists working for Red China and the Soviet Union capture and brainwash a young American solider, turning him into an assassin.
RELEASE: October, UA
AVAILABILITY: VHS, LD, DVD

Seven Days in May — 1964 (120 mins)

PRODUCER: Edward Lewis, Seven Arts Productions, Joel Productions, A John Frankenheimer Production
SCRIPT: Rod Serling, from Fletcher Knebel and Charles W. Bailey's novel
PHOTOGRAPHY (B & W): Ellsworth Fredericks
EDITOR: Ferris Webster
MUSIC: Jerry Goldsmith

CAST: Burt Lancaster (Scott), Kirk Douglas (Jiggs Casey), Fredric March (Lyman), Ava Gardner (Eleanor), Edmond O'Brien (Senator Clark), Martin Balsam (Paul Girard), George Macready (Christopher Todd), Whit Bissell (Senator Prentice), John Houseman (Admiral Barnswell), Andrew Duggan (Mutt Henderson)
SUMMARY: A coup is thwarted when an Army general's assistant learns about the plot and brings it to the attention of the sitting president.
RELEASE: February, Paramount
AVAILABILITY: VHS, LD, DVD

The Train—1965 (133 mins)

PRODUCER: Jules Bricken, Les Productions Artistes Associes
SCRIPT: Franklin Coen (credited), Frank Davis (credited), Walter Bernstein (uncredited), Ned Young (uncredited), Howard Dimsdale (uncredited), from Rose Valland's *Le front de l'art: defense de collections francaises 1939-1945*
PHOTOGRAPHY (B & W): Jean Tournier, Walter Wottitz
EDITOR: David Bretherton.
MUSIC: Maurice Jarre
CAST: Burt Lancaster (Labiche), Paul Scofield (von Waldheim), Jeanne Moreau (Christine), Suzanne Flon (Miss Villard), Michel Simon (Papa Boule), Wolfgang Preiss (Herren), Albert Rémy (Didont).
SUMMARY: French Resistance fighters prevent Nazi soldiers from looting an art museum.
RELEASE: March, UA
AVAILABILITY: VHS, LD, DVD

Seconds—1966 (106 mins)

PRODUCER: Edward Lewis, Douglas & Lewis Productions
SCRIPT: Lewis John Carlino, from David Ely's novel
PHOTOGRAPHY (B & W): James Wong Howe
EDITOR: Ferris Webster, David Webster
MUSIC: Jerry Goldsmith
CAST: Rock Hudson (Tony Wilson), John Randolph (Arthur Hamilton), Salome Jens (Nora), Will Geer (Old Man), Jeff Corey (Mr. Ruby), Richard Anderson (Dr. Innes), Murray Hamilton (Charlie), Wesley Addison (John)
SUMMARY: Problems develop after a businessman undergoes plastic surgery and assumes a new identity.
RELEASE: September, Paramount
AVAILABILITY: VHS, LD, DVD

Grand Prix—1966 (179 mins)

PRODUCER: Edward Lewis, Joel Productions, A Douglas & Lewis Production
SCRIPT: Robert Alan Aurthur (credited), William Hanley (uncredited)
PHOTOGRAPHY (COLOR): Lionel Lindon.
EDITOR: Henry Berman
MUSIC: Maurice Jarre
CAST: James Garner (Pete Aron), Yves Montand (Jean-Pierre Sarti), Toshiro Mifune (Izo Yamura), Brian Bedford (Scott Stoddard), Eva Marie Saint (Louise Frederickson), Jessica Walter (Pat), Antonio Sabato (Nino Barlini), Françoise Hardy (Lisa), Genevieve Page (Mme Sarti)

SUMMARY: Formula One drivers experience danger and romance as they compete in races around the world.
RELEASE: December, MGM
AVAILABILITY: VHS, DVD

The Fixer—1968 (132 mins)

PRODUCER: Edward Lewis, A John Frankenheimer-Edward Lewis Production
SCRIPT: Dalton Trumbo, from Bernard Malamud's novel
PHOTOGRAPHY (COLOR): Marcel Grignon
EDITOR: Henry Berman
MUSIC: Maurice Jarre
CAST: Alan Bates (Yakov Bok), Dirk Bogarde (Bibikov), Ian Holm (Grubeshov), David Warner (Count Odoevsky), Hugh Griffith (Lebedev), Elizabeth Hartman (Zinaida), Georgia Brown (Marfa)
SUMMARY: A Jewish handyman wins international sympathy after he is imprisoned for a murder he did not commit.
RELEASE: December, MGM
AVAILABILITY: VHS

The Extraordinary Seaman—1969 (79 mins)

PRODUCER: Edward Lewis, John H. Cushingham, John Frankenheimer Productions
SCRIPT: Phillip Rock, Hal Dresner, based on Rock's novel
PHOTOGRAPHY (COLOR): Lionel Lindon
EDITOR: Fredric Steinkemp
MUSIC: Maurice Jarre
CAST: David Niven (Finchhaven), Faye Dunaway (Mrs. Winslow) Alan Alda (Krim), Mickey Rooney (Oglethorpe), Jack Carter (Toole)
SUMMARY: In the final weeks of World War II, a group of shipwrecked sailors discovers a boat which is captained by a ghost.
RELEASE: January, MGM
RATING: G

The Gypsy Moths—1969 (106 mins)

PRODUCER: Hal Landers, Bobby Roberts, A John Frankenheimer-Edward Lewis Production
SCRIPT: William Hanley, from James Drought's novel
PHOTOGRAPHY (COLOR): Phillip Lathrop
EDITOR: Henry Berman
MUSIC: Elmer Bernstein
CAST: Burt Lancaster (Rettig), Gene Hackman (Browdy), Scott Wilson (Malcolm), Deborah Kerr (Elizabeth Brandon), William Windom (Allen Brandon), Bonnie Bedelia (Annie), Sheree North (Waitress)
SUMMARY: Film charts the hours leading up to and following a professional skydiver's death in a Kansas town.
RELEASE: August, MGM
AVAILABILITY: DVD
RATING: M

I Walk the Line—1970 (96 mins)

PRODUCER: Harold D. Cohen, John Frankenheimer Productions / An Edward Lewis Production
SCRIPT: Alvin Sargent, from Madison Jones' *An Exile*
PHOTOGRAPHY (COLOR): David M. Walsh
EDITOR: Harold F. Kress
MUSIC: Johnny Cash
CAST: Gregory Peck (Tawes), Tuesday Weld (Alma), Ralph Meeker (McCain), Estelle Parsons (Ellen-Haney), Lonny Chapman (Bascomb), Charles Durning (Hunnicutt)
SUMMARY: A middle-aged sheriff falls in love with the teenaged daughter of moonshiner.
RELEASE: October, Columbia
AVAILABILITY: DVD
RATING: GP

The Horsemen—1971 (110 mins)

PRODUCER: Edward Lewis, A John Frankenheimer-Edward Lewis Production
SCRIPT: Dalton Trumbo, from Joseph Kessel's novel
PHOTOGRAPHY (COLOR): Claude Renoir
EDITOR: Harold F. Kress
MUSIC: Georges Delerue
CAST: Omar Sharif (Uraz), Jack Palance (Tursen), Leigh Taylor-Young (Zereh), David De (Mukhi), Peter Jeffrey (Hayatal)
SUMMARY: After injuring his leg in a sporting match, a young man struggles through a mountain pass to return to his father's home.
RELEASE: June, Columbia
AVAILABILITY: VHS, DVD
RATING: GP

Impossible Object—1972 (110 mins)

PRODUCER: Robert Bradford, A Franco-London Film-Euro International Production
SCRIPT: Nicolas Mosley, from his novel
PHOTOGRAPHY (COLOR): Claude Renoir
EDITOR: Albert Jurgenson
MUSIC: Michel Legrand
CAST: Alan Bates (Harry), Dominique Sanda (Natalie), Evans Evans (Elizabeth), Laurence De Monaghan (Cleo), Michel Auclair (Georges)
SUMMARY: A writer leaves his wife for a French woman and moves to Morocco, where the child they have together drowns.
RELEASE: Screened at Cannes May 14, 1973; released theatrically in Spain by Izaro Films in 1978.
AVAILABILITY: VHS, as *Story of a Love Story*

The Iceman Cometh—1973 (239 mins)

PRODUCER: Ely Landau, The American Film Theatre
SCRIPT: Thomas Quinn Curtiss, from Eugene O'Neill's play

PHOTOGRAPHY (COLOR): Ralph Woolsey
EDITOR: Harold Kress
CAST: Lee Marvin (Hickey), Fredric March (Harry Hope), Robert Ryan (Larry Slade), Evans Evans (Cora), Nancy Dawson (Pearl), Hildy Brooks (Margie), Bradford Dillman (Willie Oban), Jeff Bridges (Don Parritt), Sorrell Brooks (Hugo), Tom Pedi (Rocky), Stephen Pearlman (Chuck)
SUMMARY: A hardware salesman upsets his friends, a group of alcoholics, when he tells them to embrace reality and forgo their dreams and fantasies.
RELEASE: October, American Express and The American Film Theatre
AVAILABILITY: DVD
RATING: PG

99 and 44/100% Dead! — 1974 (97 mins)

PRODUCER: Joe Wizan, 20th Century–Fox
SCRIPT: Robert Dillon
PHOTOGRAPHY: Ralph Woolsey
EDITOR: Harold F. Kress
MUSIC: Henry Mancini
CAST: Richard Harris (Harry Crown), Edmond O'Brien (Uncle Frank), Bradford Dillman (Big Eddie), Ann Turkel (Buffy), Catherine Baumann (Baby), Chuck Connors (Marvin "Claw" Zuckerman), David Hall (Tony)
SUMMARY: A hitman comes to the aid of a mobster friend.
RELEASE: June, 20th Century-Fox
AVAILABILITY: VHS
RATING: PG

French Connection II — 1975 (118 mins)

PRODUCER: Robert L. Rosen, 20th Century-Fox
SCRIPT: Robert Dillon, Laurie Dillon, Alexander Jacobs, Pete Hamill (uncredited)
PHOTOGRAPHY (COLOR): Claude Renoir
EDITOR: Tom Rolf
MUSIC: Don Ellis
CAST: Gene Hackman (Popeye Doyle), Fernando Rey (Charnier), Bernard Fresson (Barthelemy), Philippe Leotard (Jacques), Jean-Pierre Castaldi (Raoul), Cathleen Nesbitt (Old Lady), Ed Lauter (General), André Penvern (bartender)
SUMMARY: A New York City detective travels to Marseilles to find a drug kingpin.
RELEASE: May, 20th Century-Fox
AVAILABILITY: VHS, LD, DVD
RATING: R

Black Sunday — 1977 (143 mins)

PRODUCER: Robert Evans, Paramount
SCRIPT: Ernest Lehman, Kenneth Ross, Ivan Moffat, from Thomas Harris's novel
PHOTOGRAPHY (COLOR): John A. Alonzo
EDITOR: Tom Rolf
MUSIC: John Williams
CAST: Robert Shaw (Kabakov), Bruce Dern (Lander), Marthe Keller (Dahlia), Fritz Weaver (Corley), Steve Keats (Moshevsky), Bekim Fehmiu (Fasil), Michael V. Gazzo (Muzi)

SUMMARY: An Israeli commando discovers a terrorist plot to sabotage the Super Bowl with a blimp.
RELEASE: March, Paramount
AVAILABILITY: VHS, DVD, LD
RATING: R

Prophecy—1979 (102 mins)

PRODUCER: Robert L. Rosen, Paramount
SCRIPT: David Seltzer
PHOTOGRAPHY (COLOR): Harry Stradling, Jr.
EDITOR: Tom Rolf
MUSIC: Leonard Rosenman
CAST: Talia Shire (Maggie), Robert Foxworth (Verne), Armand Assante (Hawks), Victoria Racimo (Ramona), George Clutesi (M'Rai), Richard Dysart (Isely), Evans Evans (Cellist).
SUMMARY: A monstrous bear, poisoned by water pollution, attacks human beings in Maine.
RELEASE: June, Paramount
AVAILABILITY: VHS, DVD
RATING: PG

The Challenge—1982 (106 mins)

PRODUCER: Robert L. Rosen and Ron Beckman, CBS Theatrical Films
SCRIPT: Richard Maxwell (credited), John Sayles (credited), Ivan Moffat (uncredited)
PHOTOGRAPHY (COLOR): Kozo Okazaki
EDITOR: John W. Wheeler
MUSIC: Jerry Goldsmith
CAST: Scott Glenn (Rick), Toshiro Mifune (Toru), Donna Kei Benz (Akiko) Atsuo Nakamura (Hideo), Calvin Jung Go (Ando), Kenta Fukasaku (Jiro)
SUMMARY: An ex-boxer aids an aging martial arts teacher as he attempts to recover a stolen sword.
RELEASE: July, Embassy
AVAILABILITY: VHS
RATING: R

The Holcroft Covenant—1985 (112 mins)

PRODUCER: Edie Landau, Ely Landau, Thorn EMI
SCRIPT: George Axelrod, Edward Anhalt, John Hopkins, from Robert Ludlum's novel
Photography (color, b&w): Gerry Fisher
EDITOR: Ralph Sheldon
MUSIC: Stanislas
CAST: Michael Caine (Noel Holcroft), Anthony Andrews (Johann), Victoria Tennant (Helden), Lilli Palmer (Althene Holcroft), Mario Adorf (Kessler), Michael Lonsdale (Manfredi), Alexander Kerst (Clausen), André Penvern (Leger)
SUMMARY: An American architect prevents a neo-Nazi cabal from gaining access to a great fortune.
RELEASE: September, Universal
AVAILABILITY: VHS, LD, DVD
RATING: R

52 Pick-Up—1986 (114 mins)

PRODUCER: Menahem Golan, Yoram Globus, Cannon
SCRIPT: Elmore Leonard, John Steppling, from Leonard's novel
PHOTOGRAPHY (COLOR): Jost Vacano
EDITOR: Robert F. Shugrue
MUSIC: Gary Chang
CAST: Roy Scheider (Mitch), John Glover (Raimy), Clarence Williams III (Bobby Shy), Robert Trebor (Leo), Ann-Margret (Barb), Vanity (Doreen), Lonny Chapman (O'Boyle), Kelly Preston (Cini)
SUMMARY: A trio of criminals meet resistance when they attempt to extort a Los Angeles businessman.
RELEASE: November, Cannon
AVAILABILITY: VHS, LD, DVD
RATING: R

Riviera—1987 (100 mins)

Director: Alan Smithee
PRODUCER: Robert L. Rosen, MTM
SCRIPT: Michael Sloan
PHOTOGRAPHY: Henri Decaë, Bernard Lutic
EDITOR: Robert F. Shugrue
CAST: Ben Masters (Kelly), Patrick Bauchau (Rykker), Elyssa Davalos (Ashley), Shane Rimmer (Doc), Jon Finch (Jeffers), Daniel Emilfork (Messenger)
SUMMARY: A retired intelligence agent investigates the murder of his former colleagues.
BROADCAST: May 31, 1987, ABC
AVAILABILITY: VHS, as *Espionage*

Dead Bang—1989 (109 mins)

PRODUCER: Steve Roth, Lorimar, A Steve Roth Production
SCRIPT: Robert Foster
PHOTOGRAPHY (COLOR): Gerry Fisher
MUSIC: Gary Chang, Michael Kamen
EDITOR: Robert F. Shugrue
CAST: Don Johnson (Jerry Beck), Tim Reid (Dixon), Penelope Ann Miller (Linda), William Forsythe (Kressler), Bob Balaban (Webly), Bobby Burns (Frank Military), Tate Donovan (John Burns)
SUMMARY: A Los Angeles deputy sheriff meets resistance from a neo-Nazi group as he investigates the murder of a police officer.
RELEASE: March, Warner Bros.
AVAILABILITY: VHS, LD, DVD
RATING: R

The Fourth War—1990 (104 mins)

PRODUCER: Wolf Schmidt, Kodiak
SCRIPT: Stephen Peters, Kenneth Ross
PHOTOGRAPHY (COLOR): Gerry Fisher

MUSIC: Bill Conti
EDITOR: Robert F. Shugrue
CAST: Roy Scheider (Knowles), Jürgen Prochnow (Valachev), Harry Dean Stanton (Hackworth), Tim Reid (Clark), Lara Harris (Elena)
SUMMARY: The personal conflict between an American and a Russian colonel nearly precipitates a war between the United States and the Soviet Union.
RELEASE: Cannon, Month
AVAILABILITY: VHS, LD
RATING: R

Year of the Gun — 1991 (111 mins)

PRODUCER: Edward R. Pressman, Initial Films
SCRIPT: David Ambrose (credited), Jay Presson Allen (uncredited), from Michael Mewshaw's novel
PHOTOGRAPHY (COLOR): Blasco Giuarto
MUSIC: Bill Conti
EDITOR: Lee Percy
CAST: Andrew McCarthy (Raybourne), Sharon Stone (Alison) John Pankow (Italo Bianchi), Valeria Golino (Lia)
SUMMARY: An American writer receives unwanted attention from a group of terrorists in Italy.
RELEASE: November, Triumph
AVAILABILITY: VHS, DVD
RATING: R

"Maniac at Large" — 1992 (30 mins)

PRODUCER: Gil Adler, HBO
SCRIPT: Mae Woods
PHOTOGRAPHY (COLOR): John Leonetti
EDITOR: Lou Angelo
MUSIC: Bill Conti
CAST: Blythe Danner (Margaret), Salome Jens (Mrs. Pritchard), Clarence Williams III (Grady), Adam Ant (Pipkin)
SUMMARY: A terrified library clerk kills people in order to calm her nerves.
BROADCAST: August 19, 1992, HBO
AVAILABILITY: VHS, DVD

Against the Wall — 1994 (111 mins)

PRODUCER: Steven McGlothen, Producers Entertainment Group, HBO Pictures
SCRIPT: Ron Hutchinson
PHOTOGRAPHY (COLOR): John Leonetti
EDITOR: Lee Percy
MUSIC: Gary Chang
CAST: Kyle MacLachlan (Michael Smith), Samuel L. Jackson (Jamaal X), Clarence Williams III (Chaka), Harry Dean Stanton (Hal Smith), Frederic Forrest (Wiesbad)
SUMMARY: After years of mistreatment, prison inmates stage an uprising, taking several guards hostage.

BROADCAST: March 26, 1994, HBO
AVAILABILITY: VHS, DVD

The Burning Season—1994 (123 mins)

PRODUCER: Thomas M. Hammel, John Frankenheimer, HBO Pictures
SCRIPT: William Mastrosimone, Michael Tolkin, Ron Hutchinson, based in part on Andrew Revkin's book *The Burning Season* and Adrian Cowell's *The Decade of Destruction*.
PHOTOGRAPHY (COLOR): John Leonetti
EDITOR: Paul Rubell
MUSIC: Gary Chang
CAST: Raul Julia (Chico Mendes), Edward James Olmos (Wilson Pinheiro), Sonia Braga (Regina), Kamala Dawson (Ilzamar Mendes), Luis Guzman (Estate Boss), Nigel Havers (Steven Keyes), Tomas Milian (Darli Alves), Gerrado Moreno (Darci Alves), Marco Rodríguez (Tavora)
SUMMARY: A rubber tapper arouses international sympathy as he attempts to save the Brazilian rain forest from greedy ranchers and corrupt government officials.
BROADCAST: September 17, 1994, HBO
AVAILABILITY: VHS

Andersonville—1996 (167 mins)

PRODUCER: David Rintels, Lansing L. Smith, Turner Pictures
SCRIPT: David Rintels
PHOTOGRAPHY (COLOR): Ric Waite
EDITOR: Paul Rubell
MUSIC: Gary Chang
CAST: Jarrod Emick (Josiah Day), Frederic Forrest (McSpadden), Ted Marcoux (Martin Blackburn), Carmen Argenziano (Hopkins), Frederick Coffin (Collins), Denis Forest (Mad Matthew), Jan Triska (Wirz), William Sanderson (Munn), William H. Macy (Chandler)
SUMMARY: A group of soldiers struggle to endure the hellish conditions of a Confederate prison camp during the Civil War.
BROADCAST: March 3 and 4, 1996, TNT
AVAILABILITY: VHS, DVD

The Island of Dr. Moreau—1996 (96 mins)

PRODUCER: Edward R. Pressman, New Line
SCRIPT: Richard Stanley (credited), Ron Hutchinson (credited), Walon Green (uncredited), from H. G. Wells' novel
PHOTOGRAPHY (COLOR): William A. Fraker
EDITOR: Paul Rubell
MUSIC: Gary Chang
CAST: Marlon Brando (Dr. Moreau), Val Kilmer (Montgomery), David Thewlis (Douglas), Fairuza Balk (Aissa), Ron Perlman (Sayer of the Law), Nelson de la Rosa (Majai), Daniel Rigney (Hyena-Swine)
SUMMARY: Using genetic engineering, a scientist strives to turn animals into human beings.

RELEASE: August, New Line
AVAILABILITY: VHS, DVD
RATING: PG-13

George Wallace—1997 (178 mins)

PRODUCER: John Frankenheimer, Julian Krainin, Turner Pictures
SCRIPT: Paul Monash, Marshall Frady, from Frady's book *Wallace*
PHOTOGRAPHY (COLOR, B&W): Alan Caso
EDITOR: Tony Gibbs
MUSIC: Gary Chang
CAST: Gary Sinise (George Wallace), Mare Winningham (Lurleen), Angelina Jolie (Cornelia), Ron Perkins (Nicholas Katzenbach), Joe Don Baker (Jim Folsom), Clarence Williams III (Archie), William Sanderson (Odum), Mark Valley (Robert Kennedy)
SUMMARY: After he is shot and paralyzed, a firebrand politician recants his racist views.
BROADCAST: August 24 and 26, 1997, TNT
AVAILABILITY: VHS, DVD

Ronin—1998 (121 mins)

PRODUCER: Frank Mancuso, Jr., UA
SCRIPT: J. D. Zeik, Richard Weisz
PHOTOGRAPHY (COLOR): Robert Fraisse
EDITOR: Tony Gibbs
MUSIC: Elia Cmiral
CAST: Robert De Niro (Sam), Jean Reno (Vincent), Natascha McElhone (Deirdre), Stellan Skarsgard (Gregor), Sean Bean (Spence), Skipp Sudduth (Larry), Michael Lonsdale (Jean-Pierre), Jonathan Pryce (Seamus)
SUMMARY: Mercenaries and terrorists fight one another over the possession of a mysterious suitcase.
RELEASE: September, MGM
AVAILABILITY: VHS, DVD
RATING: R

Reindeer Games—2000 (99 mins)

PRODUCER: Marty Katz, Bob Weinstein, Chris Moore, Dimension Films, Marty Katz Productions
SCRIPT: Ehren Kruger
PHOTOGRAPHY (COLOR): Alan Caso
EDITOR: Tony Gibbs, Michael Kahn
MUSIC: Alan Silvestri
CAST: Ben Affleck (Rudy), Gary Sinise (Gabriel), Charlize Theron (Ashley), Clarence Williams III (Merlin), Dennis Farina (Jack Bangs), James Frain (Nick), Danny Trejo (Jumpy), Donal Logue (Pug)
SUMMARY: An ex-car thief is forced by a gang of crooks to help them rob a casino.
RELEASE: February, Dimension
AVAILABILITY: VHS, DVD
RATING: R

"Ambush" — 2001 (6 mins)

PRODUCER: Robyn Boardman, Aristides McGarry, Anonymous Content
SCRIPT: Andrew Kevin Walker
PHOTOGRAPHY: Newton Thomas Sigel
EDITOR: Robert Duffy
MUSIC: Michael Wandmacher
CAST: Clive Owen (driver), Tomas Milian (passenger), Franklin Jones (bandit)
SUMMARY: A professional driver shields a jewelry thief from a pack of bandits.
AVAILABILITY: DVD and BMW's website (http://www.bmwusa.com/uniquelybmw/
   bmw_art/films)

Path to War — 2002 (165 mins)

PRODUCER: Guy Riedel, Avenue Pictures/Edgar J. Scherick Associates
SCRIPT: Daniel Giat
PHOTOGRAPHY (COLOR): Stephen Goldblatt
EDITOR: Richard Francis-Bruce
MUSIC: Gary Chang
CAST: Michael Gambon (Lyndon Johnson), Donald Sutherland (Clark Clifford), Alec
   Baldwin (Robert McNamara), Phillip Baker Hall (Everett Dirksen), Bruce McGill
   (George Ball), James Frain (Dick Goodwin), Felicity Huffman (Lady Bird Johnson),
   Frederic Forrest (Gen. Earl "Bus" Wheeler), Tom Skerritt (Gen. William Westmore-
   land), John Aylward (Dean Rusk), Chris Eigeman (Bill Moyers), Curtis McClarin
   (Martin Luther King Jr.), Gary Sinise (George Wallace)
SUMMARY: The United States' escalating involvement in Vietnam damages Lyndon John-
   son's presidency.
BROADCAST: May 18, 2002, HBO
AVAILABILITY: DVD

Chapter Notes

Introduction

1. Staff, "Bird Man of Alcatraz," 20 Jun 1962.

2. Vincent Canby, "*The Manchurian Candidate*," 17 Sep 1962.

3. John Thomas, "The Smile on the Face of the Tiger," *Film Quarterly*, Winter 1965-1966, pp. 2-13; Charles Higham, "Frankenheimer," *Sight & Sound*, Spring 1968, p. 91.

4. *The Cinema of John Frankenheimer* (New York: A.S. Barnes, 1969), p. 15.

5. *The American Cinema* (New York: Dutton, 1968), p. 193.

6. Collected in Kael's *Going Steady* (Boston: Little, Brown, 1970), p. 206.

7. "Terror over the Superbowl," 1 Apr 1977.

8. David Quinlan, *The Illustrated Guide to Film Directors* (London: Batsford, 1983), p. 103.

9. Ephraim Katz, et al., eds. *The Film Encyclopedia* (New York: HarperCollins, 2000), p. 490.

10. "A Tippling Detective vs. a Low I.Q. Mob," *The New York Times*, 25 Mar 1989.

11. "The Director as Survivor," *Los Angeles Times*, 5 Nov 1989. Frankenheimer also won an Emmy in 2002 for his fifth and final cable television feature, *Path to War*.

12. Roy Loynd, "Against the Wall," 21 Mar 1994.

13. In 1998, as well, *The Manchurian Candidate* was selected for the AFI's "100 Greatest American Movies" list (#67).

14. "Ronin: Real Tough Guys, Real Derring-Do," 25 Sep 1998.

15. "'Reindeer Games': Wild Sledding," 25 Feb 2000.

16. "Impossible Cinema," Nov/Dec 2002, p. 49.

17. Yoram Allon, et al., eds. *Contemporary North American Film Directors: A Wallflower Critical Guide* (New York: Wallflower, 2002), p. 183.

18. Elliott Stein, "They Stand Alone," 23 Sep 2003.

19. "Dialogue on Film: John Frankenheimer," *American Film*, Mar 1989, p. 20.

One: Biography

1. See Charles Champlin, *John Frankenheimer: A Conversation* (Burbank: Riverwood, 1995), p. 3. "Frankenheimer grew up in New York City and Long Island, the son of a Jewish stockbroker, but was brought up Catholic by his Irish American mother. He went to a Catholic military academy and wanted to be a priest at age 13." Quoted from Rita Kempley, "An Old Hand's Sure Touch," *The Washington Post*, 20 Feb 2000. Frankenheimer lost his faith when he was a teenager: see Gerald Pratley, *The Films of Frankenheimer: Forty Years in Film* (Bethlehem, PA: Lehigh UP, 1998), p. 4. On several occasions, Frankenheimer makes use of Christian and Catholic imagery, often in a mocking manner. The assassin Raymond

Shaw dresses as a priest in *The Manchurian Candidate*. A pastor gives last rites to Arthur Hamilton in *Seconds*. A cardinal consorts with gangsters in *99 and 44/100% Dead!*. Statuettes of the Virgin Mother are made out of plastic explosive in *Black Sunday*. The central character in *The Island of Dr. Moreau* rides around in vehicle that resembles Pope John Paul II's "popemobile." In *The Burning Season*, however, Frankenheimer purposefully links the film's hero with biblical martyrs and saints.

2. The names of Frankenheimer's siblings are Richard and Jean. See Bernard Weinraub, "Obituary," *The New York Times*, 7 Jul 2002.

3. Charles Higham interviewed Frankenheimer for *Sight and Sound* in 1968. Higham adapted the interview and included it in *The Celluloid Muse* (London: Angus & Robertson, 1969), which he co-edited with Joel Greenberg. All subsequent citations refer to the interview with Higham as it appears in *Celluloid Muse*. The quotation cited here is taken from p. 72.

4. Quoted in *Conversation*, op. cit., pp. 3–4

5. *Muse*, op. cit., p. 72.

6. *Conversation*, op. cit., p. 3.

7. "On Screen: John Frankenheimer," *Horizon*, Mar 1963, p. 35.

8. *Conversation*, op. cit., p. 5; and see *Forty Years*, op. cit., pp. 4, 5.

9. *Muse*, op. cit., p. 73.

10. *Forty Years*, op. cit., p. 5.

11. *Muse*, op. cit., p. 73.

12. William Grimes, "A Director's Debt to a Hereford Cow," *The New York Times*, 18 Jan 1996.

13. *Conversation*, op. cit., pp. 7, 211, 8.

14. *Muse*, op. cit., p. 74.

15. Frankenheimer claimed that Ford encouraged him to find work in television: "If I were you," the director said," and if I were starting out today...I'd get into television. That's what it's all about." Quoted in *Conversation*, op. cit., p. 9. "[Frankenheimer's] first experience with film occurred as a U.S. Air Force lieutenant assigned to make documentaries for the military during the Korean War. After that, he landed a job as an assistant to the renowned director John Ford. When Ford took ill, he advised Franken-

heimer to seek work in New York. He did — and was hired as an assistant director at CBS." From the press kit prepared by Kodiak Films for *The Fourth War* in 1990.

16. See *Conversation*, op. cit., p. 11. The marriage was annulled: see Joyce Haber, "Frankenheimer a Hothead with an Up-Down Record," *Los Angeles Times*, 18 Jul 1971.

17. *Muse*, op. cit., p. 74.

18. *Forty Years*, op. cit., pp. 6–7.

19. *Muse*, op. cit., p. 75.

20. *Conversation*, op. cit., pp. 13-14.

21. *Muse*, op. cit., pp. 76, 75.

22. *Forty Years*, op. cit., p. 8.

23. *Conversation*, op. cit., pp. 18, 19, 22. See also *Forty Years*, op. cit., p. 8.

24. Bernstein had been blacklisted and was obliged to use pseudonyms. See *Forty Years*, op. cit., p. 8 and *Conversation*, op. cit., pp. 18-19.

25. *Conversation*, op. cit., p. 22.

26. "Frankenheimer Live," *Film Comment*, Nov/Dec 2002, p. 48.

27. See *Forty Years*, op. cit., pp. 8–9.

28. *Muse*, op. cit., pp. 77–78.

29. Richard Coe, "Well-Told Tale of Teen-Agers," *The Washington Post*, 9 May 1957; Staff, "The Young Stranger," *Variety*, 20 March 1957.

30. *Forty Years*, op. cit., pp. 8–9.

31. "Someone once asked me, 'How were you able to do such quality stuff then, compared to what television does now?' The answer is that most people didn't own a television set in those days. Owning a TV set was a kind of elitist thing, and we had an elitist audience." Quoted in *Conversation*, op. cit., p. 40.

32. Manulis discusses the creation of *Playhouse 90* on Emery's documentary *The Directors: John Frankenheimer*. Written by Rod Serling, "The Forbidden Area" is also notable because of the pessimistic manner in which it depicts military leadership, a trait it shares with a number of films Frankenheimer would later direct, particularly his political thrillers of the Sixties. Vahimagi described the show as

> a Cold War scare story in which an apparent atomic attack by the Russians has the Pentagon high brass on the edge of panic but eventually turns out to be a minor sabotage plot. A talky drama played out mainly

in the corridors of the Pentagon, with its ominous fantasies of impending and military disaster, it introduced the theme of paranoia that would be further advanced in *The Manchurian Candidate* and *Seven Days in May*. From "Frankenheimer Live," op. cit., p. 48. "The Forbidden Area" was broadcast on October 4, 1956. During the four years Frankenheimer was affiliated with *Playhouse 90*, he worked with several actors he would later recruit for his features, including Mickey Rooney (*The Extraordinary Seaman*), Edmond O'Brien (*Seven Days in May*, 99 and 44/100% Dead), Whit Bissell (*Bird Man of Alcatraz, The Manchurian Candidate, Seven Days in May*), Jack Palance (*The Horsemen*) and Martin Balsam (*Seven Days in May*). The expressive visuals and thematic depth which characterized Frankenheimer's television work aroused the interest of both critics and peers. In 1957, for instance, a profile of the director at work was published in *Time*: see "Backstage *at Playhouse 90*," 2 Dec 1957. Several of his programs were nominated for awards, as well, and one of these, "The Comedian," won a Best Single Program Emmy in 1958. Industry players began to show interest, and during this period he became friends with the writer George Axelrod and the producers John Houseman and David O. Selznick. Of his friendship with Selznick, Frankenheimer told Pratley: "It was almost a father-son relationship. He would look at all my television shows and criticize them; he would tell me what he thought was good and bad." *Forty Years*, op. cit., p. 27. Frankenheimer would also work with Selznick on an adaptation of Scott Fitzgerald's novel *Tender is the Night*. He claimed that when Selznick left the project, 20th Century–Fox decided to replace the young director with the veteran Henry King. See *Muse*, op. cit., p. 78. King took over direction in February 1961, however, and Selznick didn't detach himself from the project until the fall of that year. See Rudy Behlmer's *Memo from David O. Selznick* (New York: Viking, 1972), pp. 471-475. In a 2000 interview, Frankenheimer talked about the debt he owed to his mentor: "Selznick was so smart in so many ways. He's not known as a maker of action films, but he taught me everything about directing a chase scene. He

said to let the audience know where everyone is, to give them a sense of geography, and then you can do anything." Quoted in Philip Wuntch, "Frankenheimer, Once a Reluctant Director, Can Boast an Enviable Career," *The Dallas Morning News*, 23 Feb 2000. Selznick helped Frankenheimer cut *The Young Savages*: see *Muse*, op. cit., p. 79.

33. *Conversation*, op. cit., pp. 44.

34. "Frankenheimer a Hothead with an Up-Down Record," op. cit.

35. In her 1989 profile "The Director as Survivor," op. cit., Easton suggested that there is a "Hemingway side [to] Frankenheimer's personality" and it "is reflected in his movies. You won't find much romance or many complex leading ladies in a Frankenheimer film. For the most part his characters are men, real men, fighting each other or some outside force trying to destroy a way of life."

36. Quoted in "John Frankenheimer: 'Nowhere To Go,'" a piece written by Jamie Allen which appeared on *CNN Online*, 25 Feb. 2000.<http://archives.cnn.com/2000/ SHOWBIZ/Movies/02/25/frankenheimer/> (18 Nov 2004).

37. Ralph Appelbaum, "The Fourth Commitment," *Films and Filming*, Nov 1979, p. 24.

38. Frankenheimer's remarks are taken from Emery's documentary, op. cit. The director had hoped to cast Marilyn Monroe as the film's lead: see Chris Chase, "At the Movies," *The New York Times*, 23 Jul 1982.

39. Chase, "At the Movies," op. cit.

40. Quoted in Garry Fishgall, *Against Type* (New York: Scribner, 1995), p. 197. A few weeks before making the offer, Hecht and his business partner Burt Lancaster had dissolved their independent production company Hecht-Hill-Lancaster, but because of a contractual obligation, the two were expected to produce four pictures for United Artists, the first of which would be this treatment of Hunter's novel. See also Kate Buford, *Burt Lancaster* (New York: Knopf, 2000), p. 200.

41. *Lancaster*, op. cit., pp. 204, 205, 206.

42. *Shelley II: The Middle of My Century* (New York: Simon and Schuster, 1989), p. 319.

43. *Lancaster*, op. cit., p. 206.

44. Quoted in Philip K. Scheuer, "Ace TV Director Back With Movie," *Los Angeles Times*, 5 Jul 1960.

45. *Lancaster*, op. cit., p. 209.

46. From the commentary Frankenheimer recorded for the DVD release of *The Manchurian Candidate*. McGraw-Hill published Condon's novel in 1959.

47. From an interview the director gave to Terry Gross, host of National Public Radio's *Fresh Air*, 6 Mar 1990.

48. *Conversation*, op. cit., p. 66. Sinatra's friendship with John Kennedy also helped the project. See J. Hoberman, "When Dr. No Met Dr. Strangelove," *Sight and Sound*, Dec 1993, p. 18:

> In September of [1961], Frank Sinatra—the most widely publicized of the president's friends—was a weekend guest at the Kennedy compound in Hyannis Port. Among other things, Sinatra used his visit to secure the president's approval for the movie that he, writer George Axelrod and director John Frankenheimer hoped to adapt from Richard Condon's lurid thriller *The Manchurian Candidate*. Sinatra had a deal with United Artists, but UA president Arthur Krim—who was also the national finance chairman for the Democratic Party—felt that the project was political dynamite.

49. Quoted in Doug Nye, "Color Him Intense," Knight Ridder/Tribune News Service, 2 Mar 1996.

50. *Conversation*, op. cit., p. 47.

51. Quoted in "Dialogue on Film," op. cit., p. 22. Random House published Gaddis' book as *Birdman of Alcatraz: The Story of Robert Stroud* in 1955. The title of the film, as it appears in the opening credits, as well as UA's promotional material, is *Bird Man of Alcatraz*.

52. *Conversation*, op. cit., p. 54.

53. See *Against Type*, op. cit., p. 209.

54. Bill Higgins, "Frankenheimer Reception Rounds Up Filmland Past," *Los Angeles Times*, 13 Nov 1989.

55. *Conversation*, op. cit., p. 54.

56. See *Lancaster*, op. cit., p. 209 and *Against Type*, op. cit., p. 209.

57. John Houseman, *Final Dress* (New York: Simon and Schuster, 1983), p. 204.

58. Staff, "All Fall Down," 21 Mar 1962.

59. While the chiefs at Metro prohibited Frankenheimer from filming in Cleveland, they did grant him permission after primary shooting was completed to head down to the Florida Keys to shoot the footage of the ocean, the causeway bridges and the old buildings which appears in the picture's vivid first reel. See *Conversation*, op. cit., p. 64 and *Forty Years*, op. cit., p. 32.

60. *Final Dress*, op. cit., pp. 207, 208–209.

61. Spivy plays the woman who runs the strip joint in *All Fall Down*.

62. *Fresh Air* interview, op. cit.

63. *Conversation*, op. cit., p. 70

64. As Louis Menand pointed out in an essay he wrote about Condon's novel for *The New Yorker* ("Brainwashed," 15 Sep 2003, p. 88), the movie "was a flop" that "failed to recover its costs." Menand may be guilty of overstatement, however. As Hoberman in "When Dr. No Met Dr. Strangelove," op. cit., has argued: "[A]lthough it has since become a part of *The Manchurian Candidate*'s mythology that it was a popular failure, the movie had supplanted *The Longest Day* as the national box office champion by Election Day 1962."

65. In his piece for *Film Quarterly*, Thomas wrote: "*The Manchurian Candidate* is the nightmare of history played for laughs.... It's not just black comedy, but the blackest black comedy ever filmed." "The Smile on the Face of the Tiger," op. cit., p. 8.

66. "Return of the 'Candidate,'" *The Washington Post*, 13 Feb 1988.

67. See Michael Schienfield, "The Manchurian Candidate," *Films in Review*, 1988, p. 539.

68. *Angela Lansbury: A Life on Stage and Screen* (New York: Birch Lane, 1996), p. 121.

69. *Muse*, op. cit., p. 62.

70. Quoted from "Seven Ways with *Seven Days in May*," *Films & Filming*, Jun 1964, pp. 9–10.

71. *Muse*, op. cit., p. 82. Frankenheimer's anger with Douglas lasted for decades. In 2000, for instance, he blasted the actor in an interview he gave to Bob Longino:

> Q: Is Kirk Douglas like he is on-screen? He seems so commanding and at the same time so completely full of himself.
> A: He manages to convey exactly the same thing in real life.
> Q: And Burt Lancaster?
> A: He was great. He was all the things Kirk Douglas wasn't and all the things Kirk Douglas wanted to be.

Quoted from "Frankenheimer Loves Film Game," *The Atlanta Journal-Constitution*, 25 Feb 2000.

72. Kirk Douglas, *The Ragman's Son* (New York: Pocket, 1988), p. 324.

73. Tony Macklin, *Voices from the Set* (Lanham: Scarecrow, 2000), p. 82.

74. The marriage was announced in the December 27, 1963 issue of *Time*. While living in Paris, the couple became acquainted with the director Jean-Pierre Melville, whose influence upon Frankenheimer is especially noticeable in *French Connection II* and *Ronin*: see Lindsay Amos, "Veteran's Still a Maestro at the Wheel of a Thriller," *New Zealand Herald*, 2 Feb 1999. Houseman talks about socializing with the Frankenheimers in Paris in *Final Dress*, op. cit., p. 284. Evans Evans appeared in several of her husband's films, beginning with *All Fall Down*, in which she plays the dancer who talks to Brandon De Wilde in the opening sequence. The others are: *Grand Prix, Impossible Object, The Iceman Cometh, Prophecy* and *Dead Bang*. She also appeared in Arthur Penn's *Bonnie and Clyde* (1967), playing a young woman who is abducted, along with her boyfriend (Gene Wilder), by the bank robbers. In a 1977 interview with the *Los Angeles Times*, the Frankenheimers talked about their marriage and its impact upon Evans' career:

> Evans: There's no pressure relationship between us. There might be if I were trying to become the world's greatest actress. But I decided early in the game there was just no way for us to put together a good marriage if I got involved in long-term commitments as an actress. I've worked in some of John's films, including *All Fall Down* and *The Iceman Cometh*. But to have a career that places him in one part of the world and me in another, simply beggars senses.
>
> Q: Doesn't absence make the heart grow fonder?
>
> Evans: Not in my book. Perhaps other people know how to work out long separations, but I think marriage is fragile and beautiful as a butterfly. It has to be treated gently. I made the deliberate decision to subordinate my career to John's. My approach might not sit well with today's women, but the reality for me is that our relationship works.
>
> Q: And you, John?
>
> John: There's no conflict here. I really

would like to see Evans do more as an actress. But above all, what works for us is that we give each other space to function as individuals.

Quoted from Marshall Bergess, "Evans and John Frankenheimer," 1 May 1977. The marriage received a blow several years later when a college student named Michael Bay contacted Frankenheimer, curious to find out if the director might be his father. Bay, who later became a successful Hollywood director himself with films like *Bad Boys* (1995), *Armageddon* (1998) and *Pearl Harbor* (2001), discussed his relationship with Frankenheimer in an interview he gave to the *Los Angeles Times*' Robert Welkos a few weeks prior to *Pearl Harbor*'s release. Welkos wrote:

> Rumors have circulated around Hollywood for years that Bay's birth father is John Frankenheimer....
>
> Bay acknowledged the rumors but is reluctant to discuss them. "Have I ever spoken to him? I've met him," Bay says of Frankenheimer. "I met him at a [Directors Guild of America] function, three, four years ago. It was just, 'Hi.'"
>
> Frankenheimer, speaking on the record for the first time about the situation, remembers the encounter at the Directors Guild. He said Bay approached him [in 1985] and asked, "Do you think it's true?"
>
> "I said, 'It's not true, Michael,'" Frankenheimer recalled.... [H]e added flatly in a recent interview, "it's absolutely, categorically untrue. We had tests done and I am not his father."
>
> Frankenheimer admitted that he had a "one-night stand" with Bay's birth mother at the Hollywood Roosevelt Hotel in the early 1960s while he was filming "Seven Days in May".... "Here's the embarrassing part," Frankenheimer continued. "I was living at the time with the woman whom I later married and am still married to. Understand, she knows about it. It's embarrassing. Did I cheat on this woman? Yes, I did. It was a one-night stand. Then I married her."

From "Marshaling All of His Forces," 20 May 2001. The accuracy of Frankenheimer's recollections about the affair is debatable. He finished *Seven Days in May* in the summer of 1963. Bay was born in February 1965.

75. *Forty Years*, op. cit., p. 58.

76. *Muse*, op. cit., p. 83.

77. Rock Hudson attended the screening and his experience is described in Sara David-

son's 1986 biography, *Rock Hudson: His Story* (New York: Morrow, 1986), pp. 142-143:

> When the film ended, the audience booed. The M.C. came on stage and said, "Mesdames et messieurs, we have a surprise: in the balcony, Monsieur Rock Hudson." It was an awkward moment for Rock, but the booing changed instantly to cheers and applause as people rose to their feet. It was disconcerting, but later Mark [Hudson's boyfriend, who attended the screening] realized, "They were applauding him for his previous films."
>
> Rock and Mark went to different parties, and met back at the Carlton Hotel at four in the morning. "Shit," Rock said. "I thought I had a hit."

78. "Dialogue on Film," op. cit., p. 24.

79. *Conversation*, op. cit., p. 97.

80. *Forty Years*, op. cit., p. 84.

81. See the program prepared for the American Cinema Editors' 46th Annual Eddie Awards, p. 6.

82. Quoted in Peter Dick, "The Grand Prix Circus, Hollywood Style," *Road and Track*, Apr 1992, p. 133.

83. Nick Spanos, "'Grand Prix' a Production Race That Went to the Wire," 3 Jun 1967. The director's beliefs were vindicated at the 1967 Academy Awards as *Grand Prix* took Oscars in the Best Editing, Best Sound and Best Sound Effects categories.

84. Staff, "MGM, Independent Film Deal Announced," *Los Angeles Times*, 28 Jan 1967.

85. Staff, "Kennedy Tactics Change Primaries," *The Washington Post*, 7 May 1968.

86. *Conversation*, op. cit., p. 113.

87. "The Director as Survivor," op. cit. See also Fred Bernstein's profile, "Director John Frankenheimer's *The Manchurian Candidate* Plays to a Full House After 26 Years," *People Weekly*, 16 May 1988, p. 130:

> On the day of the 1968 California primary, Bobby was relaxing at the director's home. Then Frankenheimer drove Kennedy to the Ambassador Hotel to greet his supporters and to celebrate the primary victory that practically guaranteed him the Democratic nomination. "I was supposed to be the guy standing next to Bobby on the podium," he says. Instead, Frankenheimer begged off to watch the speech on a TV monitor in the archway. As he watched, Sirhan Sirhan, Kennedy's assassin, brushed by him. "It was like *Manchurian Candidate*...I felt this shaking inside of me." Just before Kennedy was fatally shot by Sirhan, Frankenheimer

went out to his car to wait for the candidate and heard the news of the tragedy on the car radio.

Also present that night (June 5) was the journalist Pete Hamill, who would later write the dialogue for *French Connection II*. Hamill recalled the experience in 2006:

> I met John Frankenheimer at the Ambassador Hotel in LA, on the night Robert Kennedy was shot. Many Kennedy supporters and campaign aides were there, too (it was an immense suite). John had made a commercial for RFK that was used in the California primary.... He and I talked for about 10 minutes, mostly politics. Later I ended up in a room with Robert Kennedy, Jack Newfield, Jimmy Breslin and Cesar Chavez. We were together until it was clear that Kennedy had won the primary and a few of us moved together to a back elevator and went down to the main floor, where a huge crowd had gathered. Not long afterwards, Kennedy went through another passage into the kitchen (I was walking backwards making notes) and then Sirhan Sirhan raised his arm, the one with a gun at the end.

Pete Hamill, "Hamill on sat," 9 Jul 2006, personal email (9 Jul 2006).

88. Macklin, op. cit., p. 91.

89. "An Old Hand's Sure Touch," op. cit. Evidence of the author's sadness, arguably, is detectable in the movie he made right after the tragedy, *The Gypsy Moths*, which tells the story of a suicidal skydiver who is overcome by the conviction that life is not worth living. Filmed in El Dorado, Kansas, the picture would be the final collaboration between Lancaster and Frankenheimer, a partnership which had produced three great films—*Bird Man of Alcatraz*, *Seven Days in May* and *The Train*—and a friendship that would last until Lancaster's death in 1994. The film also marked the final pairing of Lancaster and Deborah Kerr, the two having appeared together in not only *From Here to Eternity* (1953), but *Separate Tables* (1958), too.

90. Mary Blume, "The Games Frankenheimer People Play," *Los Angeles Times*, 28 Jun 1970.

91. Quoted in *Forty Years*, op. cit., p. 106. Sharif had signed on to the play the lead in *The Last Valley* (1971).

92. *Conversation*, op. cit., p. 121.

93. See Garry Fishgall, *Gregory Peck* (New York: Scribner, 2002), p. 271. Audiences, ev-

Notes — Chapter One 219

idently, were not interested in watching the aging Peck play against type and the picture failed at the box office. In 2006, Columbia released this forgotten movie on DVD in an effort apparently to capitalize on the popularity of *Walk the Line*, 20th Century–Fox's Oscar-winning biopic about Johnny Cash and his wife June Carter.

94. *Conversation*, op. cit., pp. 127-129. Frankenheimer's claim that Howe stepped down because of illness may be spurious. In a piece Vincent LoBrutto wrote for *American Cinematographer*, he claims that Howe "walked off the project" because he found the director to be too meddlesome over camera placements and shots. LoBrutto cites an interview Howe gave to W.S. Eyman for *Take One* in the early Seventies. See LoBrutto, "The Surreal Images of *Seconds*," Nov 1997, p. 103.

95. *Forty Years*, op. cit., p. 123.

96. "Honor and 'The Horsemen,'" *The New York Times* 22 Jul 1971.

97. See Macklin, op. cit, p. 78 and "Frankenheimer Given Triomphe Film Award," *Los Angeles Times*, 18 Dec 1971.

98. *Conversationn*, op. cit., p. 129.

99. For nine months, Frankenheimer apprenticed just outside of Paris in a restaurant owned by the celebrated chef Michel Guerard: see Roderick Mann, "Frankenheimer Speeds On," *Los Angeles Times*, 26 Sep 1986. His interest in cooking arose after he lost his taste for automobile racing. He and Evans discussed this development in the 1977 interview they gave to the *Los Angeles Times*, op. cit.:

> Evans: ...John and I had both been driving racing cars as a hobby. We sat down to breakfast one morning in Paris and our attention was riveted by a pair of side-by-side stories. One headline reported *World champion racing driver dies at age 28* and the other informed us *Famous gourmet and wine connoisseur dies at age 93*.
>
> John: The message was loud and clear. I sold my Ferrari and went straight to the Cordon Bleu. I'd always been interested in cooking, but this—if you'll pardon the pun—really *bleu* my mind. I spent three months studying there and followed up with a tour of Europe, studying with the great chefs. I'd exchanged the high-powered tension of the highway for the great fun of the kitchen.

100. *Forty Years*, op. cit., p. 127

101. See Roy Flannagan, "Nicholas Mosley," *Review of Contemporary Fiction*, Fall 2002, p. 72.

102. Charles Champlin, "A Year of Triumph for Frankenheimer," *Los Angeles Times*, 9 Jan 1974.

103. Charles Champlin, "Frankenheimer Flying High Again," *Los Angeles Times*, 10 Apr 1977.

104. "Impossible Object," 22 May 1973.

105. Quoted from "A Year of Triumph for Frankenheimer," op. cit. See also *Forty Years*, op. cit., p. 127. The film did have a brief run in Spanish theaters in 1978.

106. Robert Cashill, "The American Film Theatre," *Cineaste*, Spring 2004, p. 75.

107. *Conversation*, op. cit., p. 133.

108. Quoted from "Filming *The Iceman Cometh*," an essay Frankenheimer published in the Jan/Feb 1974 issue of *Action*, p. 37. Readers can find a copy of this article in *Forty Years*, pp. 141-143. All citations used here, however, refer to the original publication.

109. Staff, "The Iceman Cometh," 24 Oct 1973.

110. From the commentary Frankenheimer recorded for the film's DVD release. Frankenheimer also took the job because he wanted, in the aftermath of *Impossible Object*, to make a movie that had a better chance of finding a large audience. As he explained to Mary Blume: "There's a great public out there and you have to reach them; otherwise you're not in the movie business." Quoted in "Fathering a 'Connection' Offspring," *Los Angeles Times*, 1 Sep 1974.

111. *Forty Years*, op. cit., p 149.

112. "Mortuary Case," 30 Sep 1974, p. 10; "99 44/100% Dead," 25 Jul 1974.

113. From correspondence with the author, op. cit.

114. "Popeye Doyle: 'French Connection II' is Very Different," *The New York Times*, 19 May 1975.

115. "Frankenheimer Flying High Again," 10 Apr 1977.

116. See *Conversation*, op. cit., pp. 147-151 and *Forty Years*, op. cit., pp. 163-165.

117. *The Kid Stays in the Picture* (New York: Hyperion, 1994), p. 283. Frankenheimer received permission to shoot footage of Super Bowl X in which the Pittsburgh

Steelers beat the Dallas Cowboys 21 to 17. The game was played on January 18, 1976.

118. *Conversation*, op. cit. 152.

119. Ralph Appelbaum, "Pop Art Pitfalls," *Films and Filming*, October 1979, p. 13.

120. From "The Golden Autumn of Old Hollywood's Boy Wonder," *The San Jose Mercury News*, 6 Oct 1991.

121. Louis B. Parks, "Veteran Director Returns to Form," 5 Mar 2000.

122. "Pop Art Pitfalls," op. cit., p. 11. See also *Forty Years*, op. cit., p. 171.

123. Roderick Mann, "Secret Film of Frankenheimer's," *Los Angeles Times*, 22 Jun 1978.

124. See Gregg Kilday, "Film Clips: A Sneaked Peek at 'Prophecy,'" *Los Angeles Times*, 10 Aug 1977 and Roderick Mann, "Frankenheimer: Prophetic Film?," *Los Angeles Times*, 24 Oct 1978. See also *Forty Years*, op. cit., p. 171.

125. "Pop Art Pitfalls," op. cit., p. 13.

126. The writer Stephen King enjoyed the film. In his collection of essays about horror movies and books *Danse Macabre* (New York: Everest, 1981), p. 197, he wrote: "I must admit here that I not only liked John Frankenheimer's *Prophecy*, I actually saw it three times."

127. Staff, "Prophecy," 13 Jun 1979.

128. Frank Rich, "Doomsday," 16 Jul 1979, p. 60.

129. "Muted Mutant in 'Prophecy,'" *Los Angeles Times*, 15 Jun 1979.

130. See Roderick Mann, "Frankenheimer — A Novel Plug for 'Destinies,'" *Los Angeles Times*, 12 Jun 1979 and *Forty Years*, op. cit., p. 285.

131. Chase, "At the Movies," op. cit.

132. "Director in Love — With Japan," *Los Angeles Times*, 21 Jul 1981.

133. *Conversation*, op. cit., p. 163. Roy Scheider discusses Frankenheimer's recovery from alcoholism with the critic Kirk Honeycutt in *Movie Talk from the Front Lines* (Jefferson, NC: McFarland, 1995), p. 283, a collection of interviews edited by Jerry Roberts and Steven Gaydos.

134. "Back to Hollywood's Bottom Rung, and Climbing," *The New York Times*, 24 Mar 1994.

135. Aljean Harmetz, "President of CBS Films Quits as Movie Plans are Reduced," *The New York Times*, 13 Mar 1982. The quote from Frankenheimer is taken from *Forty Years*, op. cit., p. 177.

136. "'Challenge' to Way of the Warrior," *Los Angeles Times*, 3 Sep 1982. Several critics responded with disdain to the film's grisly content: see Janet Maslin, "Frankenheimer's Challenge," *The New York Times*, 23 Jul 1982 and Richard Corliss, "Masochists," *Time*, 9 Aug 1982, p. 58–59.

137. See Roderick Mann, "Frankenheimer Speeds On," *Los Angeles Times*, 26 Sep 1982 and *Conversation*, op. cit., p. 166.

138. Shot on videotape at the Moore Theater in Seattle, the production featured Tommy Lee Jones in the lead, as well as performances from Tuesday Weld and Lonny Chapman, who'd both worked with the director on *I Walk the Line*. Chapman would again collaborate with Frankenheimer on *52 Pick-up* and *Reindeer Games*. See David Crook, "The Play Must Go On," *Los Angeles Times*, 25 May 1982.

139. See *Forty Years*, op. cit., p. 185 and Roderick Mann, "5 on the Ludlum Exchange," *Los Angeles Times*, 17 Jun 1980.

140. *Forty Years*, op. cit., p. 185.

141. Bernard Weinraub, "James Caan Rises from the Ashes of His Career," *The New York Times*, 7 Nov 1991.

142. *What's It All About* (New York: Random House, 1992), p. 466.

143. *Forty Years*, op. cit., p. 185.

144. Ibid., pp. 187-189.

145. Ibid., pp. 195.

146. "'52 Pickup': Film Noir Idea Gone Gray," *Los Angeles Times*, 17 Nov 1986.

147. See *Forty Years*, op. cit., p. 200.

148. "The Director as Survivor," op cit.

149. Staff, "The Fourth War," *Variety*, 1 Jan 1990.

150. Glenn Lovell wrote in a commemorative piece which was published a few days after Frankenheimer's death: "[H]is Cold War Thriller 'The Fourth War' was instantly dated by the fall of the Berlin Wall." *The San Jose Mercury News*, "Director Left Legacy of Fearless Filmmaking," 11 Jul 2002.

151. "A Pair of Cold Warriors Who Are Frozen in Place," *The Philadelphia Inquirer*, 26 Mar 1990.

152. "The Fourth War," *Chicago Reader*, 23 Mar 1990.

153. "Roy Scheider in a Parable of the Cold War," *The New York Times*, 24 Mar 1990.

154. "John Frankenheimer to Direct Commercial through Gibson, Lefebvre, Gartner," *Back Stage*, 16 Sep 1988, p. 4.

155. Quoted in Clyde Haberman, "Italy's Bullet-Scarred 70's Return," *The New York Times*, 6 Jun 1991. See also *Forty Years*, op. cit., p. 211. In his review of the picture, Ebert noted:

> The hero of John Frankenheimer's "Year of the Gun" is trapped in the same situation that Alfred Hitchcock found so useful: He is an innocent man, wrongly accused. This is the stuff of nightmares. He has lived blamelessly, but a combination of circumstances have [sic] conspired to make him look blatantly guilty. And nobody can see more clearly how guilty he seems, than the innocent man himself.

"Year of the Gun," *Chicago Sun-Times*, 1 Nov 1991. David Ambrose received credit for writing the film's script, but Frankenheimer claimed that Jay Presson Allen — who penned Hitchcock's *Marnie* (1964) — significantly re-worked the narrative: see *Conversation*, op. cit., p. 181.

156. Weinraub noted in "Back to Hollywood's Bottom Rung, and Climbing," op. cit.: "[T]he decline in the number and quality of the scripts he was offered [contributed] to a downhill professional decline."

157. See *Forty Years*, op. cit., p. 230. "Maniac at Large," the title of the episode Frankenheimer directed, was adapted from a story which originally appeared in 1955 in an illustrated magazine called *Crime SuspenStories*.

158. Ibid., p. 238. See also John O'Connor, "Unlikely Allies in a Dangerous Place and Time," *The New York Times*, 26 Mar 1994 and also Michael McCall, "From 'Alcatraz' to 'Attica,'" *Los Angeles Times*, 20 Jun 1993. In spite of the tragedy which had occurred there the state of New York never closed the Attica Correctional Facility.

159. "Unforgettable Prison Drama," *Los Angeles Times*, 26 Mar 1994.

160. "Against the Wall," 21 Mar 1994.

161. "Maligned Director Back in Driver's Seat," Knight Ridder/Tribune News Service, 25 Sep 1998.

162. John Hartl, "Frankenheimer Directs Dark Tale," *The Seattle Times*, 23 Aug 1998.

163. See David Hughes, *The Greatest Sci-Fi Movies Never Made* (London: Titan, 2001), pp. 233–234.

164. "An Old Hand's Sure Touch," op. cit.

165. "Director Identifies with Gun-for-Hire," 25 Sep 1998.

166. "Frankenheimer Puts Thrills First," *The Washington Times*, 25 Sep 1998.

167. See Bruce Newman, "History in the Remaking," *Los Angeles Times*, 17 Aug 1997. See also Staff, "Career Revived," *The Bergen Record*, 19 Apr 1996 and *Forty Years*, op. cit., p. 271.

168. Ray Richmond, "Wallace Kin Take TNT Biopic to Task," *Variety*, 3 Jan 1997.

169. See "History in the Remaking," op. cit. and Amy Hetzer, "George Wallace 'The Movie' Stirs Anger in Alabama," Reuters, 19 Jan 1997.

170. Chris Kaltenbach, "Frankenheimer Relishes Work for Small Screen," *The Baltimore Sun*. 28 Sept. 1998. See also Barry Koltnow, "Hollywood Samurai," *The Orange County Register*, 25 Sep 1998.

171. "Hollywood Samurai,", op. cit.

172. "Frankenheimer Relishes Work for Small Screen," op. cit.

173. Ron Magid, "Samurai Tactics," *American Cinematographer*, Oct 1998, pp. 34–36.

174. Quoted in Kaltenbach, op. cit.

175. "Samurai Tactics," op. cit., p. 34.

176. Quoted from Lawrence Gelder, "Footlights," *The New York Times*, 25 Feb 1998. See also Nancy Tartaglione, "Disgusted De Niro Vows Self-exile from France," *Variety*, 26 Feb 1998.

177. "Abstractly Expressive," 21 Sep 1998, p. 100.

178. "Frankenheimer may get 'Dirty,'" *The Hollywood Reporter*, 14 Oct 1998.

179. Monica Roman, "Frankenheimer reins 'Games' for Dimension," 11 Nov 1999.

180. Benedict Carver, "Frankenheimer, Miramax Pact," 21 Jul 1999, *Variety*.

181. From commentary recorded for the "Director's Cut" version of the film which Dimension released on DVD in 2001. Also see Longino's "Frankenheimer Loves Film Game," op. cit. and Arnold's "Frankenheimer Puts Thrills First," *The Washington Times*, 18 Feb. 2000.

182. "John Frankenheimer's Reindeer

Games is Anything But Boring," *New York Observer*, 6 Mar 2000.

183. Just before he left for Canada, Frankenheimer signed a non-exclusive contract with TNT "to both direct and produce an unspecified number of movies" for the network. Quoted from John Dempsey, "TNT locks up Frankenheimer," *Variety*, 15 Mar 1999. See also "Frankenheimer Loves Film Game," op. cit.

184. Giat discusses these aspects of the production in an interview he recorded for HBO; a copy of the conversation appears on the DVD edition of the film which HBO released in 2003. At one point Giat says: "[D]elving into this subject I came to see very clearly that the first front of this war was the threshold of the Cabinet room across which a small group of men debated our policy and made decisions."

185. See Giat, HBO interview, op. cit. See also Bernard Weinraub, "A Timely Film on Lyndon Johnson and Viet Nam," *The New York Times*, 3 Dec 2001.

186. Hugh Hart, "LBJ's Troubled 'Path to War,'" *San Francisco Chronicle*, 12 May 2002.

187. From an interview featured on the website *Time.com* created for the film: "Q&A With John Frankenheimer," <http://www.time.com/time/classroom/vietman/ga.html> (17 Nov 2004).

188. See interview Frankenheimer recorded for HBO, which can be found on the DVD edition of the film. See also Giat's HBO interview, op. cit. and "LBJ's Troubled 'Path to War,'" op. cit. and "A Timely Film on Lyndon Johnson and Viet Nam," op. cit.

189. Tom Shales, "HBO's Powerful 'Path to War': The Drama that was LBJ," *The Washington Post*, 18 May 2002.

190. Jeff Guinn, "HBO's 'Path to War' Accentuates the Negative," *Fort Worth Star-Telegram*, 18 May 2002.

191. Laura M. Holson "Enough Trouble to Make your Head Spin," *The New York Times*, 22 Feb 2004

192. From Frankenheimer's death certificate.

Two: Problems at Home

1. *Muse*, op. cit., p. 88
2. *Conversation*, op. cit., p. 64.

3. Berry-Berry's unusual name is never explained in the movie. But Herlihy discusses its origin and meaning in his novel. "[S]ome men claimed it was a disease. The flat truth is that it came from some foolishness of [his mother Annabel]: as a baby, the boy's cheeks were astonishingly red; as she plucked them in quick succession she would say *berry berry berry*, to make the child giggle." *All Fall Down* (New York: Dell 1960), p. 26

4. "'All Fall Down' Film Second-Class Inge," *Los Angeles Times*, 6 Apr 1962.

5. "All Fall Down," *The New York Times*, 12 Apr 1962.

6. *The Sexiest Man Alive* (New York: HarperCollins. 2002), p. 72.

7. "The nymph Echo fell in love with the handsome Narcissus, who was too proud to love anyone. The grieving Echo pined away until she was only a voice, heard in the mountains." Quoted from Richard Cavendish, *An Illustrated Encyclopedia of Mythology* (New York: Crescent, 1984), p. 138.

8. "A Love Story that Doesn't Die," Mary Blume, *Los Angeles Times*, 8 Oct 1972

9. "Iceman Cometh," *Variety*, op. cit.

10. Frederic Ives Carpenter, *Eugene O'Neill* (New York: Twayne, 1964), p. 154.

11. "Movie Review," 29 Oct 1973.

12. "Filming 'The Iceman Cometh,'" op. cit., p. 37.

13. Richard Schickel, "Famous Plays, Famous Players," *The New York Times*, 13 April, 2003.

14. "Filming 'The Iceman Cometh,'" op. cit., p. 37.

15. Ibid., p. 35.

Three: The Physical Challenge

1. See "The Grand Prix Circus, Hollywood Style," op. cit., pp. 130-136. See also *Conversation*, op. cit., p. 97 and Philip K. Scheuer, "'Grand' Film Will Be Authentic," *Los Angles Times*, 15 Dec 1964.

2. Frankenheimer and his screenwriters drew heavily from stories described in Robert Daley's *The Cruel Sport* (New York: Bonanza Books, 1963). See Betty Martin, "Race Film in Stretch Run," *Los Angeles Times*, 29 Jul 1966.

3. *Forty Years*, op. cit., p. 62.

4. "Grand Prix," *The New York Times*, 22 Dec 1966.

5. See Kevin Thomas, "Racing Thrills," *Los Angeles Times*, 29 Oct 1966.

6. Stephen Farber, "The Spectacle Film: 1967" *Film Quarterly*, Summer 1967, p. 18.

7. *Variety*, 1 Jan 1966.

8. Quoted in "Race Film in Stretch Run," op. cit. and *Forty Years*, op. cit., p. 63.

9. "The Spectacle Film: 1967," op. cit., p. 17.

10. *Forty Years*, op. cit., p. 88.

11. "'Gypsy Moths': Dead Air," *The Washington Post*, 19 Nov 1969; "Barnstorming Parachutists," *The New York Times*, 29 Aug 1969.

12. "The Gypsy Moths," *Chicago Sun-Times*, 17 Nov 1969.

13. *Forty Years*, op. cit., p. 112.

14. Ibid.

15. The building in which Hideo works and lives is actually the Kyoto International Conference Hall.

16. From "Filmmakers on Film: John Sayles on Yojimbo," *The Daily Telegraph* (UK), 13 Jul 2002. Donaldson's observations correspond with remarks Frankenheimer made about the film's themes in an interview he gave to Pat Broeske: "This was a chance to do a modern Samurai movie. Also, I saw it as the story of a man who finds himself, as well as commitment. I saw it as a film about ancient Japan versus modern Japan, technology versus ideals." Quoted in "...I'm a filmmaker...I like to work...," *Films in Review*, Feb 1983, p. 100.

17. Readers will find that *The Challenge* is to a degree indebted to Sydney Pollack's *The Yakuza* (1974), as well. Both pictures focus upon the friendship that develops between American and Japanese protagonists; both were shot by the cinematographer Kozo Okazaki; both make use of the surreally designed Kyoto International Conference Hall. Pollack was a friend of Frankenheimer. The two had worked together in live television and Frankenheimer had hired Pollack, who was then an actor and an acting coach, to work with the boys who played the toughs in *The Young Savages*: see *Against Type*, op. cit., p. 208 and *Lancaster*, op. cit., p. 207. See also Baxter's essay about Frankenheimer

in the *International Dictionary of Films and Filmmakers* (Chicago: St. James Press, 1990), p. 184: "*The Challenge* [is] a stylish Japanese romp in the style of *The Yakuza*." *The Yakuza*, we should also note, opens with titles that explain what the word "yakuza" means, that it refers to gangsters. Frankenheimer's other "Japanese" film *Ronin* opens in the same manner, telling viewers that "ronin" are, in effect, self-employed warriors.

18. Alain Silver discusses the *bushido* code at length in *The Samurai Film* (South Brunswick and New York: A.S. Barnes and Co., 1977), pp. 19–27.

Four: Threats to Freedom

1. Rallies, parades and crowd scenes appear often in Frankenheimer's cinema, showing up in *Seven Days in May*, *99 and 44/100 Percent Dead!*, *Black Sunday*, *The Burning Season*, *George Wallace* and *Path to War*. Divided families appear frequently in several films, too, including *The Young Stranger*, *All Fall Down*, *52 Pick-Up*, *Dead Bang* and *The Fourth War*.

2. "The Manchurian Candidate," *The New York Times*, 25 Oct 1962.

3. "Frankenheimer's 'Candidate' a Big Winner," *Los Angeles Times*, 28 Oct 1962.

4. "The Manchurian Candidate," *Chicago Sun-Times*, 11 Mar 1988.

5. "'Candidate' Runs Again and Wins," *The New York Times*, 24 Apr 1988.

6. "From Failure to Cult Classic," *Time*, 21 Mar 1988, p. 84.

7. "Paranoid Illusions," *Chicago Reader*, 11 Mar 1988.

8. Quoted from *The Manchurian Candidate* (London: BFI, 2002), p. 48. On the artists who influenced him, Frankenheimer told Higham:

> As far as perspective is concerned, Gauguin has taught me more than any book could, and he was influenced by Japanese painters in his turn; Japanese painters taught me about perspective. You look at Kurosawa's films, with the long lenses he uses, and you can learn more from him than from anybody. Among photographers, I learned most from Robert Frank, Ernst Haas, Eisenstadt, and Werner Bischof. I learned from these men that

every rule, so far as composition was concerned, was made to be broken. You read Eisentein's film books and they're fine, but what you don't read is that you can break the rules, if you want to.

Hitchcock influenced me deeply as well. Any American director who says he isn't influenced by him is out of his mind. René Clement was a very great influence also. And, of course, Welles: from the photographic point of view he made just about the perfect film in *Citizen Kane*.
Quoted in *Muse*, op. cit., p. 75.

9. In "When Dr No Met Dr Strangelove," op. cit., p. 19, Hoberman says that Axelrod modeled the film's "matter-of-fact integration of dreams, flashbacks and waking reality" after Resnais' *Hiroshima*.

10. *Voices from the Set*, op. cit., p. 82.

11. *Muse*, op. cit., p. 84.

12. *Lancaster*, op. cit., p. 238.

13. *Voices from the Set*, op. cit. p. 84.

14. In spite of its schedule and cost problems, *The Train* earned a profit for UA: see *Lancaster*, op. cit., pp. 238–240.

15. In 2000, Frankenheimer was asked by *The Wall Street Journal* to list his favorite films. The five selections he made are: Clement's *Purple Noon* (1960), Rosselini's *Open City* (1946), Bergman's *Smiles of a Summer Night* (1955), Hitchcock's *Shadow of a Doubt* (1943) and Pontecorvo's *Battle of Algiers* (1965), of which he said: "Talk about creating realism: There isn't one foot of stock footage in that movie, yet it's one of the most realistic movies you ever saw." "Talking Head: John Frankenheimer," 24 Mar 2000. With its irregular combatant characters who use cunning to frustrate the German army, *The Train* resembles *The Guns of Navarone* (1961), *The Great Escape* (1963) and *Von Ryan's Express* (1965), all shot during the same period. Unlike these pictures, however, *The Train* was filmed in black and white.

16. *Voices from the Set*, op. cit., p. 85.

17. Ibid. Arguably, the men's antipathy anticipates the sort that develops between the American and Russian colonels in *The Fourth War*.

18. See *Forty Years*, op. cit., p. 166 and *Conversation*, op. cit., p. 147.

19. The film is fictitious, but Black September was an actual terror group which

gained notoriety after its operatives kidnapped and murdered several Israeli athletes during the 1972 Olympics—the incident which in part inspired Spielberg's *Munich* (2005).

20. Jeff Simon suggested in "Man Behind the 'Candidate,'" *The Buffalo News*, 25 Jul 2004 that *Black Sunday* "come[s] the closest of any American film to anticipating the events of September 11, 2001." The parallels between art and history upset Frankenheimer, and in the weeks immediately following the 9/11 attack, the director told Glenn Lovell that

he now wants nothing to do with terrorist movies. "It would be irresponsible to do one right now—I'm just sick of it," the director says. "These are tricky times," he adds. "I don't think anybody really knows what to do right now."
Quoted in "Action Films: Do They Have a Future?," *The San Jose Mercury News*, 23 Sep 2001.

21. Canby, op. cit.; Arnold, "A Dogged 'Black Sunday,'" *The Washington Post*, 1 Apr 1977.

22. The sequence was actually filmed in Morocco.

23. Staff, "Black Sunday," 23 Mar 1977.

24. Spielberg's *Munich* received similar criticism. *Munich* and *Black September* both feature musical scores composed by John Williams.

25. Op. cit., 284.

26. Staff, "The Holcroft Covenant," 31 Sep 1985.

27. "Crying out for the Truth," *The Sunday Times* (UK), 22 Sep 1985.

28. *Forty Years*, op. cit., p. 189.

29. *Conversation*, op. cit., p. 181.

30. "A Journalist, His Novel and Trouble in 70's Rome," *The New York Times*, 1 Nov 1991.

31. "Year of the Gun Shooting Blanks," *The Washington Post*, 1 Nov 1991.

32. "Year of the Gun," *The Washington Post*, 7 May 1992.

33. Raybourne at one point compares the book he's writing with Frederick Forsyth's *The Day of the Jackal*, the 1971 novel upon which Fred Zinneman's 1973 film is based.

34. "Nobody's pure here," noted *The Boston Globe*'s Jay Carr. "Year of the Gun," 1 Nov 1991.

35. "Year of the Gun," 1 Nov 1991.
36. "Year of the Gun," op. cit.

Five: Oligarchs and Bullies

1. From commentary Frankenheimer recorded for the film's release on laser disc in 1996.

2. Critics have noted the narrative's similarities with the Faust story since the picture's release. In 1966, Sam Lessner wrote:

> A college production of Goethe's "Faust" which he directed in 1951 has paid off for John Frankenheimer in his latest film, "Seconds." The movie stars Rock Hudson as a man who undergoes a complete physical transformation to re-live his life and strongly suggests the classic and tragic "Faust" story.

Quoted from "'Faust' Comes Back to 'Seconds' Director," *Los Angeles Times*, 14 Nov 1966. And Glenn Lovell referred to the old story, too, when he interviewed Frankenheimer in 1991:

> Most underrated film?
> "Probably 'The Gypsy Moths'... I love that movie. I love the cast — Lancaster, Deborah Kerr. I love the sense of place: Middle America. And I love that theme of the individual and how he functions and what it takes to survive.... From a commercial standpoint I think '52 Pick-Up'...is a really good movie. I think that movie is going to hold up years from now."
> And what about "Seconds," your 1966 Faustian thriller with Rock Hudson?
> "People think it's a classic now. So, no, I don't think its underrated.... It was depressing. I meant it to be a positive movie, though. It says, 'You are what you are; you can't change that.'"
> That sounds like a personal credo.
> "Right. I identify with that, obviously. I've always felt that I had to stand for what I believed in. I always had to take a stand."

Quoted from "The Golden Autumn of Old Hollywood's Boy Wonder," *The San Jose Mercury News*, 6 Oct 1991.

3. *Conversation*, op. cit., p. 95.
4. From Frankenheimer's commentary.
5. "Pop Art Pitfalls," op. cit., p. 11.
6. The argument might be made that the mothers who appear in *All Fall Down*, *Bird Man of Alcatraz* and *The Manchurian Candidate* are monsters of a sort, too. Referring to the maternal protagonists in these pic-tures, Combs claimed: "Mother is the monster who spawns sociopathic sons in all three films." From "Impossible Cinema," op. cit., p. 46.

7. "Pop Art Pitfalls," op. cit., p. 12.
8. "Frankenheimer's 'Prophecy': Mercury, Lukewarm," *The New York Times*, 15 Jun 1979.
9. Claudia Puig, "'Burning Season' Emerges from the Ashes," *Los Angeles Times*, 16 Sep 1994.
10. See "'Burning Season' Emerges from the Ashes," op. cit. See also *Forty Years*, op. cit., pp. 246–247.
11. Benjamin Svetkey, "Rain-forest Crunch," *Entertainment Weekly*, 16 Sep 1994, p. 19.
12. Quoted in Susan King, "Chico and the Land," *Los Angeles Times*, 11 Sep 1994. See also *Conversation*, op. cit., p. 195.
13. "Chico and the Land," op. cit.
14. "Little Guy as Hero: The Death of Chico Mendes," *The New York Times*, 16 Sep 1994.
15. "The Burning Season," Variety, 12 Sep 1994.
16. "The Burning Season," 16 Sep 1994, p. 98.
17. "Chico and the Land," op. cit.
18. In his article about Mendes which appeared in *Vanity Fair*, Alex Shoumatoff discussed the South American custom of giving a person notice that his death is imminent. Chico, he says, lived in

> one of those parts of Brazil where...when someone calls you up and tells you that you going to die, it is not so much a threat as a statement of fact. You have been, in the Portuguese term, *anunciado*. The *anuncio*...is a form of torture. You increase the pleasure of killing your victim by first destroying him psychologically.

"Murder in Brazil," Apr 1989, p. 184.

19. "The Island of Dr. Moreau," *People Weekly*, 9 Sep 1996, p. 17; Todd McCarthy, "The Island of Dr. Moreau," *Variety*, 23 Aug 1996.
20. David Ansen, "Brando Plays God," *Newsweek*, 2 Sep 1996, p. 66.

Six: Faulty Command

1. *Muse*, op. cit., p. 82.
2. Scott is a realization, arguably, of the

fears President Eisenhower articulated when he famously said:

> In the councils of government, we must guard against the acquisition of unwarranted influence, whether sought or unsought, by the military-industrial complex. The potential for the disastrous rise of misplaced power exists and will persist. We must never let the weight of this combination endanger our liberties or democratic processes.

From the farewell address the president gave on January 17, 1961.

3. See Stephen Farber, "The Extraordinary Seaman," *Film Quarterly*, Spring 1969, p. 60: "*The Extraordinary Seaman* is the film John Frankenheimer directed before *The Fixer*, but due to studio jitters about the satiric use of World War II newsreel footage, its release was delayed for more than a year." See also *Forty Years*, op. cit., pp. 72–73. Shooting was fraught with problems, too. Alan Alda recalled the experience in his memoir, *Never Have Your Dog Stuffed* (New York: Random House, 2006), pp. 129-130:

> [F]ilming it was a disaster from the first moment. We shot it outside a town called Coatzocoalcos, on a river that wound through a thick jungle. Members of the crew were carried out on stretchers with typhoid. The river was so full of unfamiliar microbes that a nick on my shin turned into a major infection.

4. See Farber, "The Extraordinary Seaman," op. cit.

5. "The Extraordinary Seaman," 22 Jan 1969.

6. *Forty Years*, op. cit., p. 72.

7. Ibid.

8. Just as *The Fourth War* ends, a quote from Albert Einstein appears on the screen, shedding some light on the film's title: "I cannot predict what breed of weapons will be employed in the waging of the Third World War; what I can predict is that the Fourth World War shall be fought with sticks and stones."

9. "'Wallace': An Epic Tragedy," *Chicago Sun-Times*, 22 Aug 1997; "Going Beyond Just Facts to Show a Hollow Soul," *The New York Times*, 23 Aug 1997.

10. "George Wallace 'The Movie' Stirs Anger in Alabama," op. cit.

11. "Fact, Fiction, and Film: Franken-

heimer's George Wallace," *Perspectives*, Jan 1998, p. 16.

12. "History in the Re-Making," op. cit.

13. "Strong Acting, Weak History," 23 Aug 1997.

14. David Kronke, "Where LBJ Went Wrong," *Daily News of Los Angeles*, 18 May 2002.

15. "HBO's Powerful Path to War," op. cit.

16. From "Interview with the Director John Frankenheimer," which appears on the film's DVD release, op. cit.

Seven: The Misuse of Force

1. Quoted in *Forty Years*, op. cit., p. 104. Flint McCain is similarly stuck. But in contrast to Tawes, who longs to break away from his bourgeois existence, Flint strives for prosperity. "We lose that still, we got nothing," he tells one of his sons. And to protect this source of revenue, he is willing to commit murder and force his daughter into semi-prostitution. But the moonshiner's dreams are also doomed. He may elude the reach of the law at the end of the film, but in doing so he is forced to abandon his still.

2. From the commentary Robert L. Rosen, the film's producer, recorded for the film's 2001 DVD release.

3. To further enhance the viewer's identification with Doyle, Frankenheimer decided against using subtitles in the film. He told Pratley: "We used the French language as a weapon against 'Popeye' Doyle. We had actors talking French, nothing to do with the plot, but he couldn't understand them and it drove him crazy. The audience couldn't understand it either and they were just as vexed." Quoted in *Forty Years*, op. cit., p. 156. Frankenheimer's treatment of Doyle and his alienation is compelling, but it's hardly ground-breaking. In 1968, Don Siegel worked with the same "culture shock" theme in *Coogan's Bluff*, which tells the story of a rural Arizona deputy who searches for a fugitive in New York City.

4. "French Connection 2," *Chicago Sun-Times*, 1 Jan 1975.

5. See *Conversation*, op. cit., p 141-143. On the commentary track Frankenheimer

recorded for the film's DVD release, he says that he hired real doctors to play the doctors who treat Popeye for his withdrawal from heroin.

6. "The Director as Survivor," op. cit.

7. Lawrence Van Gelder, "At the Movies: A New Candidate for Frankenheimer," *The New York Times*, 19 Aug 1988.

8. Lane, op. cit.

9. Oscar Ratti and Adele Westbrook, *Secrets of the Samurai* (Boston: Tuttle, 1973), p. 119.

10. From commentary Frankenheimer recorded for the film's 1999 DVD release.

11. To capitalize on this popularity, MGM released a "deluxe" two-disc edition of the film in 2006, which includes documentaries about the making of *Ronin* as well as commentary from the picture's director of photography Robert Fraisse.

Eight: Outsiders

1. Philip K. Scheuer, "Ace TV Director Back with Movie," 5 Jul 1960.

2. Collected in *5001 Nights at the Movies* (New York: Holt, Rinehart and Winston, 1982), p. 670.

3. *Lancaster*, op. cit., p. 199.

4. On two occasions, Frankenheimer links the lawyer's zealotry with blindness. The director cuts ironically to a shot of a statue of Justice with a blindfold drawn over her eyes, for instance, just after Bell commits himself to the case. Then, much later, when Bell is attacked in the subway and loses control of his temper, he is literally blinded by the lack of light in the car.

5. "99 and 44/100% Dead!," 6 Jun 1974.

6. Quoted in Andrea Karnes, et al, "Roy Lichtenstein," *Modern Art Museum of Fort Worth: 110 Masterworks* (London: Third Millennium, 2002), p. 255.

7. *Forty Years*, op. cit., p. 194.

8. See Alain Silver's "Son of *Noir*: Neo-Film Noir and the Neo-B Picture," collected in *Film Noir Reader* (New York: Limelight, 1999), p. 331.

9. Frankenheimer directed a version of Clifford Odet's *Clash By Night* for *Playhouse 90* on June 13, 1957.

10. "'52 Pick-Up,' A No-Frills Thriller," 7 Nov 1986.

11. Quoted from *Front Lines*, op. cit., p. 278.

12. *Conversation*, op. cit., p. 13.

13. The incest theme also materializes in *All Fall Down*, *The Manchurian Candidate* and *The Holcroft Covenant*.

14. Gary Arnold, "Frankenheimer Puts Thrill First," *The Washington Times*, 18 Feb 2000.

15. Written by Robert L. May and Johnny Marks, the song first became popular in 1949 when it was released by the singer Gene Autry.

16. Terry Lawson, "Veteran Director Always has a Story to Tell," *Detroit Free Press* 23 Feb 2000.

17. Cynthia Fuchs, "Interview with John Frankenheimer director of *Reindeer Games*," *PopMatters*, <http://www.popmatters.com/film/interviews/frankenheimer-john.shtml> (12 Nov 2004).

18. Anthony Kaufman, "INTERVIEW: John Frankenheimer Keeps Playing 'Games,'" *IndieWIRE*, 25 Feb 2000, <http://www2.indiewire.com/people/int_Frankenheimer_> Jo_2A67C.html (15 Nov 2004).

19. In the interview he gave to Lawson, op. cit., Frankenheimer compared Ashley to the character Jane Greer played in Jacques Tournier's 1947 *noir*, *Out of the Past*.

Nine: Prisoners

1. *Lancaster*, op. cit., p. 208.

2. "'Bird Man' Notable Study of Prison Life," 4 Jul 1962.

3. "Bird Man of Alcatraz," op. cit.

4. "Bird Man of Alcatraz," 19 Jul 1962.

5. See *Lancaster*, op. cit., p. 214.

6. *Forty Years*, op. cit., p. 79.

7. Vincent Buist, "Western Movie Crews Flock to East Europe," 3 Feb 1968.

8. See *Conversation*, op. cit., p. 107.

9. "'The Fixer' Put Through Hollywood Mill," 9 Dec 1998.

10. "The Fixer," 20 Nov 1968.

11. "'The Fixer' on Screen of the Fox Lido," 11 Dec 1968.

12. "The Fixer," *Chicago Sun-Times*, 25 Dec 1968

13. *Conversation*, op. cit., p. 107.

14. "A Virtuoso Role in a Russian Jail," 6 Dec 1968, p. 14.

15. "Inside the Walls," *Los Angeles Times*, 20 Mar 1994.

16. See Michael McCall, "On Location: From 'Alcatraz' to 'Attica,'" *Los Angeles Times*, 20 Jun 1993:

> As for tackling a subject that previously has been made into a TV movie, Frankenheimer contends that the HBO film comes from a different point of view. "They did it from a book by Tom Wicker," he said of "Attica" and the bestseller it drew upon, "A Time to Die." "It was from the viewpoint of a journalist. Ours is based on the story from a man who was there, a man who was a central character in the worst prison riot in the history of our country."

17. "'Andersonville' Script Caught Busy Director," op. cit. Winant became friends with Frankenheimer in the early Sixties. As John Houseman's assistant, she worked on both *Playhouse 90* and *All Fall Down*.

18. Doug Nye, "'Andersonville' Director John Frankenheimer Talks About Miniseries," Knight Ridder/Tribune News Service, 28 Feb 1996.

19. "Andersonville Parts I & II," 26 Feb 1996.

20. "Disgrace in a Profusion of Detail," *The New York Times*, 2 Mar 1996.

21. "History Escapes Drama," 3 Mar 1996.

22. "Forward," *Andersonville* (Baton Rouge: Louisiana State University P, 1996), p. viii.

23. "Andersonville, A Symbol of Wartime Suffering and Brutality," *The New York Times*, 3 Mar 1996.

Appendix: Two Short Films

1. *Forty Years*, op. cit., p. 230.

2. Ibid.

3. Sandy Hunter, "Cruising for Content," *Boards*, 1 Jul 2001, p. 12.

4. Michael Goldman, "Effecting BMW Shorts," *Millimeter*, Jul 2001, p 13.

5. Erika Milvy, "BMW at Intersection of Art and Commerce," *Los Angeles Times*, 4 May 2001.

6. "Honk if You've Seen These Online Films," 26 Jun 2001.

7. Jon Silberg, "BMW Hits the Infobahn," *American Cinematographer*, Spring 2001, pg. 86.

Bibliography

Alda, Alan. *Never Have Your Dog Stuffed*. New York: Random House, 2006.

Allon, Yoram, et al., eds. *Contemporary North American Film Directors: A Wallflower Critical Guide*. New York: Wallflower, 2002.

Amburn, Ellis. *The Sexiest Man Alive*. New York: HarperCollins, 2002.

AuWerter, Russell. Interview. *Action*, May-June 1970, pp. 6–9.

Behlmer, Rudy, ed. *Memo from David O. Selznick*. New York: Viking, 1972.

Bond, Jeff, and Lukas Kendall. Liner Notes. *All Fall Down/The Outrage*, CD. Hollywood: Film Score Monthly, 2003.

Bonham, Joe. "*Prophecy*: The New Breed of Monsters." *Fangoria*, Oct 1979, pp. 48–51.

Brodie, John. "Deliverance [profile of John Frankenheimer and John Boorman]." *Gentlemen's Quarterly*, Oct. 1998, pp. 175-178.

Buford, Kate. *Burt Lancaster*. New York: Knopf, 2000.

Caine, Michael. *What's It All About?* New York: Random House, 1992.

Carpenter, Frederic Ives. *Eugene O'Neill*. New York: Twayne, 1964. P. 154.

Carruthers, Susan. "'The Manchurian Candidate' (1962) and the Cold War Brainwashing Scare." *Historical Journal of Film, Radio and Television*, March 1998, pp. 75–94.

Casty, Alan. "Realism and Beyond: The Films of John Frankenheimer." *Film Heritage*, Winter 1966–67, pp. 21-32.

Cavendish, Richard. *An Illustrated Encyclopedia of Mythology*. New York: Crescent, 1984.

Champlin, Charles. *John Frankenheimer: A Conversation*. Burbank: Riverwood, 1995.

Clifford, Clark, and Richard Holbrooke. *Counsel to the President: A Memoir*. New York: Random House, 1991.

Combs, Richard. "A Matter of Conviction." *Sight and Sound*, 1979, p. 231.

Condon, Richard. *The Manchurian Candidate*. New York: McGraw-Hill, 1959.

Cook, Bruce. "The War Between the Writers and the Directors: Part II: The Directors." *American Film*, June 1979, pp. 49–53, 61.

_____. "Directors of the Decade: John Frankenheimer." *Films and Filming*, February 1984, pp. 16-18.

Corman, Roger. *How I Made a Hundred Movies in Hollywood and Never Lost a Dime*. New York: Random House, 1990.

Cowell, Adrian. *Decade of Destruction*. New York: Henry Holt, 1990.

Daley, Robert. *The Cruel Sport*. New York: Bonanza, 1963.

Davidson, Sara, and Rock Hudson. *Rock Hudson: His Story*. New York: Morrow, 1986.

The Directors: John Frankenheimer, DVD. Directed by Robert J. Emery. New York: Win-Star, 1999.

Douglas, Kirk. *The Ragman's Son*. New York: Simon & Schuster, 1988.

Drought, James. *The Gypsy Moths*. Norwalk, CT: Skylight, 1964.

Edelman, Rob, and Audrey E. Kupferberg. *Angela Lansbury: A Life on Stage and Screen*. New York: Carol, 1996.

Ely, David. *Seconds*. New York: Pantheon, 1963.

Evans, Robert. *The Kid Stays in the Picture*. New York: Hyperion, 1994.

Farber, Stephen. "*Seconds* [review]." *Film Quarterly*, Winter 1966-1967, pp. 25–28.

Fishgall, Garry. *Against Type*. New York: Scribner, 1995.

_____. *Gregory Peck*. New York: Scribner, 2002.

Frady, Marshall. *Wallace*. New York: World, 1968.

Frankenheimer, John. "Criticism as Creation." *Saturday Review*, 26 Dec. 1964, pp. 12–13.

_____. "Director Commentary." In "Ambush." *The Hire*, DVD. Directed by John Frankenheimer. 2002; BMW of North America: BMW Films , 2001.

_____. "Director Commentary." In *Andersonville*, DVD. Directed by John Frankenheimer. 1996; Burbank: Turner Entertainment, 2003.

_____. "Director Commentary." In *French Connection II*, DVD. Directed by John Frankenheimer. 1975; Beverly Hills, CA: 20th Century–Fox, 2001.

_____. "Director Commentary." In *The Gypsy Moths*, DVD. Directed by John Frankenheimer. 1969; Burbank: Warner, 2002.

_____. "Director Commentary." In *The Holcroft Covenant*, DVD. Directed by John Frankenheimer. 1985; Santa Monica, CA: MGM, 1999.

_____. "Director Commentary." In *The Manchurian Candidate*, DVD. Directed by John Frankenheimer. 1962; Santa Monica: MGM, 2004.

_____. "Director Commentary." In *Reindeer Games*, DVD, director's edition. Directed by John Frankenheimer. 2000; Burbank: Buena Vista, 2001.

_____. "Director Commentary." In *Ronin*, DVD. Directed by John Frankenheimer. 1998; Santa Monica: MGM, 1999.

_____. "Director Commentary." In *Seven Days in May*, DVD. Directed by John Frankenheimer. 1964; Burbank: Warner, 2000.

_____. "Director Commentary." In *The Train*, DVD. Directed by John Frankenheimer. 1964; Santa Monica: MGM, 1999.

_____. "Fredric the Great — But He Didn't Know It [eulogy for Fredric March]." *Los Angeles Times*, 27 Apr. 1975.

_____. Interview. In *Path to War*, DVD. Directed by John Frankenheimer. 2002; HBO: Santa Monica, 2003.

_____. Interview by Terry Gross. *Fresh Air*. National Public Radio, 6 Mar. 1990.

_____. "Style Cramps Film Directors' Style." *Los Angeles Times*, 27 Dec. 1964.

Gaddis, Thomas. *Birdman of Alcatraz: The Story of Robert Stroud*. New York: Random House, 1955.

Giat, Daniel. Interview. In *Path to War*, DVD. Directed by John Frankenheimer. 2002; HBO: Santa Monica, 2003.

Harris, Thomas. *Black Sunday*. New York: Putnam, 1975.

Hawes, William. *The American Television Drama: The Experimental Years*. University: University of Alabama Press, 1986.

Herlihy, James Leo. *All Fall Down*. New York: Dell, 1960.

Higham, Charles, and Joel Greenberg, eds. *The Celluloid Muse*. London: Angus & Robertson, 1969.

Hillstrom, Laurie Collier. *International Directory of Films and Filmmakers 2: Directors*. 2nd ed. Chicago: St. James, 1997.

Houseman, John. *Final Dress*. New York: Simon & Schuster, 1983.

Hughes, David. *The Greatest Sci-Fi Movies Never Made*. London: Titan, 2001.

Hunter, Evan. *A Matter of Conviction*. New York: Simon & Schuster, 1959.

Jones, Madison. *An Exile*. New York: Viking, 1967.

Kael, Pauline. "The Fixer." In *Going Steady*. Boston: Little, Brown, 1970.

_____. "The Young Savages." In *5001 Nights at the Movies*. New York: Holt, Rinehart and Winston, 1982.

Karnes, Andrea, et al. *Modern Art Museum of Fort Worth: 110 Masterworks*. London: Third Millennium, 2002.

Katz, Ephraim, et al., eds. *The Film Encyclopedia*. 4th ed. New York: HarperCollins, 2000.

King, Stephen. *Danse Macabre*. New York: Everest, 1981.

Knebel, Fletcher, and Charles W. Bailey II. *Seven Days in May*. New York: Harper & Row, 1962.

Leonard, Elmore. *52 Pick-Up*. New York: Delacorte, 1974.

Logevall, Fredrik. "The Biggest Hawk After All [review of *Path to War*]." *Diplomatic History*, June 2004, pp. 459–462.

Madsen, Axel. "99 and 44/100% Dead." *Sight and Sound*, Winter 1973–74.

Marcus, Greil. *The Manchurian Candidate*. London: BFI, 2002.

Martin, Nancy Guild. "Architectural Digest Visits: Mr. and Mrs. Frankenheimer." *Architectural Digest*, Feb. 1983, pp. 82–90.

Mewshaw, Michael. *Year of the Gun*. New York: Atheneum, 1984.

Moore, Robin. *French Connection II*. New York: Dell, 1975.

Oppenheimer, Jean. "Down Under in Jungleland." *American Cinematographer*, Sept. 1996, pp. 44–52.

Pratley, Gerald. *The Cinema of John Frankenheimer*. New York: A.S. Barnes, 1969.

_____. *The Films of Frankenheimer: Forty Years in Film*. Bethlehem, PA: Lehigh University Press, 1998.

Quinlan, David. *The Illustrated Guide to Film Directors*. London: Batsford, 1983.

Ratti, Oscar, and Adele Westbrook. *Secrets of the Samurai*. Boston: Tuttle, 1973.

Revkin, Andrew. *The Burning Season*. New York: Houghton Mifflin, 1990.

Rintels, David. *Andersonville*. Baton Rouge, LA: Gideon, 1996.

Rock, Phillip. *The Extraordinary Seaman*. New York: Meredith, 1967.

Rosen, Robert. Producer Commentary. In *French Connection II*, DVD. Directed by John Frankenheimer. 1975; Beverly Hills: 20th Century–Fox, 2001.

Sarris, Andrew. *The American Cinema*. New York: Dutton, 1968.

Seltzer, David. *Prophecy*. New York: Ballantine, 1979.

Silver, Alain. *The Samurai Film*. New York: A.S. Barnes, 1977.

_____, and Elizabeth Ward, eds. *Film Noir: An Encyclopedic Reference to the American Style*. 3rd ed. New York: Overlook, 1992.

_____, and James Ursini, eds. *Film Noir Reader*. New York: Limelight, 1996.

Stanbrook, Alan. "Laurence Harvey." *Films and Filming*, May 1964, pp. 42–46.

Sturcken, Frank. *Live Television: The Golden Age of 1946-1958 in New York*. Jefferson, NC: McFarland, 1990.

Tobias, Scott. "Interview: John Frankenheimer." *The Onion*. 16 Feb. 2000.

Wells, H.G. *The Island of Dr. Moreau*. London: Heinemann, 1896.

Wicking, Christopher, and Tise Vahimagi. *The American Vein: Directors and Directions in Television*. New York: Dutton, 1979.

Winters, Shelley. *Shelley II: The Middle of My Century*. New York: Simon & Schuster, 1989.

Zoller Seitz, Matt. "Those High-tech Shoot-em-ups Got the Formula from 'The Train.'" *The New York Times*, 30 Apr. 1995.

Index

233